Contents

Publisher's Note

The Penguin Guide to the States and Union Territories of India incorporates the latest official figures available on 1 August 2005. All data made available or modified after this date will be incorporated in the next edition of the book.

India—Physical Map

India—Political Map

STATES

Andhra Pradesh

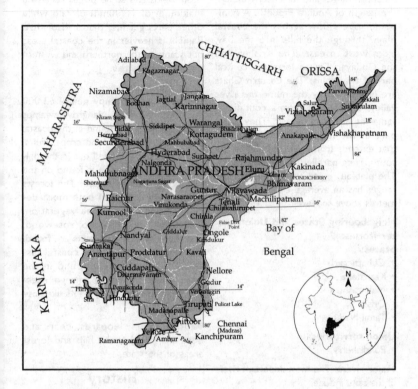

Key Statistics

Capital: Hyderabad.
Area: 276,754 sq. km.
Population: Total: 76,210,007
Male: 38,527,413
Female: 37,682,594
Population density: 275 per sq. km.
Sex ratio: 978 females per 1000 males.
Principal languages: Telugu, Urdu, Hindi.
Literacy rates: Total: 60.5%
Male: 70.3%
Female: 50.4%

Government

Governor: Sushilkumar Shinde. He assumed office on 1 November 2004.

Chief Minister: Y.S. Rajasekhar Reddy (INC). He was sworn in on 14 May 2004.

Geography

Physical characteristics: Andhra Pradesh has three main physiographic regions: a coastal plain lying in the eastern part of the state, the Eastern

Ghats, which form the western flank of the coastal plain, and a plateau west of the Eastern Ghats. The coastal plain extends from the Bay of Bengal to the mountain ranges and runs nearly the entire length of Andhra Pradesh. A number of rivers flow across the coastal plain, through the hills into the bay, from west to east. The Krishna and the Godavari Deltas form the central part of the plains. The Eastern Ghats are broken up by the numerous river valleys and do not form a continuous range in Andhra Pradesh. They are a part of the larger mountain system that extends from central India to the south, lying parallel to the east coast. The plateau region to the west of the ranges has an average elevation of 500 metres above sea level.

Neighbouring States and Union territories:
States:
• Chhattisgarh
• Karnataka
• Maharashtra
• Orissa
• Tamil Nadu

Union territories:
• Pondicherry

Major rivers: The most important rivers of the state include:
• Krishna
• Godavari
• Musi
• Penneru
• Tungabhadra

Climate: In Andhra Pradesh, the summer is from March to June, the rainy season from July to September and the winter from October to February. Maximum and minimum temperatures in most parts of the state range from 23°C to 28°C and from 10°C to 12°C respectively. The coastal plain region experiences very warm summers with

temperatures rising to 42°C in some places. Summers are cooler and winters colder still in the plateau region. Rainfall is largely due to the south-west monsoon winds and some places receive a maximum of 1,400mm of rain while other parts get less than half of that. Rainfall is heavier in the coastal areas but scanty in the northern and western parts of the plateau.

Flora and Fauna:
Flora: Forests occupy nearly 63,000 sq. km. in the state. Mangrove swamps and palm trees are found in the coastal plain. Cultivation of food crops, fruits, and tobacco are carried out in the deltas. Thorny vegetation is found on the hills of the plateau region. The forests in the state consist of both moist deciduous and dry savanna vegetation. Plants like teak, bamboo, rosewood, and those bearing wild fruits are found. Cashew is grown in the coastal districts. Common trees found in the state include the banyan, mango, neem and pipal and flowering plants like rose and jasmine.

Fauna: Tigers, leopards, bears and deer are found in the hills and forest areas of the state.

History

Although references to people called 'Andhras', who lived south of the central Indian mountain ranges, can be found in Sanskrit writings dating back to about 1000 BC, the earliest definitive historical evidence of the Andhras dates only from the times of the Mauryan dynasty, around the third century BC. Emperor Asoka had sent Buddhist missions to the Andhras. Around the first century AD, the Satakarnis (or the Satavahanas) came to power. They were one of the most well known Andhra dynasties and ruled over almost the entire Deccan Plateau. They even established trade relations with Rome. In the eleventh century, large expanses of Andhra were united under the reign of the eastern Chalukyas. The Kakatiya dynasty of Warangal spread Andhra power in the twelfth and thirteenth centuries. Their regime witnessed the rise of the Andhras as a commercial power to parts of South-East Asia. Muslim invasion of south India led to the downfall of Warangal in 1323. However, the rise of the kingdom of Vijayanagar to the south-west of Warangal prevented Muslim domination to some extent. The Vijayanagar kingdom is often regarded as the greatest kingdom in Andhra history. Its greatest ruler was Krishna Deva Raya who reigned from 1509 to 1529. However, the glory of the Vijayanagar kingdom came to an end when it succumbed to an alliance of the neighbouring Muslim states in 1565.

In 1687, the Mughal emperor Aurangzeb invaded Golconda and annexed it to the Mughal Empire. The Mughals appointed 'Nazims' as agents of the Mughal emperor. For about thirty-five years the Nazims ruled the area. Then came the Asaf Jahi Nizams.

When the Europeans arrived in India and gained power, the Nizams of Hyderabad sought their help against their rivals. In this process, they acquired French and later British support. In exchange, the British acquired vast stretches of land from the Nizams. Over a period of time the British gained control over most parts of Andhra territory and only parts of the Telugu-speaking areas, the Telangana region, remained with the Nizams. Even the French acquired a few towns.

At the time of Independence in 1947, the Nizams held sway over Hyderabad and desired to gain independence. Hyderabad was then one of the most prosperous of the princely states and had substantial armed forces. For this purpose, Nizam Osman Ali enlisted the help of Kasim Razvi of the Ittehadul Muslimeen and its private army, the Razakars. Even as the Hindus of the state campaigned to join India, the Nizam banned the Congress party in the state. As 15 August 1947 approached, negotiations between India and the Nizam reached a stalemate as Osman Ali refused to join India. Meanwhile, the Nizam's police, the Razakars and the supporters of the Nizam perpetrated a reign of terror in the state. On 29 November 1947, Hyderabad signed a Stand Still Agreement with India. It established a period of status quo. Hyderabad was allowed to maintain the status that existed between the British and the Nizam before 15 August 1947. The Nizam sent representations to other nations to seek their support and even approached the United Nations Security Council.

The Indian armed forces launched Operation Polo on 13 September 1948. It ended just over 100 hours later, when the Nizam asked his forces to cease fire, allowed Union troops into the Hyderabad territories and banned the Razakars. On 18 September, the Hyderabad Army surrendered and Major General J.N. Chaudhuri of the Indian Amy was appointed Military Governor of the state. The merger of Hyderabad state with the Indian Dominion followed. In January 1950, M.K. Vellodi, a Senior Civil Servant, was appointed the Chief Minister of the State. The first General Elections were held in 1952 and B. Rama Krishna Rao became the first popularly elected Chief Minister.

Meanwhile, the demand for a separate Andhra state gained momentum. To complicate matters, a local Gandhian leader, Potti Sreeramulu, fasted to death in 1953. On 1 October 1953, the Andhra state, which included the Telugu-speaking districts of the former Madras state, was formed with its capital at Kurnool. Andhra Pradesh was formed on 1 November 1956 when the erstwhile state of Hyderabad was split up and its Telugu-speaking districts were joined to the Andhra state. Neelam Sanjiva Reddy was the first Chief Minister of Andhra Pradesh.

In 1960, 221.4 square miles in the Chingleput and Salem districts of Madras state were transferred to Andhra Pradesh in exchange for 410 square miles from Chittoor district.

Politics

Andhras were greatly agitated over the developments in the state of Hyderabad during the years 1946–48. The Nizam was very anxious to become independent and he insisted that Hyderabad should be the third dominion. Meanwhile, the Hindus of Hyderabad state who accounted for 93 per cent of its population launched the 'Join India' movement with the cooperation of a few patriotic Muslims for the integration of the state with the rest of the country. The state Congress leaders, led by Swami Ramanand Tirtha, involved themselves wholeheartedly in the movement. As the state Congress was banned by the Nizam, its leaders conducted their activities from places like Vijayawada and Bombay. The Communists on their part organized village defence squads to protect the villagers from the attacks of the Nizam Police and Razakars. All negotiations between the Nizam's Dominions and the Indian Union proved abortive. The Government of India tried to make the Nizam see reason and sign the Instrument of Accession with India. After tortuous negotiations, the Nizam finally entered into a 'Stand Still Agreement' on 29 November 1947 with India for one year to maintain status quo, which existed between the British and the Nizam before 15 August 1947. In the meanwhile, the Nizam sent a delegation to the UNO to refer the Hyderabad case to the Security Council.

The Government of India decided to curb these tendencies by launching a 'Police Action' against the Nizam. On 13 September 1948 'Police Action' on Hyderabad commenced. The Indian Army, led by Major-General J.N. Chaudhuri entered the state from five directions and the military action was a brilliant success. On 23 September the Nizam withdrew his complaint in the Security Council. The merger of Hyderabad Dominions into the Indian Union was announced.

Major-General J.N.Chaudhuri took over as Military Governor of Hyderabad and stayed in that position till the end of 1949. In January 1950, M.K. Vellodi, a senior civil servant, was made the Chief Minister of the state and the Nizam was designated 'Raj Pramukh'. After the 1952 General Elections, the first popular ministry headed by B. Rama Krishna Rao took charge of the state.

On 19 October 1952, a popular freedom fighter, Patti Sriramalu, undertook a fast unto death over the demand for a separate Andhra and expired after fifty-eight days. His death was followed by three days of rioting, demonstrations, hartals and violence all over Andhra. The government immediately gave in and conceded the demand for a separate state of Andhra. The Andhra state was created in October 1953 and strengthened the general demand for linguistic states.

Andhras had also long cherished a demand for the formation of Visalandhra, since the people of Hyderabad state were unanimous in their demand for the trifurcation of their state. Andhras hoped that the outlying Telugu areas in Orissa, Madhya Pradesh, Mysore and Madras would be incorporated in the greater Andhra. The States Reorganisation Commission, set up by the Government of India in December 1953, who heard the views of different organizations and individuals, though convinced of the advantages of Visalandhra, however, favoured the formation of a separate state for Telangana.

This report of the S.R.C. led to an intensive lobbying both by the advocates of Telangana and Visalandhra. The Communists reacted sharply and announced that they would resign their seats in the Hyderabad legislative assembly and contest elections on the issue. In the Hyderabad legislative assembly, a majority of the legislators supported Visalandhra. The Congress High Command favoured Visalandhra and prevailed upon the leaders of the Andhra state and Telangana to sort out their differences, who, thereupon, entered into a 'Gentlemen's Agreement'. One of the main provisions of the Agreement was the creation of a 'Regional Council' for Telangana for its all round development. The enlarged state formed by merging nine Telugu-speaking districts into Andhra state with its eleven districts, totalling twenty districts was named 'Andhra Pradesh' with its capital at Hyderabad. It was inaugurated on 1 November 1956 by Jawaharlal Nehru. Three more districts were added later; the state presently has twenty-three districts.

Neelam Sanjiva Reddy became the first Chief Minister of Andhra Pradesh; he later rose to the position of the President of India. Consequent on his becoming the President of the All India Congress Committee, he resigned the post of Chief Minister on 10 June 1960 and was succeeded by D. Sanjivaiah, from the Scheduled Castes. After the 1962 General Elections, N.Sanjiva Reddy again became the Chief Minister of the state on 12 March 1962. But he relinquished the Chief Ministership in 1964 on moral grounds consequent on the adverse verdict of the Supreme Court in the Kurnool Transport Nationalization case. He was succeeded by Kasu Brahmananda Reddy on 29 February 1964. He was in the office till 30 September 1971.

During the years 1969 and 1972, Andhra Pradesh was rocked by two political agitations popularly known as the 'Telangana' and the 'Jai Andhra' Movements respectively.

Telangana agitation was started by the people of the region when they felt that the Andhra leaders had flouted the Gentlemen's Agreement which facilitated the formation of Andhra Pradesh. The agitation took a new turn when the Congress legislators from Telangana supported the movement. Dr Channa Reddy formed the Telangana Praja Samiti to lead the movement. But by November 1969, there was a split in the Praja Samiti when dissident Congress legislators realized that the Prime Minister Indira Gandhi was not in favour of a separate Telangana. The movement slowly petered out. In September 1971, Brahmananda Reddy, the then Chief Minister, resigned his position to make room for a leader from Telangana to become the Chief Minister. On 30 September 1971, P.V. Narasimha Rao became the Chief Minister. The Telangana Praja Samiti was dissolved and its members rejoined the Congress.

During 1972, another agitation known as the Jai Andhra Movement was launched in the Andhra region. The agitation was a sequel to the Telangana agitation, which demanded that only 'Mulkis' should be appointed to the posts in Telangana including Hyderabad city. 'Mulki' was defined as one who was born in the state of Hyderabad or resided there continuously for fifteen years and had given an affidavit that he abandoned the idea of returning to his native place. Even after the formation of Andhra Pradesh, the Mulki rules continued to be in force in the Telangana region. As these rules stood in the way of the people of the Andhra region to compete for the posts, their validity was challenged in the High Court. A full bench of the High Court held that the Mulki rules were not valid and operative after the formation of Andhra Pradesh. But on an appeal by the state government, the Supreme Court declared on 3 October 1972 that the Mulki rules were valid and were in force.

The judgement created a great political crisis in the state. The people of the Andhra region felt that they were reduced to the status of second class citizens in their own state capital. They felt that the only way to uphold their dignity was by severing their connection with Telangana and started a movement for the separation of the Andhra region from Andhra Pradesh. As the agitation continued, President's Rule was imposed in the state on 10 January 1973. Finally, a political settlement was arrived at under the aegis of the central government. On 10 December 1973, President's Rule in the state was revoked and a popular ministry with Jalagam Vengala Rao as the Chief Minister was inducted. With this, normalcy returned and the state enjoyed political stability. In the General Elections held in February 1978 for the Legislative Assembly, the Congress swept the polls and Dr M. Channa Reddy became the sixth Chief Minister. Owing to some factional squabbles in the party, Dr Channa Reddy resigned in October 1980 and was succeeded by T. Anjaiah, who remained in office only for one year and four months. In February 1982, he was replaced by Bhavanam Venkataram, who in turn was replaced by K.Vijaya Bhaskara Reddy in September 1982. Thus Andhra Pradesh was administered by four Chief Ministers in four years.

N.T. Rama Rao, a leading figure of the film world formed a regional party called 'Telugu Desam' in January 1983 and contested the elections to the Andhra Pradesh Legislative Assembly held in 1983. His party became victorious and Rama Rao was sworn in as the tenth Chief Minister of the state. But, on 16 August 1984, Nadendla Bhaskara Rao, a cabinet colleague of Rama Rao, succeeded in becoming the Chief Minister by engineering the dismissal of Rama Rao by the then Governor. However, Rama Rao was reinstated on 16 September 1984 consequent on the severe criticism on the action of the Governor. In the elections of March 1985, Rama Rao proved that he continued to enjoy the confidence of people by winning an absolute majority in the House.

The Congress returned to power in the 1989 general elections to the state Legislature with a good majority. During the following five years, three Chief Ministers, Dr M. Channa Reddy, N. Janardhana Reddy and K.Vijaya Bhaskara Reddy held the reins of power. The discontentment of the Telugu public was reflected in pushing the Congress out and handing over the power again to the Telugu Desam Party in 1994. In 1995 N.T. Rama Rao was succeeded by N. Chandrababu Naidu, of the same party. He was in office till 14 May 2004. In 2004, the Congress swept back to power and Y.S. Rajashekhara Reddy was sworn in as the Chief Minister.

Culture

One of the six classical dance forms of India, Kuchipudi, is indigenous to Andhra Pradesh. The state is also well known for its banjara embroidery, bidri metalwork, Budithi metalwork and Dokra metal craft. Nirmal in Adilabad district is famous for its Nakash craftsmen, who specialize in painting scenes from the *Mahabharata* and the *Ramayana*. The state is also known for its Ikat textiles. Besides these, Andhra Pradesh is also reputed for its wood and stone carvings, kalamkari fabrics, puppets, toys, dolls and filigree work.

Fairs and festivals: Hindu festivals such as Dasara, Deepavali, Sri Ramanavami, Krishna Janmastami, Vinayaka Chavithi (Ganesh Chaturthi) and Maha Sivarathri are celebrated in the state. But the celebrations of Ugadi (Telugu New Year's day), Sankranti, Dasara and Vinayaka Chavithi in the state are unique.

Economy, Industry and Agriculture

Economy: The net state domestic product at current prices for 2002–03 (provisional) was Rs 143,975 crores. The per capita net state domestic product at current prices for 2002–03 (provisional) was Rs 18,661.

Minerals and industry: The significant industries of the state include IT industry, auto-component manufacturing, chemical synthesis and process engineering, and horticulture. Smaller industries that have developed in the state from locally available agricultural raw materials include rice flour, rice-bran oil,

soaps and detergents, cardboard and other packaging materials, paints and varnishes, and cattle feed.

Minerals found in the state include oil and natural gas, coal, limestone, iron ore, manganese, gold, diamonds, asbestos, ball clay, fire clay, graphite, dolomite, quartz, tungsten, feldspar and silica sand. Much of the state's mineral resources remain unexploited.

Agriculture: Production of food grains dominates agriculture in Andhra Pradesh and forms the mainstay of the state's economy. The state is one of the leading producers of rice and tobacco in the country. Sugarcane is also produced in the state. Other agricultural commodities now grown in different parts of Andhra Pradesh include pulses (peas, beans and lentils), chili peppers, castor beans, sorghum, groundnut and cotton, as well as fruits like mangoes, grapes, bananas and oranges.

Power: Andhra Pradesh has one of the highest installed power capacities in the country.

Education

Prominent educational institutions of Andhra Pradesh include:
• Andhra University (Vishakhapatnam)
• Central Institute of English and Foreign Languages (Hyderabad)
• Dr B.R. Ambedkar Open University (Hyderabad)
• Dravidian University (Chitoor)
• University of Hyderabad (Hyderabad)
• Jawaharlal Nehru Technological University (Hyderabad)
• Kakatiya University (Warangal)
• Maulana Azad National Urdu University (Hyderabad)
• Nagarjuna University (Guntur)
• Nizam's Institute of Medical Sciences (Hyderabad)
• N.T.R. University of Health Sciences (Vijayawada)

- Osmania University (Hyderabad)
- Potti Sreeramulu Telugu University (Hyderabad)
- Rashtriya Sanskrit Vidyapeetha (Tirupati)
- Sri Krishnadevaraya University (Anantapur)
- Sri Sathya Sai Institute of Higher Learning (Prasanthinilayam)
- Sri Padmavati Mahila Visvavidyalayam (Tirupati)
- Sri Vinkateswara Institute of Medical Sciences (Tirupati)

Tourism

Major tourist attractions:

1. Hyderabad: Charminar, Salarjung Museum, Hussein Sagar Lake, Durgam Ceruvu (Secret Lake), Shamirpet Lake, Qutb Shahi Tombs, Statue of Lord Buddha in Hussein Sagar Lake, Golconda Fort.

2. Tirupati: Lord Venkateswara Temple, Sri Agastheswara Swamy Temple, Govindarajaswami Temple, Goddess Alamelumanga Temple, Kodandarama Swamy Temple.

3. Vishakhapatnam: Simhachalam Temple, Rishikonda Beach, Dolphin's Nose.

4. Chittor: Horsley Hills, Chandragiri Fort, Lord Venkateswara Temple, Sri Venkateswara Sanctuary, Govindarajaswami Temple.

5. Cuddapah: Bhagavan Mahavir Government Museum, Chand Phira Gumbadh, Gandikota Fort.

6. Vijayawada: Prakasam Barrage, Kanakadurga Temple, St. Mary's Church, Moghalrajapuram caves, Hazrat Bal Mosque, Kondapalli Fort, Victoria Jubilee Museum.

Airports:
International:
- Hyderabad
Domestic:
- Rajahmundry

- Tirupati
- Vijaywada
- Vishakhapatnam
- Warangal
- Cuddapah
- Donakonda
- Nadrigul

National Parks

- Kasu Brahma Reddy National Park in Hyderabad district (1.42 sq. kms)

- Mahavir Harina Vanasthal National Park in Rangareddi district (14.59 sq. kms)

- Mrugavani National Park in Rangareddi district (3.6 sq. kms)

- Sri Venkateshwara National Park in Chittoor

- Cuddapah districts (353.62 sq. kms)

Administration

Legislature: Andhra Pradesh has a unicameral legislature with only the legislative assembly. The assembly has 295 seats including 39 seats reserved for SCs, 15 seats reserved for STs and one member who is nominated from the Anglo-Indian community.

The current party position is as follows:

Name of Party	Seats
Indian National Congress	185
Telugu Desam Party	47
Telangana Rashtra Samithi	26
Communist Party of India (Marxist)	9
Communist Party of India	6
All India Majlis-E-Ittehadul Muslimeen	4
Bharatiya Janata Party	2
Janata Party	2
Bahujan Samaj Party	1
Samajwadi Party	1
Independent	11
Nominated	1
Total	**295**

Judiciary: The seat of the Andhra Pradesh High Court is in Hyderabad. The present acting Chief Justice is Bilal Nazki.

Districts:

District	Area (sq. km)	Population	Headquarters	Urban Agglomerations
Adilabad	16128	2,479,347	Adilabad	Adilabad
Anantapur	19130	3,639,304	Anantapur	Anantapur
Chittoor	15151	3,735,202	Chittoor	Madanapalle, Tirupati
Cuddapah	15359	2,573,481	Cuddapah	Cuddapah
East Godavari	10807	4,872,622	Kakinada	Kakinada, Rajahmundry
Guntur	11391	4,405,521	Guntur	Narasaraopet
Hyderabad	217	3,686,460	Hyderabad	Hyderabad
Karimnagar	11823	3,477,079	Karimnagar	Ramagundam, Karimnagar
Khammam	16029	2,565,412	Khammam	Kothagudem, Khammam
Krishna	8727	4,218,416	Machilipatnam	Vijayawada
Kurnool	17658	3,512,266	Kurnool	Adoni, Kurnool, Nandyal
Mahbubnagar	18432	3,506,876	Mahbubnagar	Mahbubnagar, Gadwal
Medak	9700	2,662,296	Sangareddy	
Nalgonda	14240	3,238,449	Nalgonda	Miryalguda, Nalgonda, Suryapet
Nellore	13076	2,659,661	Nellore	Guduru, Kavali, Nellore
Nizamabad	7956	2,342,803	Nizamabad	
Prakasam	17626	3,054,941	Ongole	Chirala, Ongole
Rangareddi	7493	3,506,670	Hyderabad	Hyderabad
Srikakulam	5837	2,528,491	Srikakulam	Srikakulam
Visakhapatnam	11161	3,789,823	Visakhapatnam	Bheemunipatnam, Visakhapatnam
Vizianagaram	6539	2,245,103	Vizianagaram	Vizianagaram
Warangal	12847	3,231,174	Warangal	Warangal
West Godavari	7742	3,796,144	Eluru	Palacole, Tanuku, Eluru, Bheemavaram

Arunachal Pradesh

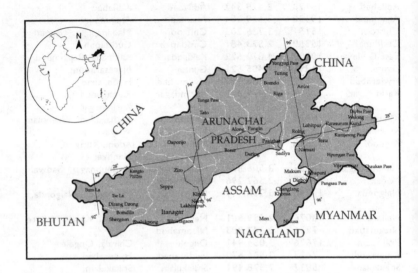

Key Statistics

Capital: Itanagar.
Area: 83,743 sq. km.
Population: Total: 1,097,968
Male: 579,941
Female: 518,027
Population density: 13 per sq. km.
Sex ratio: 893 females per 1000 males.
Principal languages: Nissi/Daffla, Nepali, Bengali.
Literacy rates: Total: 54.3%
Male: 63.8%
Female: 43.5%

Government

Governor: S.K. Singh. He was sworn in on 16 December 2004.

Chief Minister: Gegong Apang (INC). He was sworn in on 16 October 2004.

Geography

Physical characteristics: Arunachal Pradesh is a land of lush green forests, deep river valleys and plateaus. The land is mostly mountainous with the Himalayan ranges lying along the northern borders criss-crossed with north-south running ranges. These divide the state into five river valleys: the Kameng, the Subansiri, the Siang, the Lohit and the Tirap. A series of foothills lie in the southernmost part of the state, rising from the Assam plains to touch altitudes of 300 to 1000 metres. These hills rise northward to the Lesser Himalayas to reach heights of more than 3000 metres. The main ranges of the Great Himalayas lie further north along the Chinese border.

Neighbouring States and Union territories:
International borders:
• Bhutan
• China
• Myanmar

States:
• Assam
• Nagaland.

Major rivers:
• The Brahmaputra, known as the Siang in Arunchal Pradesh, and its tributaries which include the
• Lohit
• Subansiri
• Dibang
• Kameng
• Tirap
• Kamla
• Siyum
• Noa-Dihing
• Kamlang

Climate: The climate of Arunachal Pradesh varies from subtropical in the south to alpine in the north. Arunachal Pradesh receives heavy rainfall varying from 1000mm in the higher altitudes to 5750mm in the foothills. Average rainfall is more than 3500mm. It is spread over eight to nine months with the exception of a dry period in winter. The average temperature ranges from 15 to 21°C during winter and 22 to 30°C during monsoon. Between June and August the temperature sometimes rises to 40–42°C (in some regions).

Flora and Fauna:
Flora: Almost 60 per cent of the state is covered with evergreen forests. Arunachal Pradesh has seven types of forests. These are: tropical, subtropical, pine, temperate, alpine, bamboo and degraded forests. Besides these forests, there are grasslands in the riverine plains and higher altitudes.

The state is home to a variety of timber species, orchids, oaks, rhododendrons, medicinal plants, ferns, bamboos and canes.

Fauna: Arunachal Pradesh has a rich wildlife population. It is home to the mithun, elephant, tiger, leopard, snow leopard, clouded leopard, white browed gibbon, red panthers, musk deer, gaur and wild buffalo. The species of primates found in the state include slow loris, hoolock gibbon, rhesus macaque, pigtailed macaque, Assamese macaque, stump-tailed macaque, and capped langur. Three species of goat-antelopes, serow, goral and takin, are found in the state. Significant species of birds found in the state are hornbill, Sclater's monal, white winged duck, Bengal florican, Temminck's tragopan and green pigeon.

History

The history of Arunachal Pradesh is rich in myths and traditions. The recorded history of this state is available only from the sixteenth century onwards. It was at this point of time that the Ahom kings began to rule Assam. The modern history of the state begins with the imposition of British rule in Assam following the Treaty of Yandaboo (1826). Between 1947 and 1962, it was a part of the North East Frontier Agency that was constitutionally a part of Assam. Because of its strategic importance, the ministry of external affairs administered Arunachal Pradesh till 1965, with the governor of Assam acting as an agent to the President of India. The administrative head was the advisor to the governor. Later, in August 1965, the ministry of home affairs gained administrative control. In 1972, it became a Union territory under the name of Arunachal Pradesh. In 1975, it got its own legislature. Arunachal Pradesh attained full-fledged statehood on 20 February 1987. At that time, Gegong Apang was its Chief Minister.

Politics

Though the history of the growth of the political process in Arunachal Pradesh dates back to 1875 when the British-India Government started to define the administrative jurisdiction by drawing an Inner Line in relation to the frontier tribes inhabiting the North Frontier Tract, the area was kept outside the purview of regular laws of the country. Thereafter, the British followed the policy of gradual penetration to bring more areas under normal administration. By the year 1946, the North East Frontier Tracts were reorganized into four Frontier Tracts namely Sadiya, Lakhimpur, Tirap and Sela Sub Agency and Subansiri area and administrated by the Governor of Assam in his discretion. By virtue of the Indian Independence Act 1947, the Government of Assam assumed administrative jurisdiction over North East Frontier Tracts and the Governor of Assam was divested of his discretionary powers. The Government of Assam administered the North East Frontier Tracts during the period 15 August 1947 to 26 January 1950.

After Independence, a sub-committee headed by Gopinath Bordoloi was appointed by the Constituent Assembly of India to recommend the future pattern of administration of the North Eastern Frontier Areas. The Bordoloi Committee recommended that since the administration had been satisfactorily established over a sufficiently wide area, the Government of Assam should take over that area by the strength of

a notification. However, for various considerations, particularly problems of communication and defiance, the Government of India decided to administer North East Frontier Tracts as an 'Excluded Area' through the Governor of Assam as an agent to the President of India. In the year 1950, the plain portions of these tracts namely, Balipara Frontier Tract, Tirap Frontier Tract, Abor Hill District and Mishimi Hills Districts were transferred to the Government of Assam. In 1951, the units of the tracts were reconstituted again and Tuensang Frontier Division was created which later merged with Nagaland. The remaining portion of the Tracts after the introduction of the North East Frontier (Administration) Regulation 1954 was designated as the North East Frontier Agency, the NEFA. Thereafter, the administration was brought under the Ministry of External Affairs and in August 1965, it was brought under the supervision and control of the Ministry of Home Affairs. It remained so till the attainment of Union Territory status by Arunachal Pradesh in 1972.

It was only in 1975 that by virtue of the enactment of 37th Constitutional Amendment Act, the Pradesh Council was constituted as a separate Legislative Assembly and a Lt. Governor was appointed as the head of the Union Territory of Arunachal Pradesh. The Pradesh Council became a provisional Legislative Assembly having 23 members during 1975 to 1978. On 13 August 1975 Prem Khandu Thungon became the first Prime Minister and he remained in power till 18 September 1979. Tomo Riba who remained in power till 3 November 1979 succeeded him. The first elected Legislative Assembly consisting of 33 members (30 elected members and 3 nominated members) was formed on 4 March 1978, which lasted only for about 20 months. In November 1979, the Assembly was dissolved and President's Rule was imposed which continued till January 1980.

On 18 January 1980 Gegong Apang became the Chief Minister. He was the Chief Minister for a record 19 years since 1980. The second general election was held in January 1980. The third general election for the Legislative Assembly was held simultaneously with the general election for the eighth Lok Sabha in December 1984 and the Assembly was constituted in January 1986. The Union Territory of Arunachal Pradesh became a full-fledged state with effect from 20 February 1987. On the persistent demand of the people of the state, the total membership in the Legislative Assembly was raised to 60 during the general election in 1990 and thus, the first legislative assembly of the state of Arunachal Pradesh was constituted. The fourth election to the Assembly was held in March 1995; that was the second legislative assembly of Arunachal Pradesh. The second legislative assembly was dissolved by the Governor on 27 July 1999, ahead of schedule of March 2000. The third legislative assembly headed by Mukut Mithi was constituted in October 1999. From 3 August 2003, the Government is again led by Shri Gegong Apang.

Culture

The various tribes of Arunachal Pradesh have their own dance forms. Some of the more popular folk dances include Roppi (Nishing Tribe), Aji Lamu (Monpa), Hiirii Khaniing (Apatani), Chalo (Nocte), Lion and Peacock dance (Monpa), Ponung (Adi), Popir (Adi), Pasi Kongki (Adi) and Rekham Pada (Nishing). Most of the dance forms of the state are group dances performed by both men and women. However there are some dance forms, such as the war dances of the Adis, Noctes and Wanchos, Igu dance of the Mishmi priests and ritualistic dance of the Buddhist tribes, that are exclusive male dances. The state has a notable tradition of bamboo and cane handicrafts, as well as pottery, carpet weaving and woodcarving. Handloom is a significant aspect of the state's culture and tradition.

Fairs and festivals: Important festivals of the state include Lossar, Si-Donyi, Mopin, Solung, Nyokum, Dree, Sipong Yong, Reh, Boori-boot, Kshyatsowai, Tamladu, Sarok, Chalo-loku, Nichido, Sangken, Mopin and Oriah. Parashuram Kund Mela (Parashuram Kund) and Malinithan Mela (Likabali) are two notable fairs of the state.

Economy, Industry and Agriculture

Economy: The net state domestic product at current prices for 2002–03 (provisional) was Rs 1747 crores. The per capita net state domestic product at current prices for 2002–03 (provisional) was Rs 15,616.

Minerals and industry: Notable among the industries of the state are timber-based industries, tourism, tea-based industries, coal mines and fruit processing plants.

Coal reserves at the Namchik–Namphuk coalfield are estimated at 90 million tonnes. Petroleum crude reserves are estimated at 1.5 million tonnes. Besides these, there are reported deposits of iron, copper, limestone, graphite, dolomite, quartzite, kyanite and mica.

Agriculture: The major crops grown in the state are rice, maize, millet, wheat, pulses and sugarcane. There are rubber, coffee and tea plantations. The state also grows banana, ginger, chillies, turmeric, pineapple, plum, orange, apple, walnut, guava, grapes and potato.

Power: Most of the state's power requirements are met by hydroelectric power plants. As a matter of fact, the hydel power potential of Arunachal Pradesh is estimated at 30,000 MW. There are a large number of mini and micro hydel power plants in the state. A certain amount of the state's power needs are met by diesel power plants.

Education

Educational institutes:
• Arunachal University (Itanagar)
• North Eastern Regional Institute of Science and Technology (Itanagar).

Tourism

Major tourist attractions: Tawang Monastery, Bhismaknagar, Malinithan, Parashuram Kund, Tipi Orchid Research Centre, Akashiganga, Gekar Sinyi (Ganaga lake), Talley Valley, Dr D. Ering Wildlife Sanctuary, Bomdila.

Airports:
• Along
• Daporijo
• Pasighat
• Teju
• Ziro.

National Parks:
• Mouling National Park in Upper Siang district (483 sq. km)
• Namdapha National Park in Changlang district (1985.23 sq. km)

Administration

Legislature: The state has a 60-seat legislative assembly, out of which 59 are reserved for STs. Elections were held in October 2004. The current party position is:

Name of Party	Seats
Indian National Congress	34
Bharatiya Janata Party	9
Nationalist Congress Party	2
Arunanchal Congress	2
Independent	13
Total	**60**

Judiciary: Arunachal Pradesh is under the jurisdiction of the Itanagar Bench of the Gauhati High Court at Guwahati, Assam. Binod Kumar Roy is the current chief justice.

Districts:

District	Area (sq. km)	Population	Headquarters	Urban Agglomerations
Changlang	4,662	124,994	Changlang	–
Dibang Valley	1,302	57,543	Anini	–
East Kameng	4,134	57,065	Seppa	–
East Siang	3,895	87,430	Pasighat	–
Kurung Kumey	NA	NA	Laying-Yangte	–
Lohit	11,402	143,478	Teju	–
Lower Subansiri	9,548	97,614	Ziro	–
Papum Pare	3,462	121,750	Yupia	–
Tawang	2,172	34,705	Tawang	–
Tirap	2,362	100,227	Khonsa	–
Upper Siang	6,590	33,146	Yingkiong	–
Upper Subansiri	7,032	54,995	Daporijo	–
West Kameng	7,422	74,595	Bomdila	–
West Siang	8,033	103,575	Along	–

Assam

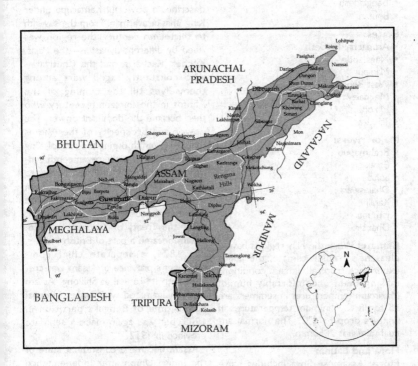

Key Statistics

Capital: Dispur.
Area: 78,438 sq. km.
Population: Total: 26,655,528
Male 13,777,037
Female: 12,878,491
Population density: 340 per sq. km.
Sex ratio: 935 females per 1000 males.
Principal languages: Assamese, Bengali,
Bodo/Boro.
Literacy rates: Total: 63.3%
Male: 71.3%
Female: 54.6%.

Government

Governor: Lt Gen. (Retd) Ajai Singh.
He was sworn in on 5 June 2003.

Chief Minister: Tarun Gogoi. He was
sworn in on 18 May 2001.

Geography

Physical characteristics: Assam can
be broadly divided into three geographical units: the alluvial Brahmaputra Valley
covering large parts of the state in the
north, the Barak Valley in the southern

part of the state, and the hilly region that separates the two valleys.

Neighbouring States and Union territories:
International borders:
• Bangladesh
• Bhutan

States:
• Arunachal Pradesh
• Nagaland
• Manipur
• West Bengal
• Meghalaya
• Mizoram
• Tripura

Major rivers:
• Brahmaputra
• Barak
• Sonai
• Dhaleswari
• Kapili
• Jamuna
• Dhansiri

Climate: While the hilly regions have a pleasant subalpine climate, the plains experience tropical climatic conditions making them uncomfortably humid. Maximum temperatures in summers are 35 to 38°C. Minimum temperatures in winters drop to 6°C. The normal annual rainfall is 2850mm.

Flora and Fauna:
Flora: Assamese flora includes bamboo, lac and valuable timber trees like sal and teak. The state's forests have about 74 species of trees, of which two-thirds are commercially exploited.

Fauna: Wildlife found in Assam includes one-horned rhinoceros, elephant, wild buffalo, wild boar, swamp deer, sambar, hog deer, sloth bear, tiger, leopard, leopard cat, jungle cat, hog badger, capped langur, hispid hare, pigmy hog and golden langur, hoolock gibbon, jackal, goose, hornbill, ibis, pelican, duck, cormorants, egret, river chats (white capped redstars), forktail, heron, fishing eagle, etc.

History

In ancient times, Assam was a part of the kingdom of Kamarupa that had its capital at Pragjyotishpura. Chinese traveller Hiuen-Tsang's account of AD 640 describes a powerful Kamarupa under King Bhaskaravarman. From the seventh to thirteenth century, the region was ruled by different dynasties—the Palas, Koches, Kacharis, and the Chutiyas—who constantly raged wars among themselves till the coming of the Ahoms in the thirteenth century who then became the dominant power. The power and prosperity of the Ahoms reached a zenith during the rule of King Rudra Singh in the late seventeenth century. It then went into a decline due to internal uprisings and invasions from Myanmar. The British drove out the Myanmar invaders and restored order. After the Treaty of Yandabo in 1826, Assam became a part of British India.

In 1874, a separate chief commissioner's province of Assam was created with its capital at Shillong. Assam was amalgamated with eastern Bengal at the time of Bengal's partition in 1905, but was again made a separate province in 1912.

Assam became a constituent state of the Indian Union after Independence and has had many states carved out of it since: Nagaland in 1963, Meghalaya and Mizoram in 1971, and Arunachal Pradesh in 1972. Assam's first Chief Minister was Gopinath Bardoloi.

Politics

The Legislature of Assam remained bicameral from 1937 to 1946. Under the India (Provincial Legislatures) Order, 1947, the Legislative Council was abolished on 14 August 1947. The Assam Legislature has been unicameral since then. In the years that followed, Assam was truncated to several smaller states.

With the changing geographical boundaries together with the shifts in the population graph of Assam, the strength of members of the Assam Legislative Assembly has fluctuated over the years. In 1952-57 it was 108, reaching still lower to 105 in 1957-62 (the Second Assembly) and then to 114 in 1967-72 (the Third Assembly) until it reached a strength of 126 members in 1972-78 (the Fifth Assembly). The present strength of the Assembly is 126. The present House, the Eleventh Assam Legislative Assembly, commenced its First Session on 30 May 2001.

The Congress(I) has ruled the state for the longest period since 1952. It lost to the Asom Gana Parishad in the 1985 Assembly elections held immediately after the Assam Accord was signed in the wake of a violent anti-foreigner agitation, which lasted from 1979 to 1985. However, the Congress(I) returned to power in 1991 and ruled the state until 1996. Gopinath Bardoloi from the Congress was the first Chief Minister of Assam who remained in office from 15 August 1947 to 6 August 1950. He was succeeded by Bishnuram Medhi of the Congress who remained in power till 1957. From 1957 to 1970 Bimali Prasad Chaliha was the Chief Minister. From 1970 to 1972 Mahendra Mohan Choudhury was the Chief Minister. He was succeeded by Sarat Chandra Sinha of the Congress who remained in power till 12 March 1978. Golap Borbora followed him as Chief Minister. In 1979 Jogendra Nath Hazarika became the Chief Minister and remained in office for three months. He was succeeded by Anwara Taimur who remained in office till 29 June 1981. From 13 January 1982 to 19 March 1982 Keshav Chandra Gogoi was the Chief Minister.

Following Indian independence in 1947, the Assamese won control of their state assembly and launched a campaign to reassert the preeminence of Assamese culture in the region and improve employment opportunities for native Assamese. This led to the alienation of some tribal districts. In addition, many in the tribal districts were demanding independence from India. Thinking it would satisfy the tribals, the Indian Government parititioned former Assamese territories into the tribal states of Nagaland, Mizoram, Meghalaya, Manipur and Arunachal Pradesh over the next twenty years. This was seen by Assamese leaders as a deliberate division of their constituency. Following the Pakistan civil war in 1971, nearly two million Bengali Muslim refugees migrated to Assam. Their illegal settlement and their electoral support for Indira Gandhi's Congress government further aggravated Assamese fears of Bengali cultural domination and central government ambitions to undermine Assamese regional autonomy. In the late 1970s and early 1980s, there were persistent disputes between the government and Assamese students and some Assamese political factions over the rights of illegal immigrants to citizenship and suffrage. The state government and the Government of India responded by the use of force to suppress the movement. Many demonstrators were killed. This led to some of India's worst communal violence since Partition towards the end of the movement.

The central government's effort to hold a constitutionally mandated election to the state assembly in 1983 led to its near total boycott, a complete breakdown of order, and the worst killings since 1947. Nearly 3000 people died in communal violence. The election proved to be a complete failure with less than 2 percent of the voters casting their votes in the constituencies with Assamese majority. The Congress formed the government and on 27 February 1983 Hiteshwar Saikia became the Chief Minister of the state.

In 1985, a treaty was signed by the Assamese and the Government of India. According to it all those foreigners who had entered Assam between 1951 and 1961 were to be given full citizenship, including the right to vote; those who had done that after 1971 were to be deported; the entrants between 1961 and 1971 were to be denied voting rights for ten years but would enjoy all other rights of citizenship. This was followed by an election. A new party, Asom Gana Parishad, formed by the leaders of anti-foreigners movement, was elected to power, winning 64 of the 126 assembly seats. Prafulla Mahanta became at the age of thirty-two the youngest Chief Minister of independent India. There was a lot of expectation among the people. The victory of the AGP did not end the controversy over Assamese nationalism. The AGP was unable to implement the accord's provisions for disenfranchising and expelling illegal aliens, in part because Parliament passed legislation making it more difficult to prove illegal alien status. The AGP's failure to implement the accord along with the general ineffectiveness with which it operated the state government undercut its popular support, and in November 1990 it was dismissed and President's Rule declared.

As the AGP floundered, other nationalist groups of agitators flourished. The United Liberation Front of Assam (ULFA) became the primary torchbearer of militant Assamese nationalism while the All Bodo Students' Union (ABSU) and Bodo People's Action Committee (BPAC) led an agitation for a separate homeland for the central plain tribal people of Assam (often called Bodos). By 1990 ULFA militants ran virtually a parallel government in the state, extorting huge sums from businesses in Assam, especially the Assamese tea industry. The ULFA was ultimately subdued through a combination of military repression and generous terms of surrender for many of its leaders. The Government of India has classified it a terrorist organization and had banned it under the Unlawful Activities (Prevention) Act in 1990. On the other hand the ABSU/BPAC-led mass agitation lasted from March 1987 until February 1993 when the ABSU signed an accord with the state government that had been under the Congress (I) control since 1991. The accord provided for the creation of a Bodoland Autonomous Council with jurisdiction over an area of 5,186 square kilometers and 2.1 million people within Assam. Nevertheless, Bodo agitation continued in the mid-1990s as a result of the demands of many Bodo leaders, who insisted that more territory be included under the Bodoland Autonomous Council.

On 30 June 1991 Hiteshwar Saikia of the Congress party became the Chief Minister for the second time and remained in power till 22 April 1996. From 22 April 1996 to 15 May 1996 Bhumidar Barman of the Congress Party was the Chief Minister of the Assam state. He was succeeded by Prafulla Kumar Mahanta on May 1996. He remained in power till 18 May 2001. In the 2001 elections the Congress(I) came back to power in Assam after five years. It defeated the four-party alliance led by Asom Gana Parishad, the party that was in power, in the 10 May Assembly elections, winning 71 of the 125 seats. The alliance, which included the AGP, the BJP, the All Bodo Students Union (ABSU) and the Autonomous State Demand Committee (United) secured 39 seats, Tarun Gogoi being sworn in the 15th Chief Minister of Assam by Governor Lt. Gen. (Retd) S.K. Sinha. Despite large-scale violence by ULFA and the National Democratic Front of Bodoland (NDFB), more than 70 per cent of the electorate exercised its franchise in largely peaceful polling. About fifty people had lost their lives in the run-up to the elections, when militants selectively attacked candidates and campaigners of almost all political parties.

Culture

Assam has a large number of tribal groups who exhibit great cultural variety. Among them are the Boro-Kacharis, Deoris, Misings, Dimassas, Karbis, Lalungs and Rabhas. The three Bihus or agricultural festivals—Rongali Bihu, Bhogali Bihu and Kongali Bihu—are an important aspect of Assamese culture. Apart from Bihu, popular dance forms include Ojapali, Satriya, Ghosa Dhemali, Ras Nritya and Bagrumba.

Handloom weaving of fine silk and cotton cloths is a popular activity. Other ethnic products include cane and bamboo articles, brass and bell metal products, pottery, woodcraft, masks, jewellery and terracotta articles.

Fairs and festivals: Important festivals and fairs are the three Bihus, Durga Puja, Bathow Puja, Kherai Puja, Ali-ai-ligang, Po-rag, Baishagu, Bohaggiyo Bishu, Jonbeel Mela and Ambubasi Mela.

Economy, Industry and Agriculture

Economy: Net state domestic product at current prices for for 2002–03 (pro-visional) was Rs 31,721 crores. The per capita net state domestic product at current prices for 2002–03 (provisional) was Rs 11.755.

Minerals and industry: Industrial scenario in Assam is dominated by two major industries: tea and oil and natural gas. Other industries include jute, silk, fertilizers, petrochemicals, paper, matchsticks, cement, iron pipes, asbestos sheets and pipes, pan masala, cosmetics, plastics processing and moulded articles, polyester yarn, acrylic yarn, sugar, plywood, handloom and handicrafts.

The mineral wealth of Assam includes coal, petroleum, limestone, granite, sillimanite, iron ore, quartzite, feldspar and clay.

Agriculture: Rice, maize, wheat, jute, cotton, sugar cane and pulses are the major crops. Important plantation crops are tea, rubber and coffee. Major horticultural crops are banana, pineapple, orange, potato, sweet potato, papaya, cabbage, onion, tapioca, arecanut, coconut, ginger, jackfruit, guava and mango.

Power: Assam has great potential for development of power sector based on hydel, oil, natural gas and coal resources. At present the Assam State Electricity Board has a total installed capacity of 574 MW.

Education

Prominent educational institutions are
• Gauhati University, Guwahati
• Dibrugarh University, Diburgarh
• Tezpur University, Tezpur;
• Assam University, Silchar
• Assam Agriculture University, Jorhat
• Indian Institute of Technology, Guwahati
• National Institute of Technology, Silchar

Tourism

Major tourist attractions:

1. Kamrup: Guwahati (Kamakhya and Bhubaneswari Temples, Basishthashram, Navagraha Temple, Gandhimandap); Hajo (Hayagriva-Madhab Temple, Poa Macca); Chandubi; Sualkuchi; Madan Kamdev.

2. Darrang: Bhairabkunda.

3. Morigaon: Pobitora Wildlife Sanctuary.

4. Nagaon: Nagaon; Batadrawa; Laokhowa Wildlife Sanctuary.

5. North Lakhimpur: Pobha Wildlife Sanctuary; Garampani.

6. Golaghat: Kaziranga National Park.

7. Tinsukia: Dibru Saikhowa National Park; Digboi (National Oil Park, War Cemetery).

8. Sonitpur: Orang Wildlife Sanctuary; Nameri National Park; Bhalukpun; Tezpur (Bamuni Hill, Hazara Tank, Chitralekha Udyan, Cole Park, Agnigarh, Da-Parbatiya, Maha Bhairav Temple).

9. Barpeta: Barpeta Satra and Kirtan Ghar; Manas National Park.

10. Sibsagar: Sibsagar (Shivadol, Vishnudol and Devidol Temples, Kareng Ghar and Talatal Ghar, Gorgaon Palace, Rang Ghar, Joysagar Tank and Temples, Charaideo).

11. NC Hills: Haflong; Jatinga; Maibong; Umrangshu.

12. Jorhat: Majuli, the world's largest riverine island.

Airports:
• Guwahati
• Tezpur
• Jorhat
• Dibrugarh
• Silchar
• North Lakhimpur.

National Parks:
• Kaziranga National Park in Golaghat, Nagaon districts (471.71 sq. km)
• Manas National Park in Barpeta, Bongaigaon districts (500 sq. km)
• Nameri National Park in Sonitpur District (200 sq. km)
• Dibru Saikhowa Naional Park in Tinsukia, Dibrugarh districts (340 sq. km)
• Orang National Park in Darrang, Sonitpur districts (78.808 sq. km).

Administration

Legislature: The Assam state legislative assembly has 126 members elected from as many constituencies. Of the 126 seats, eight are reserved for scheduled castes and 16 for scheduled tribes. The term of the current assembly ends on 29 May 2006. The present party position is as follows:

Name of Party	Seats
Indian National Congress	71
Asom Gana Parishad	20
Bharatiya Janata Party	8
Nationalist Congress Party	3
Autonomous State Demand Committee (United)	2
All India Trinamool Congress	1
Samata Party	1
Samajwadi Party	1
Independents	19
Total	**126**

Judiciary: The Gauhati High Court, Guwahati, is the high court of Assam, Nagaland, Meghalaya, Manipur, Tripura, Mizoram, and Arunachal Pradesh. The present chief justice is Binod Kumar Roy.

Districts:

District	Area (sq. km)	Population	Headquarters	Urban Agglomerations
Barpeta	3245	1,642,420	Barpeta	
Bongaigaon	2510	906,315	Bongaigaon	Bongaigaon
Cachar	3786	1,442,141	Silchar	Silchar
Darrang	3481	1,503,943	Mangaldoi	
Dhemaji	3237	569,468	Dhemaji	
Dhubri	2798	1,634,589	Dhubri	
Dibrugarh	3381	1,172,056	Dibrugarh	Dibrugarh
Goalpara	1824	822,306	Goalpara	
Golaghat	3502	945,781	Golaghat	
Hailakandi	1327	542,978	Hailakandi	
Jorhat	2851	1,009,197	Jorhat	Jorhat
Kamrup	4345	2,515,030	Guwahati	Guwahati
Karbi Anglong	10434	812,320	Diphu	
Karimganj	1809	1,003,678	Karimganj	
Kokrajhar	3169	930,404	Kokrajhar	
Lakhimpur	2277	889,325	North Lakhimpur	
Marigaon	1704	775,874	Marigaon	
Nagaon	3831	2,315,387	Nagaon	Lumding, Nagaon
Nalbari	2257	1,138,184	Nalbari	
North Cachar Hills	4888	186,189	Haflong	
Sibsagar	2668	1,052,802	Sibsagar	
Sonitpur	5324	1,677,874	Tezpur	Tezpur
Tinsukia	3790	1,150,146	Tinsukia	Digboi, Tinsukia

Bihar

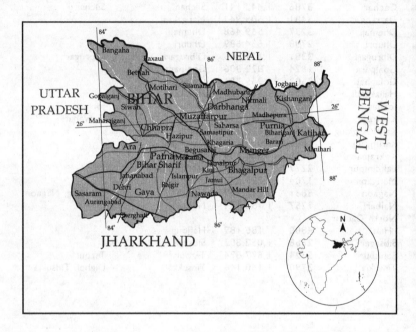

Key Statistics

Capital: Patna.
Area: 94,163 sq. km.
Population: Total: 82,998,509
Male: 43,243,795
Female: 39,754,714.
Population density: 880 per sq. km.
Sex ratio: 919 females per 1000 males.
Principal languages: Hindi, Urdu, Santhali.
Literacy rates: Total: 47%
Male: 59.7%
Female: 33.1%.

Government

Governor: Buta Singh. He was sworn in on 3 November 2004.

Chief Minister: None. The state is under President's Rule.

Geography

Physical characteristics: Located in the eastern part of the country, Bihar is a landlocked state. The outlet to the sea is through the port of Kolkata. The river Ganga flows through the middle of the Bihar plain from west to east and divides it into two halves.

Bihar lies midway between the humid West Bengal in the east and the sub-humid Uttar Pradesh in the west, which gives it a transitional position in terms of climate.

The north Gangetic Plain consist of a flat alluvial region, and are prone to floods. The Kosi river, due to its tendency to cause dangerous floods, was previously referred to as the 'Sorrow of Bihar', before the construction of artificial embankments.

The soil in the Bihar plain is composed mainly of new alluvium, which is mostly non-chalky and heavy-textured (clay and clay loam) towards the east, and chalky and light-textured (mostly sandy loam) towards the west of the Old Burhi Gandak river.

Apart from floods, another hazard is that this region lies in the Himalayan earthquake zone. The earthquakes of 1934 and 1988 caused widespread damage here.

In the south, the Gangetic Plain is more diversified than in the north. Many hills rise from the level alluvium that constitutes the Gangetic Plain. Except for Son, all the rivers are small, and their water is diverted into irrigation channels. The soil of the land is usually made up of older alluvium.

The Kaimur Plateau lies in the extreme northwest. It consists of nearly horizontal sandstone strata that are underlain by limestone. The soil of the plateau is typically red, and is sandy in the Damodar valley.

Neighbouring States and Union territories:
International border:
Nepal

States:
- West Bengal
- Uttar Pradesh
- Jharkhand

Major rivers:
- Ganga
- Kamla-Balan
- Mahananda
- Saryu (Ghaghra)

- Gandak
- Budhi Gandak
- Bagmati

Climate: Bihar's climate is in keeping with the Indian subcontinent's climatic pattern. Due to its great distance from the sea, Bihar enjoys a continental monsoon type of climate.

There are many factors that affect its climate. For one, the Himalayan mountains in the north affect the distribution of monsoon rainfall in Bihar. It records an average annual rainfall of about 1200mm.

Also, Bihar extends from 22° to 27°N latitude, i.e. in the tropical to subtropical region.

The cold weather season in Bihar lasts from December to February. Summer lasts from March to May. The southwest monsoon lasts from June to September, and the retreating southwest monsoon from October to November.

Flora and Fauna:
Flora: Deciduous forests in the state can be found in the sub-Himalayan foothills of Someshwar and the Dun ranges in Champaran. These forests are also largely made of grass, reeds and scrub. Other important trees include Semal, Khair, shisham, *Cedrela Toona*, and *Shorea robusta* (sal). These places register a rainfall of above 1600 mm, which is responsible for the presence of sal forests in certain areas.

Fauna: Many wildlife sanctuaries and reserves can be found in Bihar. Sambar, gaur, nilgai, munjtac, elephants, tigers and the Indian wolf are some of the animals that can be seen in the sanctuaries. The birds, fish and reptiles consist of species common throughout peninsular India.

History

The history of Bihar dates back to the dawn of human civilization. The earliest myths and legends of Hinduism are associated with Bihar, including the Sanatana (eternal) Dharma. Sita, the consort of Lord Rama, is believed to have been a princess from Bihar.

In the 3rd century BC, the state was part of Ashoka's kingdom.

During the British rule in India, Bihar was a part of the Bengal Presidency and governed from Calcutta, and was separated from it in 1912. Together with Orissa, Bihar formed a single province, until the Government of India Act of 1935, which made Orissa into a separate province, and led to the formation of the province of Bihar as an individual administrative unit of British India.

At the time of independence in 1947, Bihar was constituted with the same geographic boundary into the Republic of India. In 1956, during the linguistic reorganization of Indian states, the south-east area of Bihar known as Purulia was separated from the state, and was added to the territory of West Bengal. Sri Krishna Sinha became the first Chief Minister of Bihar.

In the year 2000, Bihar was bifurcated and the state of Jharkhand was carved out.

Politics

At the time of Independence in 1947, Bihar was constituted with the same geographic boundary into the Republic of India. In 1956, during the linguistic reorganization of Indian states, the south-east area of Bihar known as Purulia was separated from the state, and was aded to the territory of West Bengal.

Bihar Legislative Assembly came into existence in 1937. The Assembly had a strength of 152 members. According to the provisions of the Constitution of India, the first general elections in the state were held in 1952. The total strength of membership in the Assembly was 331, including one nominated member. It was reduced to 318 during the second general elections. In 1977, the total number of elected members of the Bihar Legislative Assembly was further raised from 318 to 324. With the creation of a separate state of Jharkhand, by an Act of Parliament titled the Bihar Reorganisation Act, 2000, the strength of the Bihar Legislative Assembly was reduced from 325 to 243 members.

The students' agitation, which began in 1974, is popularly known as the Jayprakash Narayan or JP movement. Today's Bihar is dominated by leaders who were once the chief actors in the JP movement—Lalu Prasad Yadav of the Rashtriya Janata Dal (RJD), Sushil Modi of the Bharatiya Janata Party (BJP), Ram Jatan Sinha of the Congress and Nitish Kumar of the Janata Dal (United). The JP movement's ideological thrust had been to fashion a new Bihar, free from corruption and casteism. The well-meaning movement catalysed some revolutionary social changes, such as inter-caste marriages and the breaking of the sacred thread worn by upper-caste Hindus. JP wanted a 'total revolution', not political change alone but also transformations in the social and cultural attitudes of the people. But it should be admitted that even today the caste factor is the most potent social and political force in the state. Elections are contested with formulations of caste-based alliances. Bihar has never been free of caste in politics. Even during the freedom movement, Bhumihars dominated politics; there were intense rivalries in Congress politics between Bhumihars and Rajputs, on the one hand, and Brahmins on the other. Even the state's greatest politicians couldn't rid themselves of narrow casteism. Veteran

Congress leader Srikrishna Sinha, the first Chief Minister of Bihar, credited with the abolition of the zamindari system, was accused by Jayprakash Narayan of promoting people from the Bhumihar caste and, thus, creating bottlenecks in the progressive evolution of politics and society.

Bihar had a Congress government from 1937. Srikrishna Sinha was the Chief Minister from 15 August 1947 to 31 January 1961. Deep Narayan Singh succeeded him on 1 February and remained in the post only for 17 days. From 18 February 1961 to 1 October 1963 Binodanand Jha of the Congress was the Chief Minister. Krishna Ballabh Sahay of the Congress Party succeeded him and remained in the post till 5 March 1967. Unexpectedly, the Congress party could not win a majority of seats in 1967 elections. A coalition government came to power under the leadership of Mahamaya Prasad Sinha of the Bharatiya Kranti Dal. On 28 January 1968 Satish Prasad Sinha of the Shoshit Dal succeeded him. On 1 February 1968 Bindeyyeshwari Prasad Mandal of the Shoshit Dal became the Chief Minister and remained in power till 23 February 1968. Bhola Paswan Shastri succeeded him and became the Chief Minister for the first time. President's Rule was imposed for the first time in the state on 29 June 1968 when Bhola Paswan Shastri, succumbing to pulls and pressures from various constituents of his Sanyukta Vidhayak Dal (SVD) resigned and asked the Governor to recommend Central rule, which lasted till 26 February 1969. Harihar Prasad Singh was the Chief Minister from 29 February 1969 to 22 June 1969. Again Bhola Paswan Shastri came to power. President's Rule was imposed again on 4 July 1969 and 9 January 1972, both times when Bhola Paswan Shastri was the Chief Minister, as he could not manage his squabbling coalition partners. Daroga Prasad Rai was the Chief Minister from 17 February 1970 to 22 December 1970. Karpoori Thakur succeeded him and remained in power till 2 June 1971. Kedar Pandey of the Congress was the Chief Minister from 19 March 1972 to 2 July 1973. Abdul Ghafoor of the Congress succeeded him and remained in power till 11 April 1975. Jagannath Mishra succeeded him. Bihar was brought under Central rule for the fourth time on 30 April 1977 when Jagannath Mishra's Congress Government was dismissed after Morarji Desai became Prime Minister. It lasted till 24 June 1977. From 24 June 1977 to 21 April 1979 Karpoori Thakur again was the Chief Minister. Ram Sundar Das succeeded him and remained in the post till 17 February 1980. With the failure of the Janata experiment and return of Indira Gandhi, she dismissed the Ram Sunder Das Ministry of Janata Party and President's Rule was imposed for the fifth time on 17 February 1980, which continued till 8 June 1980. After the end of the Central rule Jagannath Mishra became the Chief Minister for the second time and remained in the position till 14 August 1983.

Chandra Shekhar Singh of the Congress succeeded him and remained in the post till 25 March 1985. Bindeshwari Dubey of the Congress was the next Chief Minister; he remained in the position till 14 February 1988. From 14 February 1988 to 11 March 1989 Bhagwat Jha Azad was the Chief Minister. Satyendra Narain Sinha, the next Chief Minister remained in power till 6 December 1989. Jagannath Mishra became the Chief Minister for the third time on 6 December 1989 and remained in power till 10 March 1990.

Laloo Prasad Yadav became the Chief Minister for the first time in 1990 and remained in power till the 1995 elections. The state again came under a brief spell of President's Rule for six days for technical reasons, as the House could not be constituted till 15 March1995 due to non-completion of the election process. The then Chief Election Commissioner T.N. Seshan, who had frequently postponed the polls on account of lack of security arrangements, fixed 19 March for the last phase of polling though the term of the Assembly was to expire on 15 March. Chief Minister Laloo Prasad Yadav was allowed to function in caretaker capacity after his resignation on 15 March and Central rule was imposed on 28 March. Shortly after winning the 1995 election, Laloo Prasad Yadav came under pressure from senior leaders in the Janata Dal and its alliance partners to resign as Chief Minister following his alleged involvement in the fodder scam. He was charge-sheeted by the Central Bureau of Investigation (CBI), but he remained in power until July 1997 when he floated the Rastriya Janata Dal, resigned as Chief Minister and appointed Rabri Devi his successor.

Rabri Devi had three tenures as Chief Minister. Her first term lasted for a little over 18 months from 25 July 1997 to 12 February 1999 and the second term lasted just about 12 months from 9 March1999 to 3 March 2000. Rabri Devi became the 30th Chief Minister of Bihar, on 11 March 2000. This was her third term as Chief Minister of Bihar. In between her second and third tenures Nitish Kumar was the Chief Minister from 3 March 2000 to 10 March 2000. Central rule was imposed for the seventh time on 12 February 1999 by the Bharatiya Janata Party (BJP)-led National Democratic Alliance (NDA) Government following the massacre of 22 people at Shankerbigha village on 25 January and killing of eleven dalits at Narainpur in naxalite-hit Jehanabad district on 10 February, which continued till 9 March 1999. However, the Congress came to the rescue of the Rashtriya Janata Dal (RJD) government led by Rabri Devi and declared to vote against the Government resolution in the Rajya Sabha, where it had the majority and the resolution was withdrawn and President's Rule revoked on 9 March 1999 after 25 days.

After the 2005 state Assembly Election it is for the 8th time that Bihar has been brought under President's Rule on 8 March 2005 as the numbers did not add up for any combination with the electorate giving a fractured verdict for the 243-member state Assembly.

Culture

Writers from Bihar like Shiva Pujan Sahay, Ram Briksha Benipuri, Raja Radhika Raman Singh, Ramdhari Slngh Dinakar, and Divakar Prasad Vidyarthy contributed greatly to Hindi literature and culture, which flourished around the mid-19th century, with Bhartendu Babu Harischandra's drama 'Harischandra'. 'Indumati' by Pundit Kishorilal Goswami was published in 1900, and is considered to be one of the very first short stories in Hindi.

Bihar also has a variety of dance forms including religious dances and the dances of the tribals and the famous Chhau dance. Karma, Jatra and Paika dances are some other important dances.

Fairs and festivals: Bihar has a long tradition of festivals. The most popular festival 'Chatt Puja', is a unique form of worship of the 'sun god'. The people of Bihar have immense faith in this festival, which is celebrated twice a year, once in 'Chaitra' (according to the Hindu Calendar, in March) and in 'Kartik' (November).

The other popular festivals include Sama-Chakeva festival, Ramnavami and the Makar Sankranti, also known as the Tila Sankranti, to mark the beginning of summer.

Economy, Industry and Agriculture

Economy: The net state domestic product at current prices in 2002–03 (advance estimate) is Rs 51,345 crores, whereas the per capita net state domestic product at current prices in 2000–03 (advance estimate) is Rs 6015.

Minerals and industry: Some of the major industries in Bihar are agro-based industries, oil refineries, textiles, engineering, and oil mills.

Industries that are dependent on agriculture are the edible oil mills located at Araria, rice mills located in Buxar Karbisganch in Purnia district, spice industires, sugar mills located at Banmankhi in Purnia district, jute mills and other agro-based industries.

One of the biggest oil refineries in the country is situated at Barauni in Bihar. It is managed and controlled by the Indian Oil Corporation Ltd, and was built in collaboration with the erstwhile Soviet Union at a cost of Rs 49.40 crores, and went into operation in 1964.

After West Bengal, Bihar is the largest producer of jute and jute textiles. This is largely due to the availability of sufficient power, raw jute, water, transportation, and cheap labour. Jute mills are located in Katihar and Muktapur in Samastipur district, and at Karsbisganj in Purnia district.

Engineering industries are located at Madora in the district of Saran, Muktapur in Samastipur district, Dumaro in Bhojpur district, and Fatuha in Patna district. Railway carriages and goods factories are located in Rohtas district at Dehri-on-Son.

Due to the availability of kendu leaves and cheap labour, biri manufacturing industries are located at Bihar Sarif in Nalanda district. Bihar is also the sixth largest producer of tobacco in the country.

The important minerals found in Bihar are limestone, pyrites, quartzite and steatite.

Agriculture: Bihar has plenty of farmlands and orchards. The important crops include paddy, sugarcane, wheat and lentils. Jute or hemp, a source of tough fibres used for 'gunny bags', are also grown. Some of the important fruits grown in the state are banana, jackfruit, mangoes, and litchis.

Paddy is the important crop in all the regions. Supplementary crops include oilseeds, pulses (legumes), barley, gram, wheat and corn (maize). Sugarcane is grown in a well-defined belt in the north-west.

Vegetables include potatoes grown near Bihar Sharif, in Patna district, which produces the best variety of seed potato in India. Other important cash crops include tobacco and chillies that are grown on the banks of the Ganga.

Power: Thermal power is the main source of electricity in the state. Hydro-electric power ranks a distant second.

Education

Prominent institutes of higher education include
• B.N. Mandal University (Madhe-pura)
• Babasaheb Bhimrao Ambedkar Bihar University (Muzaffarpur)
• Jai Prakash Vishwavidyalaya (Chapra)
• Kameshwar Singh Darbhanga Sanskrit University (Darbhanga)

- Lalit Narayan Mithila University (Darbhanga)
- Magadh University (Bodh Gaya)
- Nalanda Open University (Patna)
- Patna University
- Rajendra Agricultural University (Samastipur)
- Tilka Manjhi Bhagalpur University (Bhagalpur)
- Veer Kunwar Singh University (Arrah)

Tourism

Major tourist attractions: Bodh Gaya, Rajgir, Nalanda, Vaishali, Pawapuri, Lauria Nandangarh, Vikramshila.

Airports:
- Patna
- Gaya

National Parks: Valmiki National Park in Pashchim Champaran district (335.65 sq. km).

Administration

Legislature: Bihar has a bicameral legislature consisting of the Vidhan Parishad and the Vidhan Sabha. The governor is appointed by the President of India and acts as the head of the state. The Chief Minister heads the council of ministers. There are 243 seats in the Vidhan Sabha, of which 39 seats are reserved for SC candidates. No seats are reserved for ST candidates.

The current party position is as follows:

Name of Party	Seats
Bharatiya Janata Party	37
Indian National Congress	10
Nationalist Congress Party	3
Communist Party of India	3
Bahujan Samaj Party	2
Communist Party of India (Marxist)	1
Rashtriya Janata Dal	75
Janata Dal (United)	55
Communist Party of India (Marxist-Leninist) (Liberation)	7
Samajwadi Party	4
Lok Jan Shakti Party	29
Independent	17
Total	**243**

Judiciary: The main seat for the judiciary is the high court of judicature at Patna. The chief justice is Ravi S. Dhawan.

Districts:

District	Area (sq. km)	Population	Headquarters	Urban Agglomerations
Araria	2,830	2,124,831	Araria	
Aurangabad	3,305	2,004,960	Aurangabad	
Banka	3,020	1,608,778	Banka	
Begusarai	1,918	2,342,989	Begusarai	Begusarai
Bhagalpur	2,569	2,430,331	Bhagalpur	Bhagalpur
Bhojpur	2,474	2,233,415	Arrah	
Buxar	1,624	1,403,462	Buxar	
Darbhanga	2,279	3,285,473	Darbhanga	
Gaya	4,976	3,464,983	Gaya	Gaya
Gopalganj	2,033	2,149,343	Gopalganj	
Jamui	3,098	1,397,474	Jamui	
Jehanabad	1,569	1,511,406	Jehanabad	
Kaimur (Bhabua)	3,362	1,284,575	Bhabua	
Katihar	3,057	2,389,533	Katihar	Katihar
Khagaria	1,486	1,276,677	Khagaria	
Kishanganj	1,884	1,294,063	Kishanganj	
Lakhisarai	1,228	801,173	Lakhisarai	
Madhepura	1,788	1,524,596	Madhepura	
Madhubani	3,501	3,570,651	Madhubani	
Munger	1,419	1,135,499	Munger	
Muzaffarpur	3,172	3,743,836	Muzaffarpur	
Nalanda	2,355	2,368,327	Biharsharif	
Nawada	2,494	1,809,425	Nawada	
Pashchim Champaran	5,228	3,043,044	Bettiah	
Patna	3,202	4,709,851	Patna	Patna
Purba Champaran	3,968	3,933,636	Motihari	Motihari
Purnia	3,229	2,540,788	Purnia	Purnia
Rohtas	3,851	2,448,762	Sasaram	
Saharsa	1,702	1,506,418	Saharsa	
Samastipur	2,904	3,413,413	Samastipur	Samastipur
Saran	2,641	3,251,474	Chapra	
Sheikhpura	689	525,137	Sheikhpura	
Sheohar	443	514,288	Sheohar	
Sitamarhi	2,200	2,669,887	Sitamarhi	Sitamarhi
Siwan	2,219	2,708,840	Siwan	
Supaul	2,410	1,745,069	Supaul	
Vaishali	2,036	2,712,389	Hazipur	

Chhattisgarh

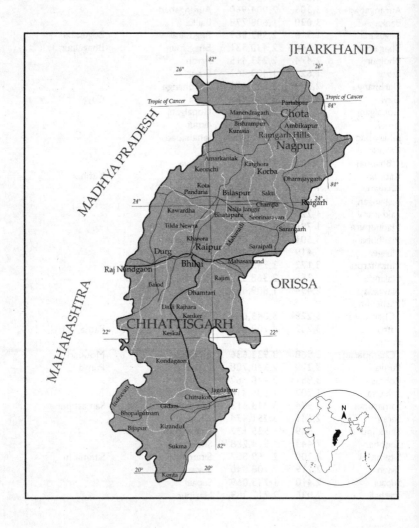

Key Statistics

Capital: Raipur.
Area: 135,191 sq. km.
Population: Total: 20,833,803;
Male: 10,474,218
Female: 10,359,585
Population density: 154 per sq. km.
Sex ratio: 989 females per 1000 males.
Principal language: Hindi.
Literacy rates: Total: 64.7%,
Male: 77.4%
Female: 51.9%

Government

Governor: Lt Gen. K.M. Seth, (Retd).
He was sworn in on 2 June 2003.

Chief Minister: Dr Raman Singh (BJP).
He was sworn in on 8 December 2003.

Geography

Physical characteristics: The state can be divided into three agro-climatic zones. These are the Chhattisgarh plains, the northern hills of Chhattisgarh and the Bastar plateau.

The Satpura mountain range lies in the northern part of the state; the plains of river Mahanadi and its tributaries lie in the central part of the state, while in the south lies the plateau of Bastar. Uttar Pradesh borders the state towards the north; Jharkhand in the north-east; Orissa in the east; Andhra Pradesh in the south and south-east; Maharashtra in the south-west and Madhya Pradesh in the west.

Neighbouring States and Union territories:
States:
• Madhya Pradesh
• Jharkhand
• Orissa
• Uttar Pradesh
• Andhra Pradesh
• Maharashtra

Major rivers: The Mahanadi and the Indravati are the two most important rivers of the state. The Narmada, the Son, the Hasdeo, the Sabari, the Sheonath, the Ib and the Arpa also provide water to the state.

Climate: Chhattisgarh has a generally sub-humid climate. It has hot, dry summers and cold winters. Annual rainfall ranges from 1200 to 1500mm.

Flora and Fauna:
Flora: Chhattisgarh has deciduous forests of two types: tropical moist deciduous forests and tropical dry deciduous forests. The state has about 22 forest subtypes. The two major tree species in the state are sal and teak. The other notable species are saja, dhawra, mahua, bija, tendu, amla, karra and bamboo.

Fauna: The notable species of animals found in Chhattisgarh are tiger, gaur, sambar, wild buffalo, hill myna, chital, nilgai, wild boar and leopard.

History

In ancient times, the region that is today Chhattisgarh was called Dakshin Kosala. Its history can be traced back to the *Ramayana* and the *Mahabharata*. It was called Ratanpur during the reign of the Mughals.

In the 10th century AD, a powerful Rajput family ruled at Tripuri, near Jabalpur. A member of the Kalchuri dynasty, Kalingraja, settled at Tuman around AD 1000. His grandson Ratanraja founded Ratanpur, which became the capital of a large part of the area now known as Chhattisgarh. This Rajput family called itself the Haihaya dynasty and it continued to rule Chhattisgarh for six centuries until about the 14th century, when it disintegrated.

In the middle ages, the Chalukya dynasty established its rule in Bastar. The Chalukya ruler Annmdev established his dynasty in Bastar in 1320.

One branch of the dynasty continued at Ratanpur, while the other settled in Raipur. At the end of the 16th century the latter branch acknowledged the domination of the Mughals.

In 1741, the Marathas attacked Chhattisgarh and destroyed the Haihaya power. In 1745, they conquered the region and deposed Raghunathsinghji, the last survivor of the Ratanpur house. In 1758, the Marathas ultimately annexed Chhattisgarh and it came directly under Maratha rule. The Maratha rule was a period of chaos and misrule, marked by widespread loot and plunder by the Maratha army. The Gonds resisted the Marathas, leading to conflicts and hostility between them. In the early 19th century, the Pindaris from Gwalior attacked and plundered the region.

In 1818, Chhattisgarh came under British control for the first time. When the province of Nagpur lapsed to the British government in 1854, Chhattisgarh was put under a deputy commissioner and Raipur made the headquarters. The tribals of Bastar resisted British overlordship and this resulted in the Halba Rebellion, which lasted nearly five years (1774–79).

A demand for a separate Chhattisgarh state was first raised in 1924 by the Raipur Congress unit. It was later raised at the Tripuri session of the Indian National Congress. In 1955, a demand for a separate state was made in the Nagpur assembly of the then state of Madhya Bharat.

On 18 March 1994, a resolution for a separate Chhattisgarh was tabled in the Madhya Pradesh Vidhan Sabha. Both the INC and the BJP supported the resolution and it was unanimously approved.

In 1998, the Union government drafted a bill for the creation of a separate state of Chhattisgarh carved out from 16 districts of Madhya Pradesh. The Madhya Pradesh assembly unanimously approved the draft bill in 1998, with some modifications.

Chhattisgarh became a separate state on 1 November 2000. Ajit Jogi was the first Chief Minister of Chhattisgarh.

Politics

The Congress government of Madhya Pradesh took the first institutional and legislative initiative for the creation of Chhattisgarh. On 18 March 1994, a resolution demanding a separate Chhattisgarh was tabled and unanimously approved by the Madhya Pradesh Vidhan Sabha. Both the Congress and the Bhartiya Janata Party supported the resolution. The election manifestos of the Congress and the BJP for both the 1998 and the 1999 parliamentary elections as well as the Madhya Pradesh assembly election of 1998 included the demand for the creation of a separate Chhattisgarh. In 1998, the BJP led union government drafted a bill for the creation of a separate state of Chhattisgarh from sixteen districts of Madhya Pradesh. This draft bill was sent to the Madhya Pradesh assembly for approval. It was unanimously approved in 1998, although with certain modifications. The union government did not survive and fresh elections were declared. The new National Democratic Alliance (NDA) government sent the redrafted Separate Chhattisgarh Bill for the approval of the Madhya Pradesh Assembly, where it was once again unanimously approved and then tabled in the Lok Sabha. This bill for a separate Chhattisgarh was passed in the Lok Sabha and the Rajya Sabha, paving the way for the creation of a separate state of Chhattisgarh. The President of

India gave his consent to the Madhya Pradesh Reorganisation Act 2000 on 25 August 2000. The Government of India subsequently set 1 November 2000 as the day on which the state of Madhya Pradesh would be bifurcated into Chhattisgarh and Madhya Pradesh. The state of Chhattisgarh came into existence on 1 November 2000. The state fulfills the long-cherished demand of the tribal people. This is the 26th state of India.

The Chhattisgarh state Legislature is unicameral, consisting of 90 members. Ajit Jogi, who had been elected unopposed as the leader of the 48-member Congress(I) Legislature Party (CLP) on 31 October, was sworn in the first Chief Minister of the state. In the 2003 Assembly elections the BJP won 50 seats in the 90-member Chattisgarh state assembly, while the ruling Congress had to content itself with a mere 37 seats. Raman Singh, president of the BJP in Chattisgarh, was sworn in as the state's Chief Minister on 7 December 2003 following the party's victorious elections.

Culture

The state is well known for its tribal art forms, dance forms and handicrafts. These include handicrafts made out of wood, bamboo, terracotta, bell metal items, wrought iron items and cotton fabrics. The state is also renowned for its Kosa silk fabric. Local dance forms include the Suga dance, Saila, Ravat Nacha and Karma.

Fairs and festivals: Besides Diwali, Dussehra and Holi, various districts have their own distinct festivals. These include Charta, Navakhana, Surhul, Mati Puja, Goncha, Madai Hareli, Pola, Cherchera, Dev Uthni, Gouri-gour and Surti Teeja.

Economy, Industry and Agriculture

Economy: The net state domestic product at current prices for 2002–03 (provisional) was Rs 25,094 crores. The per capita net state domestic product at current prices for 2002–03 (provisional) was Rs 11,893.

Minerals and industry: The famous Bhilai Steel Plant is located in this state. Apart from this, there are cement plants, food-processing plants, engineering works, chemical plants, plastics units, and fabrication units.

The minerals mined in the state include iron ore, coal, corundum, bauxite, diamond, gold, dolomite, limestone, tin and granite.

Agriculture: The most important crops are paddy, maize, pulses like tur and kulthi, kodo-kutki, small millets, oilseeds like sunflower, groundnut, soyabean and niger. The state also produces jowar, gram, urad, moong and moth in the rabi season.

Power: Most of the state's power comes from thermal power plants, while hydroelectric plants generate the rest.

Education

Educational institutes: The most well known among the institutes of higher education in the state are
• Pandit Ravishankar Shukla University (Raipur)
• Guru Ghasidas University (Bilaspur)
• Indira Gandhi Agriculture University (Raipur)
• Indira Kala Sangeet University (Khairagarh)
• Jawaharlal Nehru Krishi Vishwavidyalaya (Jabalpur)
• Rani Durgavati Vishwavidyalaya (Jabalpur)

Tourism

Major tourist attractions: Chitrakot Waterfalls, Bastar dist.; Tirathgarh Falls, Bastar dist.; Kutumsar Caves and Kailash Gufa, Bastar dist.; Danteshwari Temple, Bastar dist.; Ratanpur, Bilaspur dist.; Mallhar, Bilaspur dist.; Deorani-Jethani Temple, Talagram, Bilaspur dist.; Maitry Bagh, Durg dist.; Amrit Dhara Waterfalls, Koriya dist.; Ramdaha Waterfalls, Koriya dist.; Gavar Ghat Waterfalls, Koriya dist.; Akuri Nala, Koriya dist.; Radha Krishna Temple, Raipur dist.; Chandi Temple, Raipur dist.; Swastik Vihar Monastery, Raipur dist.; Anand Premkuti Vihar Monastery, Raipur dist.; Maa Bambleshwari Temple, Dongargarh, Rajnandgaon dist.; Thinthini Patthar, Surguja dist.

Airports:
- Raipur
- Bilaspur

National Parks:
- Indravati National Park in Dantewada dist. (1,258.37 sq. km)
- Sanjay National Park in Surguja and Koriya dists (1,471.13 sq. km)
- Kangerghati National Park in Kanker dist. (200 sq. km)

Administration

Legislature: Chhattisgarh has a unicameral legislature. There are 90 seats in the Legislative Assembly, of which 10 are reserved for SCs and 34 for STs. The tenure of the present House ends on 21 December 2008. The current party position is:

Name of Party	Seats
Bharatiya Janata Party	50
Indian National Congress	37
Bahujan Samaj Party	2
Nationalist Congress Party	1
Total	**90**

Judiciary: Chhattisgarh High Court is at Bilaspur. Ananga Kumar Patnaik is the chief justice.

Districts:

District	Area (sq. km)	Population	Headquarters	Urban Agglomerations
Bastar	14,974	13,02,253	Jagdalpur	Jagdalpur
Bilaspur	8,270	19,93,042	Bilaspur	Bilaspur, Mungeli
Dantewada	17,634	7,19,065	Dantewada	
Dhamtari	3,385	7,03,569	Dhamtari	
Durg	8,549	28,01,757	Durg	Dalli-Rajhara, Durg, Bhilainagar
Janjgir-Champa	3,852	13,16,140	Janjgir	
Jashpur	5,838	7,39,780	Jashpur	
Kanker	6,506	6,51,333	Kanker	Kanker
Kawardha	4,223	5,84,667	Kawardha	Kawardha
Korba	6,599	10,12,121	Korba	
Koriya	6,604	5,85,455	Baikunthpur	Chirmiri
Mahasamund	4,789	30,09,042	Mahasamund	
Raigarh	7,086	12,65,084	Raigarh	Raigarh
Raipur	13,083	30,09,042	Raipur	Raipur, Tilda Newra
Rajnandgaon	8,068	12,81,811	Rajnandgaon	
Surguja	15,731	19,70,661	Ambikapur	Ambikapur

Goa

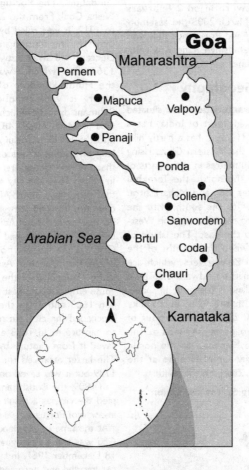

Key Statistics

Capital: Panaji.
Area: 3,702 sq. km.
Population: Total: 1,347,668
Male: 687,248
Female: 660,420

Population density: 363 per sq. km.
Sex ratio: 961 females per 1000 males.
Principal languages: Konkani, Marathi, Kannada.
Literacy rates: Total: 82.32%
Male: 88.88%
Female: 75.51%

Government

Governor: S.C. Jamir. He became the governor on 2 July 2004.

Chief Minister: Pratapsingh R. Rane (INC) was sworn in on 2 February 2005. On 4 March 2005 the assembly was dissolved and President's Rule was declared. Pratapsingh Rane was reinstated on 7 June.

Geography

Physical characteristics: Goa, situated on the Konkan coast of India, has a coastline of 131 km. It has a partly hilly terrain, with the Western Ghats rising to nearly 1200 metres in some parts of the state. In the north, the Terekhol river separates Goa and Maharashtra. Karnataka lies to the south, with the Arabian Sea to the west and the Western Ghats to the east. The island of Goa lies between the mouths of the Mandovi and Zuari rivers, which are connected on the landward side by a creek. The island is triangular in shape, with a cape in the form of a rocky headland that divides the harbour of Goa into two parts—Aguada at the mouth of the Mandovi, on the north, and Mormugao or Marmagao at the mouth of the Zuari, on the south.

Neighbouring States and Union territories:
States:
• Maharashtra
• Karnataka

Major rivers:
• Mandovi
• Zuari

Climate: Summer temperatures vary from 24°C to 32.7°C. Winter temperatures vary from 21.3°C to 32.2°C. Rainfall 3200mm (June–September).

History

Goa first appears in the Puranas as 'Gove', 'Govapuri', and 'Gomant'. The medieval Arab geographers called it 'Sindabur'. The Portuguese called it 'Velha Goa'. From the 2nd century AD to 1312, it was ruled by the Kadamba dynasty. The Muslim invaders of the Deccan held sway between 1312 and 1367, after which it was annexed by the Hindu kingdom of Vijayanagar. Later, it was conquered by the Bahmani dynasty, which founded Old Goa in 1440. After 1482, Goa passed into the hands of Yusuf Adil Khan, the king of Bijapur. It was during his reign that the Portuguese first reached India. In March 1510 the city surrendered to the Portuguese under Afonso de Albuquerque. A violent struggle between the Portuguese and Yusuf Adil Khan ensued, but the Portuguese had the last laugh. Goa was the first territorial possession of the Portuguese in Asia. It later became the capital of the entire Portuguese empire in the East.

In 1603 and 1639 the Dutch Navy blockaded the city, but never managed to capture it. In 1683 a Mughal army saved it from capture by the Maratha. The latter attacked the area again in 1739 but it was saved once again.

In 1809, the British temporarily occupied the city, as a result of Napoleon's invasion of Portugal.

At the time of independence in 1947, Goa was still a Portuguese colony. On 18 December 1961, Indian military forces invaded and occupied Goa, Daman, and Diu. They were incorporated into the Indian Union in 1962. On 30 May 1987, Goa was granted statehood, Daman and Diu remaining as a separate Union territory. Goa's first Chief Minister was Pratapsingh Rane.

Politics

Portuguese rule was so oppressive and exploitative that during 450 years of Portuguese rule, there were forty armed revolts in Goa. Although these revolts were put down with a heavy hand, the urge for freedom could not be suppressed forever. A movement for the liberation of Goa gained momentum in the 1900s. The main leaders of the movement were Tristao Bragansa Cunha, Purushottam Kakodkar, Laxmi Kant Bhembre, Divakar Kakodkar and Dayanand Bandodkar. The liberation movement became stronger after Indian independence in 1947.

India's new government claimed Goa in 1948. In 1955, nonviolent protesters attempted a peaceful annexation. The resulting casualties led to a breakdown of relations between India and Portugal. Indian troops invaded Goa in December 1961. Within three days Goa was integrated into India in a near bloodless operation—'Operation Vijay' on 19 December 1961. The other Portuguese territories of Daman and Diu were also taken over at around the same time and thus was formed the 'Union territory of Goa, Daman and Diu' which became a part of the Indian Union. Initially the liberated territory was under the army administration of Lt. Gen. Candeth, the Military Governor who was assisted by the Chief Civil Administrator. On 8 June 1962, the military government gave place to civil rule. The Lt. Governor formed an informal Consultative Council consisting of 29 nominated members to assist him in the administration of the territory. Goa attained full statehood on 30 May 1987 when Daman and Diu retained separate identity as a Union Territory.

In 1963 the Maharashtrawadi Gomantak Party, which had won the first Assembly elections, was led by Dayanand Bandodkar. On 20 December 1963 the first Chief Minister of Goa, Daman and Diu (Union Territory), Dayanand Bandodkar was sworn in. He had three tenures as the Chief Minister of Goa, Daman and Diu. Bhausaheb Bandodkar was the Chief Minister from 20 December 1963 to 2 December 1966. His second tenure was from 5 April 1967 to 23 March 1972. His third tenure was from 23 March 1972 till his death on 12 August 1973. The Maharashtrabadi Gomantak Party believed in the merger of Goa with neighbouring Maharashtra as they believed in the similarities of culture but at the same time underscored Konkani as being an under-developed dialect of Marathi. The United Goans party had the exact opposite view; they believed in retaining and preserving Goa's unique identity. They were led by Dr Jack Sequeira. They firmly believed that Konkani was an independent language and not a dialect of Marathi. The party insisted on maintaining its unique historical identity of its own with statehood as its long term goal, without being a part of neighbouring Maharashtra. On 16 January 1967 an opinion poll was held and the unanimous opinion of the people was to retain Goa's unique identity and not to merge with Maharashtra. The United Goans party won the elections by 34,021 votes.

After the death of Dayanand Banodkar his daughter, Shashikala Kakodkar was subsequently voted into power and she became the Chief Minister (India's first woman to do so). She was in power until April 1979. After a brief eight months of President's Rule, elections were held in January 1980. For the first time, the MG party was voted out of power and the mainstream Congress party came to power with the election of Pratapsingh Rane of the Congress party as Chief Minister. This was the first time the Congress party had made an entry into Goa's political scene. A scion of the Rane family of Sattari, Pratapsingh Rane remained in power, winning the election again in 1985 and 1990. Goa attained another political milestone by becoming a state on 30 May 1987. Daman and Diu remained as a separate Union territory. Pratapsingh Rane was sworn in as the first Chief Minister of the new Goa state. In 1992 Konkoni was declared as the official language of the state of Goa.

On 27 March 1990 Churchill Alemao of United Goans Democratic Party took over as the Chief Minister of Goa. His rule lasted for 18 and a half days till 14 April 1990. From 14 April 1990 to 14 December 1990, Dr Luis Proto Barbosa was the Chief Minister of Goa, followed by President's Rule. On 25 January 1991 Ravi Naik took over as the Chief Minister and was the CM till 18 May 1993. Ravi Naik was followed by Dr Wilfred or Willy D'Souza from 18 May 1993 to 2 April 1994. Shri Ravi Naik came back as the CM from 2 April 1994, to 8 April 1994. Ravi Naik's second tenure as the CM lasted for six and a half days. Once again Dr Wilfred D'Souza was the CM from 8 April 1994 to 16 December 1994. Pratapsingh Rane's fifth tenure as the Chief Minister of Goa came on 16 December 1994 and lasted till 29 July 1998. Dr Wilfred D'Souza came for the third time as the Chief Minister from 29 July 1998 to 23 November 1998. On 26 November 1998 Luizinho Faleiro took over as the Chief Minister and ruled till 8 February 1999 followed by President's Rule. On 9 June 1999 once again Luizinho Faleiro took over as the CM till 24 November 1999. From 24 November 1999 to 24 October 2000

Francisco Sardinha was the Chief Minister. From 24 October 2000 to 3 June 2002 Manohar Parrikar of the Bharatiya Janata Party was the Chief Minister. Parrikar's second tenure as the CM was from 3 June 2002 till 2 February 2005. Again Pratapsingh Rane was sworn in as Chief Minister on 2 February 2005. President's Rule was proclaimed on 4 March, but Pratapsingh Rane returned as Chief Minister on 7 June 2005.

Culture

Goa is well known for its folk dances like Dhalo, Fugdi, Mando, Corridinho and performing folk arts like Khell-Tiatro and Jagar-perani. It is also well known for rosewood and teak furniture, terracotta figurines, brass items and jewellery designs. Folk paintings of Goa mostly depict scenes from the *Mahabharata*, the *Ramayana* and the Puranas and also scenes from the New Testament. Goa is also an important centre for Konkani literature.

Fairs and festivals: The Goan Hindu community celebrates Ganesh Chathurti, Krishna Janmashtami, Rakshabandhan, Gudi Padwa, Diwali, Dussehra, Holi, and Ramnavmi.

In Goa, the most widely celebrated festival is Ganesh Chaturthi, or Chovoth. In the month of Phalgun, Goa celebrates Holi, or Shigmoutsav. In the month of Shravan, the town of Vasco celebrates Vasco Saptah. The Lairai Jatra takes place in early May. The Goa Carnival is usually celebrated in the month of February or March.

Economy, Industry and Agriculture

Economy: The net state domestic product at current prices (new series) in 2001–02(quick estimate) was Rs 6,736 crores. The per capita net state domestic product at current prices (new series) in 2001–02 (quick estimate) was Rs 49,673. At Rs 45,000, Goa has the highest per capita income in India.

Minerals and industry: There are over 5000 small-scale industrial units in the state. Mineral resources of the state include bauxite, iron ore and ferro-manganese.

Agriculture: Rice, millets and pulses are the most widely grown food grains. Coconuts, cashew nuts and oilseeds are also grown.

Education

Educational institutes: Prominent institutes of higher education include
• Goa University
• National Institute of Oceanography
• National Institute of Water Sports
• Goa Institute of Management
• Indian Council of Agricultural Research.

Tourism

Major tourist attractions: Calangute Beach, Colva Beach, Dona Paula Beach, Miramar Beach, Anjuna Beach, Palolem Beach, Vagator Beach, Arambol Beach, Agonda Beach, Basillica of Bom Jesus, Se Cathedral, Church of St Francis of Assisi, Dudhsagar Waterfalls, Aguada Fort.

Airports:
• Goa
• Mormugao.

National Parks: Bhagwan Mahavir (107 sq. km).

Administration

Legislature: Goa has a unicameral legislature, with a legislative assembly. There are 40 seats in the assembly, including one seat reserved for SCs. The term of the current assembly expires on 11 June 2007. The present party position in the assembly is as follows:

Name of Party	Seats
Bharatiya Janata Party	17
Indian National Congress	16
United Gomantwadi Democratic Party	3
Maharashtrabadi Gomantak Party	2
Nationalist Congress Party	1
Independent	1
Total	**40**

Judiciary: Goa falls under the jurisdiction of the Goa bench of the Mumbai High Court. The chief justice is Dalveer C. Bhandari. There is one district court and other subordinate courts.

Districts:

District	Area (sq. km)	Population	Headquarters	Urban Agglomerations
North Goa	1,736	757,407	Panaji	Panaji
South Goa	1,966	586,591	Margao	Margao, Mormugao

Gujarat

Key Statistics

Capital: Gandhinagar.
Area: 196,024 sq. km.
Population: Total: 50,671,017
Male: 26,385,577
Female: 24,285,440
Population density: 258 per sq. km.
Sex ratio: 920 females per 1000 males.
Principal languages: Gujarati, Hindi, Sindhi.

Literacy rates: Total: 69.1%
Male: 79.7%
Female: 57.8%

Government

Governor: Nawal Krishna Sharma. He was sworn in on 24 July 2004.

Chief Minister: Narendra Damodardas Modi. He was sworn in on 22 December 2002.

Geography

Physical characteristics: One of the most striking geographical features of the state is the Rann of Kutch, a vast salt marsh that stretches for about 18,000 sq km. In the dry season, it is a sandy salt plain prone to dust storms, but during the rainy season even light rainfall floods the Rann and the region becomes an island.

The expansive Kathiawar Peninsula lies to the south of Kutch, between the Gulf of Kutch and the Gulf of Khambhat. This is another arid region and the coastal region gives way to a low area of wooded hilly region in the central part. The rivers of the state are mostly seasonal streams. The north-eastern part of the state is primarily a region of plains and low hills. The highest point in the state is in the Girnar Hills (1,117 metres).

Neighbouring States and Union territories:

International border:
• Pakistan

States:
• Rajasthan
• Maharashtra
• Madhya Pradesh

Union territories:
• Daman and Diu
Dadra and Nagar Haveli

Major rivers:
• Narmada
• Tapti
• Mahi
• Sabarmati
• Banas
• Bhadar are the most important rivers.
Other rivers include
• Heran
• Orsang
• Karad
• Saidak
• Mohar
• Vatrak

Climate: The climate in Gujarat varies from humid in the coastal areas, to very hot in areas like Kutch. It can get extremely hot in the summers and extremely cold in the winters.

The climate of Gujarat is moist in the southern districts and dry in the northern region. The state's climate can be divided into a winter season from November to February, a summer season from March to May and a south-west monsoon season from June to September.

Flora and Fauna:
Flora: Roughly 10 per cent of the area of Gujarat is under forest cover. The state's flora includes dry deciduous forests, moist deciduous forests, grasslands, wetlands and marine ecosystems.

Fauna: Gujarat is home to some rare species. The Asiatic lion is found only in the Gir Forest, while the wild ass is found in the Rann of Kutch. Besides these, the great Indian bustard, the world's only four-horned antelope, the black buck, the dugong and the boralia are all found in different habitats across the state.

History

The settlements of Lothal, Rangpur, Amri, Lakhabaval and Rozdi in Gujarat have been linked with the Indus Valley Civilization.

Asokan rock edicts of around 250 BC show that in ancient times, the region that is today Gujarat came under the rule of the Mauryan dynasty. After the fall of the Mauryan empire, Gujarat came under the rule of the Sakas between AD 130–390. At its height, the Sakas held sway over what is today Malwa, Saurashtra, Kutch and

Rajasthan.

In the 4th and 5th centuries, Gujarat constituted a part of the Gupta empire. The Guptas were succeeded by the Maitraka dynasty of the kingdom of Valabhi. The Maitrakas ruled over Gujarat and Malwa for three centuries. The Maitraka dynasty was succeeded by the Gurjara-Pratiharas of Kannauj, who ruled during the 8th and 9th centuries. Following the Gurjara-Pratiharas came the Solanki dynasty, which was followed by the Vaghela dynasty. In about 1297, Ala-ud-Din Khalji, the sultan of Delhi, defeated Karnadeva Vaghela and the area came under Muslim influence. In 1401, Zafar Khan, whom the Tughluqs had appointed governor of the province, declared independence. His grandson Ahmad Shah, founded Ahmedabad in 1411. From the end of the 16th century to the mid-18th century, Gujarat was under Mughal rule. Then came the Marathas, who overran the region in the mid-18th century.

In 1818, Gujarat came under the administration of the British East India Company. After the Revolt of 1857, the area became a province of the British crown and was divided into Gujarat province and numerous smaller states.

When India became independent, all of Gujarat except for the states of Kutch and Saurashtra was included in Bombay state. In 1956, the provinces of Kutch and Saurashtra were also included.

On 1 May 1960, Bombay state was bifurcated into present-day Gujarat and Maharashtra. Jivraj Mehta was the state's first Chief Minister.

Politics

After Independence, British-ruled Gujarat and several princely states were clubbed together to form the state of Bombay. The States Reorganisation Act was passed by Parliament in November 1956. Bombay state was enlarged by merging the states of Kutch and Saurashtra and the Maratha-speaking areas of Hyderabad with it. The strongest reaction against the SRC's report and the States Reorganisation Act came from Maharashtra where widespread rioting broke out and eighty people were killed in Bombay city in police firings in January 1956. Under pressure, the government decided in June 1956 to divide the Bombay state into two linguistic states of Maharashtra and Gujarat with Bombay city forming a separate, centrally administered state. This move too was, however, opposed by the people both of Maharashtra and Gujarat. The government finally agreed in May 1960 to bifurcate the state of Bombay into Maharashtra and Gujarat, with Bombay city being included in Maharashtra, and Ahmedabad being made the capital of Gujarat.

On bifurcation of the Greater Bombay state on 1 May 1960, under the Bombay Reorganization Act, 1960, the new state of Gujarat came into existence and the Gujarat Legislative Assembly, composed of 132 members of Bombay Legislative Assembly elected from the constituencies of Gujarat was formed. Gujarat state has only one house, i.e. the Legislative Assembly.

The Congress dominated Gujarat's corridors of power for most of the time from 1960 to 1995. Jivraj N. Mehta, a minister twice in the Government of Bombay (1949 and 1952–60) became the first Chief Minister of Gujarat. He resigned due to dissolution of the old Legislative Assembly, which was separated from the ex-Bombay state. Balwantray Mehta was the Chief Minister from 19 June 1963 to 20 September 1965. During the Indo-Pak war in 1965, he and his wife Sarojben took off in a small plane to inspect the Gujarat-Pakistan border. A Pakistani aircraft shot down his plane in Kutch resulting in his martyrdom on 19 September 1965. The Ministry resigned in the wake of the demise of the Chief Minister. Hitendra K. Desai became the next Chief Minister on 20 September 1965. His ministry resigned in the wake of general elections on 4 March 1967. Again he came to power on 5 March 1967 and remained in the post till 6 April 1971. He resigned after losing majority in the Legislative Assembly. Hitendra K. Desai dissolved the assembly following defections from his party. President's Rule was imposed in Gujarat on 12 May 1971. President's Rule was revoked on 17 March 1972. Ghanshyambhai C. Oza became the Chief Minister on 17 March 1972 and remained in power till 17 July 1973. Chimanbhai J. Patel succeeded him on 18 July 1973. Besides being a member of the 3rd, 4th and 6th Gujarat Legislative Assemblies (1967–71, 1972–74 and 1980–85), he remained a Leader of Opposition in Gujarat Assembly for a long time after 1985. His first stint as CM ended on 9 February 1974 when his ministry resigned following recommendation for President's Rule in the state. President's Rule was revoked on 18 June 1975. Babubhai J. Patel, a known freedom fighter was the Chief Minister from 18 June 1975 to 12 March 1976. He was Deputy Minister, PWD, Transport and Home of Bombay state from 1952–56 and Minister for Planning, Power and Housing in 1956. His ministry resigned after the legislative assembly passed a cut-motion for deduction of one rupee on the demands of civil supplies. Again President's Rule was imposed on 12 March 1976. President's Rule was revoked on 24 December 1976. Madhavsinh F. Solanki

was the Chief Minister from 24 December1976 to 10 April 1977. A fourtime Chief Minister (24-12-1976 to 10-04-1977, 07-06-1980 to 10-03-1985, 11-03-1985 to 06-07-1985 and 10-12-1989 to 04-03-1990), he was the most respected of the Congress rulers of Gujarat. During his illustrious political career he had also been the Leader of the Opposition in Gujarat Assembly during 1975–76 and 1977–80. He became the first CM to have completed full term of five years since the inception of Gujarat. Babubhai J. Patel was the Chief Minister from 11 April 1977 to 17 February 1980. President's Rule followed and it was revoked on 6 June 1980. Madhavsinh F. Solanki became the Chief Minister and on 10 March 1985 the ministry resigned due to general elections.

Amarsinh Chaudhary became the Chief Minister on 6 July 1985. An ardent Congress supporter, he is known among the most influential of the Congress leaders in the state. Madhavsinh F. Solanki again became the Chief Minister. The Ministry resigned due to General Elections. Chimanbhai Patel was the Chief Minister from 4 March 1990 to 17 February 1994. The ministry resigned following the demise of the Chief Minister. Chhabildas Mehta took over as Chief Minister after the death of Chimanbhai Patel. The ministry resigned following announcement of elections on 14 March 1995. Keshubhai Savdasbhai Patel's first stint as CM began on 14 March1995 but could last only till 21 October 1995. He came back as the Chief Minister on 4 March 1998 but had to quit on BJP high command's directive on 6 October 2001 following irregularities in relief works after the 2000 quake that had killed thousands of people. Sureshchandra Rupshanker Mehta was the Chief Minister from 21 October

1995 to 19 September 1996. Sureshchandra Mehta is one of the most respected leaders of the BJP with a wide support base in the state. A lawyer by profession, he had been Cabinet Minister twice—in 1990 and 1995, before becoming the CM in 1996. He resigned due to President's Rule being imposed in the state. President's Rule was revoked on 23 October 1996. Shankersinhji Laxmansinhji Vaghela was the Chief Minister from 23 October 1996 to 27 October 1997. He led a rebellion in BJP and split the party in 1996. Dilipbhai Ramanbhai became the Chief Minister on 28 October 1997 and remained in power till 4 March 1998. Narendra Damodardas Modi took over as the 14th Chief Minister of Gujarat on 7 October 2001 after Keshubhai Patel stepped down on the directive of the BJP high-command. The imposition of President's Rule on five occasions so far and frequent outbreaks of communal violence have played a vital role in shaping the state's politics over the years. In February 2002, about 58 people (apparently mostly Hindus) died in a train fire in Godhra, Gujarat. A sleeper coach in the train Sabarmati Express, coming from Faizabad and proceeding towards Ahmedabad caught fire a few minutes after it left the Godhra railway station on 27 February 2002. The coach that was ravaged in the fire was occupied predominantly by members and sympathizers of the Sangh Parivar, called Kar Sevaks who were returning after a pilgrimage to Ayodhya. This incident was a precursor to a spate of widepsread riots in the state, which lasted nearly three months.

Culture

Gujarat is famous for its 'Garba' dance form, which is performed on Navratri.

The state is also famous for its 'bandhni' tie-and-dye technique, Patola saris, toys of Idar, perfumes of Palanpur, the handloom products of Konodar and woodwork from Ahmedabad and Surat.

Fairs and festivals: The festivals of the state include the International Kite Festival of Ahmedabad, Somnath Festival, Navratri, Tarnetra Festival and Janmastami.

Economy, Industry and Agriculture

Economy: The net state domestic product at current prices for 2002–03 (provisional) was Rs 114,405 crores. The per capita net state domestic product at current prices for 2002–03 (provisional) was Rs 22,047.

Minerals and industry: The important minerals found in the state are bauxite, manganese, limestone, lignite, bentonite, dolomite, crude oil, granite, silica, china clay and fireclay.

The major industries in the state are petrochemicals, engineering, electronics, chemicals and fertilizers. Surat is an important centre for the diamond trade while Anand is home to Amul, the milk giant.

Agriculture: Major food crops in the state are rice, wheat, jowar, bajra, maize, tur, gram and groundnut. The most important non-food crops are cotton and tobacco.

Power: Gujarat gets its power mainly from thermal power plants, as well as partially from nuclear and hydroelectric power plants.

Education

Educational institutes: Notable institutes for higher education in the state include the

- Indian Institute of Management (Ahmedabad)
- Gujarat University (Ahmedabad)
- Gujarat Agricultural University (Sardar Krushinagar)
- Maharaja Sayaji Rao University (Vadodara)
- North Gujarat University (Patan) • •
- Saurashtra University (Rajkot)
- Indian Institute of Rural Management (Anand)
- Mudra Institute of Communications (Ahmedabad)

Tourism

Major tourist attractions: Mandvi Beach, Palitana Temple, Hatheesing Temple, Akshardham Temple, Somnath Temple, Sasan Gir, Modhera Sun Temple, Lothal, Bala Sinor, Saputara Hill Station.

Airports:
International: Ahmedabad.
Domestic:
- Bhuj
- Kandla
- Jamnagar
- Keshoo
- Bhavnagar
- Rajkot
- Vadodara
- Palanpur. Porbandar.

National Parks:
- Marine National Park and Sanctuary in Jamnagar dist. (162.89 sq. km and 295.03 sq. km respectively)
- Gir National Park and Sanctuary in Junagadh dist. (258.71 sq. km and 1153.42 sq. km respectively)
- Velavadhar National Park in Bhavnagar dist. (34.08 sq. km)
- Vansda National Park in Valsad dist. (23.99 sq. km).

Administration

Legislature: Gujarat has a unicameral legislature. There are 182 seats of which 13 are reserved for SCs and 26 for STs. The tenure of the present house ends on 26 December 2007.

The party position in the current Vidhan Sabha is as follows:

Name of Party	Seats
Bharatiya Janata Party	128
Indian National Congress	49
Janata Dal	2
Independents	2
Vacant	1
Total	**182**

Judiciary: The High Court of Gujarat is at Ahmedabad. The chief justice is Bhawani Singh, sworn in on 25 August 2003.

Districts:

District	Area (sq. km)	Population	Headquarters	Urban Agglomerations
Ahmedabad	8,086	5,808,378	Ahmedabad	Ahmedabad, Dholka
Amreli	7,397	1,393,295	Amreli	Amreli
Anand	2,940	1,856,712	Anand	Anand, Khambhat
Banas Kantha	10,757	2,502,843	Palanpur	Palanpur
Bharuch	6,527	1,370,104	Bharuch	Anklesvar, Bharuch
Bhavnagar	9,980.9	2,469,264	Bhavnagar	Bhavnagar, Mahuva
Dohad	3,646.1	1,635,374	Dohad	Dohad
Gandhinagar	2,163.4	1,334,731	Gandhinagar	Ahmadabad, Kalol
Jamnagar	14,125	1,913,685	Jamnagar	Jamnagar
Junagadh	8,846	2,448,427	Junagadh	Junagadh, Mangrol, Veraval
Kutch	45,652	1,526,321	Bhuj	Bhuj
Kheda	4,218.8	2,023,354	Nadiad	Dakor, Nadiad
Mahesana	4,382.8	1,837,696	Mahesana	Kadi, Mahesana, Vijapur, Visnagar
Narmada	2,755.5	514,083	Rajpipla	
Navsari	2,209.2	1,229,250	Navsari	Bilimora, Navsari
Panch Mahals	5,219.9	2,024,883	Godhra	Godhra, Halol, Kalol
Patan	5,730.4	1,181,941	Patan	Patan, Sidhpur
Porbandar	2,297.8	536,854	Porbandar	Porbandar, Ranavav
Rajkot	11,203	3,157,676	Rajkot	Gondal, Morvi, Rajkot
Sabar Kantha	7,390	2,083,416	Himatnagar	Idar
Surat	7,657	4,996,391	Surat	Surat
Surendranagar	10,489	1,515,147	Surendranagar	Wadhwan
The Dangs	1,764	186,712	Ahwa	
Vadodara	7,549.5	3,639,775	Vadodara	Padra, Vadodara
Valsad	3,034.8	1,410,680	Valsad	Valsad

Haryana

Key Statistics

Capital: Chandigarh.

Area: 44,212 sq. km.

Population: Total: 21,144,564
Male: 11,369,953
Female: 9,780,611

Population density: 477 per sq. km.

Sex ratio: 861 females per 1000 males.

Principal languages: Hindi, Punjabi, Urdu.

Literacy rates: Total: 67.9%
Male: 78.5%
Female: 55.67%

Government

Governor: A.R. Kidwai. He became governor on 5 July 2004.

Chief Minister: Bhupinder Singh Hooda (INC). He was sworn in on 5 March 2005.

Geography

Physical characteristics: Haryana is surrounded by Himachal Pradesh in the north, Punjab in the west, Uttar Pradesh in the east and Delhi and

Rajasthan in the south. The state has four main geographical features: (i) The Shivalik hills in the north, source of main seasonal rivers; (ii) The Ghaggar–Yamuna plain, which is divided into two parts—the higher one called 'Bangar' and the lower one 'Khadar'; (iii) A semi-desert plain, bordering the state of Rajasthan and (iv) The Aravalli Hills in the south, a dry area with uneven landscape.

Neighbouring States and Union territories:

States:
- Rajasthan
- Punjab
- Uttar Pradesh
- Uttaranchal
- Himachal Pradesh

Union territories:
- Chandigarh
- Delhi

Major rivers: The Yamuna, Haryana's only perennial river, flows along the eastern boundary of the state. Ghaggar, the main seasonal river, flows along the northern boundary. Some other important seasonal rivers are Markanda, Tangri and Sahibi.

Climate: Haryana has very hot summers with maximum temperatures going up to 50°C in May and June in some areas. December and January are the coldest, minimum temperatures dropping as low as 1°C in parts of the state.

Rainfall is varied with the Shivalik region receiving the most rain and the Aravalli region being the driest. Nearly 80 per cent of the total rainfall occurs in the monsoon season, from July to September. The tributaries of the Yamuna and Ghaggar cause occasional floods.

Flora and Fauna:

Flora: Forests, mostly thorny dry deciduous forest, cover about 3.5 per cent of the total area. Common trees are babul, neem, shisham, pipal and banyan.

Fauna: Animals and birds found in the state include: leopard, jackal, the Indian fox, barking deer, sambar, chital, black buck, wild boar, seh or Indian porcupine, blue jay, northern green barbet, coppersmith, rose-ringed parakeet, kingfisher, Indian krait and Russell's viper.

History

The word 'Hariana' occurs in a Sanskrit inscription dated AD 1328. The region now known as Haryana was the scene of many important battles in Indian history. These include the three battles of Panipat: the first in 1526, when Babur defeated Ibrahim Lodi to establish Mughal rule in India; the second in 1556, when Emperor Akbar's army defeated the Afghans; and the third in 1761, when Ahmad Shah Abdali defeated the Marathas.

In 1803, the area included in the present state was ceded to the British East India Company and was subsequently transferred to the North-Western Provinces in 1832. Haryana became a part of Punjab in 1858, and remained so well after independence. Demands for states on a linguistic basis started to gain momentum in the early 1960s. On 1 November 1966, with the passage of the Punjab Reorganization Act, Haryana became the 17th state of India. Bhagwat Dayal Sharma was the first Chief Minister of the state.

Politics

In 1956, the states of PEPSU had been merged with Punjab, which remained a trilingual state having three language speakers—Punjabi, Hindi and Pahari—within its borders. In the Punjabi speaking part of the state, there was a strong demand for carving out a separate Punjabi Suba (Punjabi-speaking state). The State Reorganisation Commission had refused to accept the demand for a separate Punjabi-speaking state on the ground that this would not solve the language problem of Punjab. Finally, in 1966, Indira Gandhi agreed to the division of Punjab into two Punjabi and Hindi speaking states of Haryana, with the Pahari-speaking district of Kangra and a part of Hoshiarpur district being merged with Himachal Pradesh. Thus Haryana was created on 1 November 1966, when PEPSU was split between a Hindu majority state and a Sikh majority state. The mostly Hindu and Hindi-speaking eastern portion of Punjab became Haryana, while themostly Sikh and Punjabi-speaking western portion remained as Punjab. Today, Haryana has the vast majority of the ethnic Hindu population. Chandigarh, on the linguistic border, was made a union territory that serves as capital of both these states.

The Haryana state Legislature is unicameral right from its inception. The Haryana Legislative Assembly, which came into existence on 1 November 1966, had 54 seats out of which 10 were reserved for the Scheduled Castes. The strength was raised to 81 members in March 1967. The number of seats in the Assembly was further raised to 90 in 1977, including 17 reserved seats. There is no nominated member.

Five Chief Ministers in this state had more than two tenures though most of them did not last the complete tenure of five years. Jat strongman Devi Lal was Chief Minister twice. The first Chief Minister of Haryana was Bhagwat Dayal Sharma who took charge when Haryana was created on 1 November 1966, after dividing Punjab. He remained in the position till 24 March 1967. He was succeeded by Rao Birendra Singh who remained in power till 21 November 1967. Congress Leader Bansi Lal assumed charge for the first time in 1968 and remained Chief Minister till 1975. He was again Chief Minister between 1987-89. His last tenure was from 1996-99. Banarsi Dass Gupta who succeeded Bansi Lal on 7 December 1975 also remained Chief Minister twice—once for two years (7 December to 21 May 1977) and once just for two months (22 May 1990 to 12 July 1990). Devi Lal succeeded him on 21 May 1977.

Devi Lal played an active and decisive role in the formation of Haryana as a separate state. In 1958 he was elected from Sirsa. In 1971 he left the Congress after being in it for 39 years. He was elected in 1974 from Rori constituency against Congress. In 1975 Emergency was declared, and Devi Lal along with all opposition leaders was sent to jail for 19 months in Hissar Jail and Mahendergarh fort. In 1977 Emergency ended and general elections were held. Devi Lal was elected on a Janata Party ticket and became the Chief Minister of Haryana. He formed Lok Dal and started a movement called Nyaya Yudh under 'Haryana Sangharsh Samiti' and became hugely popular among the masses. In the 1987 state elections, the alliance led by Ch. Devi Lal won a record victory winning 85 seats in the 90-member house. Congress was routed in the state winning only 5 seats. Chaudhary Devi Lal became the Chief Minister of Haryana for the second time. He remained in power till 2 December 1989.

Bhajan Lal first became Chief Minister on 28 June 1979. In 1982, he opted for mid-term polls and came back to the post. He continued till 1985. He was again Chief Minister from 23 July 1991 to 11 May 1996. Chautala has served the state four times as Chief

Minister. It was on 2 December 1989 that he first assumed the office of Chief Minister and he remained in power till 22 May 1990. It was again on 12 July 1990, 22 March 1991 and 24 July 1999 that he assumed the office of Chief Minister. He was elected unanimously as the President of the Haryana Unit of Indian National Lok Dal in 1999. He remained President of Haryana State Janata Dal and National General Secretary of the Samajwadi Janata party. He also served as Secretary General of the Samajwadi Janata Party and Chief of the Kisan Kamgar Cell of All India Lok Dal. Hukam Singh was the Chief Minister of the state from 17 July 1990 to 22 March 1991.

Bhupinder Singh Hooda took oath on 5 March 2005 as the 19th Chief Minister of Haryana since the state was formed in 1966. Hooda of the Congress party replaced Om Prakash Chautala of the Indian National Lok Dal (INLD) whose party was routed in the recent state Assembly polls.

Culture

Haryana has a tradition of folklore expressed through mimes, dramas, ballads and songs such as Phag dance, Loor, Saang, Chupaiya and so on.

Fairs and festivals: Prominent festivals of Haryana are Holi, Diwali, Teej, Gugga Pir and Sanjhi. Popular fairs include Gopal-Mochan fair, Masani fair and Surajkund crafts fair. The Mango Festival and the Kurukshetra Festival are other popular annual events.

Economy, Industry and Agriculture

Economy: The net state domestic product at current prices for 2002–03 (provisional) was Rs 57,937 crores. The per capita net state domestic product at current prices for 2002–03 (provisional) was Rs 26,632.

Minerals and industry: The manufacturing sector's contribution to the state economy was 21.3 per cent during 1998–99. Major industries include passenger cars, motorcycles, tractors, sanitary ware, GI pipes, scientific instruments and gas stoves. In thirty years, the number of large and medium units has gone up from 162 to 1023, while the number of small-scale units increased from 4500 to 80,000. In recent years, many multinational companies have set up Business Process Outsourcing (BPO) operations in Gurgaon. Major minerals of the state are limestone, dolomite, china clay and marble.

Agriculture: Apart from meeting its own requirements, Haryana contributes about 45 lakh tonnes of food grain (mostly wheat and paddy) to the Central pool each year. Other important crops are sugarcane, cotton and maize.

Animal husbandry is a significant component of agriculture in the state. Apart from the 'Murrah' breed of buffaloes, the state regularly supplies eggs, layer-chicks and broilers to other Indian states.

Power: Most of Haryana's power is generated by thermal power plants. The rest comes from hydroelectric plants.

Education

Educational institutes: Notable institutions include the
• Maharshi Dayanand University (Rohtak)
• Kurukshetra University (Kurukshetra)
• Guru Jambheshwar University (Hissar)
• Chaudhary Charan Singh Agriculture University (Hissar)
• National Dairy Research Institute (NDRI) (Karnal)

Tourism

Major tourist attractions: Surajkund, Kurukshetra, Panipat.

Airports: Chandigarh.

National Parks: Sultanpur National Park in Gurgaon dist. (1.43 sq. km).

Administration

Legislature: The state has a unicameral legislature with 90 members. Out of this 17 seats are reserved for SCs. The tenure of the current house ends on 8 March 2005. The current party position is as follows:

Name of Party	Seats
Indian National Congress	67
Indian National Lok Dal	9
Bharatiya Janata Party	2
Bahujan Samaj Party	1
Nationalist Congress Party	1
Independents	10
Total	**90**

Judiciary: The seat of the Punjab and Haryana High Court is at Chandigarh. The current chief justice is D.K. Jain.

Districts:

District	Area (sq. km)	Population	Headquarters	Urban Agglomerations
Ambala	1,574	1,013,660	Ambala	Ambala
Bhiwani	4,778	1,424,554	Bhiwani	
Faridabad	2,151	2,193,276	Faridabad	
Fatehabad	2,538	806,158	Fatehabad	
Gurgaon	2,766	1,657,669	Gurgaon	Gurgaon
Hisar	3,983	1,536,417	Hisar	Hisar
Jhajjar	1,834	887,392	Jhajjar	Bahadurgarh
Jind	2,702	1,189,725	Jind	
Kaithal	2,317	945,631	Kaithal	
Karnal	2,520	1,274,843	Karnal	Karnal
Kurukshetra	1,530	828,120	Kurukshetra	Thanesar
Mahendragarh	1,859	812,022	Narnaul	
Panchkula	898	469,210	Panchkula	Pinjore
Panipat	1,268	967,338	Panipat	Panipat
Rewari	1,582	764,727	Rewari	
Rohtak	1,745	940,036	Rohtak	Rohtak
Sirsa	4,277	1,111,012	Sirsa	
Sonipat	2,122	1,278,830	Sonipat	Sonipat
Yamunanagar	1,768	982,369	Yamunanagar	Yamunanagar

Himachal Pradesh

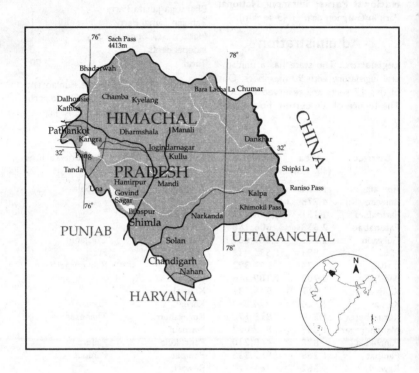

Key Statistics

Capital: Shimla.
Area: 55,673 sq. km.
Population: Total: 6,077,900
Male: 3,087,940
Female: 2,989,960
Population density: 109 per sq. km.
Sex ratio: 968 females per 1000 males.
Principal languages: Hindi, Punjabi,
  Kinnauri.
Literacy rates: Total: 76.5%
Male: 85.3%
Female: 67.4%

Government

Governor: Vishnu Sadashiv Kokje. He assumed the office of the governor on 8 May 2003.

Chief Minister: Virbhadra Singh (INC). He was sworn in on 6 March 2003.

Geography

Physical characteristics: Almost completely mountainous, with altitudes varying from 350 m to 6,975 m above sea level, Himachal Pradesh can be divided into five zones: (i) Wet sub-temperate zone (parts of Kangra, Mandi and Chamba districts); (ii) Humid sub-temperate zone (Kullu and Shimla districts; parts of Mandi, Solan, Chamba, Kangra and Sirmaur districts); (iii) Dry temperate alpine highlands (parts of Lahaul and Spiti district); (iv) Humid subtropical zone (Sirmaur district; parts of Chamba, Solan and Kangra districts); and (v) Sub-humid subtropical zone (parts of Kangra district).

Neighbouring States and Union territories:
International border:
China

States:
• Jammu and Kashmir
• Uttaranchal
• Punjab
• Haryana
• Uttar Pradesh

Major rivers:
• Sutlej
• Beas
• Ravi
• Chenab
• Yamuna

Climate: The climate varies from hot and humid in the valley areas to freezing cold in the alpine zone, which remains under snow for five to six months a year. Temperatures range from 40°C in plains during summer to −20°C in the alpine zone during winters. The average annual rainfall is about 1600mm.

Flora and Fauna:
Flora: Vegetation varies from dry scrub forests at lower altitudes to alpine pastures at higher altitudes. Between these two extremes, there are zones of mixed deciduous forests with deodar, chil, oak, bamboo, kail, spruce and fir.

Fauna: Wildlife found in Himachal Pradesh includes musk deer (the state animal), himalayan tahr, brown bear, snow leopard, ibex, western tragopan, sambhar, barking deer, wild boar, ghoral, leopard, monal (the state bird), cheer, snow cock and white crested kaleej.

History

The earliest known inhabitants of this mountainous region were a tribe called Dasas and later, Aryans. Successive Indian empires such as the Mauryans, the Kushans, the Guptas and the Mughals exercised varying degrees of control over the area. British domination of the region followed the Anglo-Sikh wars of the 1840s and continued for the next 100 years. After independence, 30 princely states were united to form the chief commissioner's province of Himachal Pradesh, which went on to become a Union territory in 1956.

With the reorganization of Punjab in 1966, Kangra and some other hill areas of Punjab were included in Himachal Pradesh, though its status remained that of a Union territory. Himachal Pradesh became the eighteenth state of the Indian Union on 25 January 1971. Yashwant Singh Parmar was the first Chief Minister.

Politics

Himachal Pradesh was formed as a union territory in 1948 by the merger of 30 former Punjabi princely states. The head was the Chief Commissioner. The first Chief Commissioner was N.C. Mehta and he was assisted by his deputy E. Penderal Moon, ICS. On 30 September 1948, an advisory council was formed for the advise of the Chief Commissioner for administrative functions. In 1951, Himachal Pradesh became a part 'C' state. Vide Section 3 of Part 'C' States Act, 1951 Himachal

Pradesh was brought under a Lt. Governor with a 36 member Legislative Assembly. First elections to the Assembly were held in 1952. In 1954 Bilaspur, another part-C state, was merged with Himachal Pradesh and the strength of its Assembly was raised to 41. Yashwant Singh Parmar became the first Chief Minister in 1952 and he remained in power till 1956.

In 1956, despite majority recommendation of the States Reorganization Commission for its merger with Punjab, Himachal Pradesh retained its separate identity, thanks to the famous dissenting note of the Chairman of the Commission, Justice Fazal Ali which found favour with the Centre. But a great price had to be paid as Himachal was made a Union Territory sans Legislative Assembly and was placed under an Administrator designated as Lt. Governor. Instead of a Legislative Assembly it was provided with a Territorial Council with limited powers. Thereafter, the people and the political leadership of the state had to literally move heaven and earth for the restoration of a democratic edifice. Their efforts finally bore fruit in 1963, when a bill was passed by the Union Parliament for providing Legislative Assemblies and Council of Ministers to certain Union Territories including H.P. It was enforced in the case of Himachal Pradesh from 1 July 1963 after receiving the President's assent. The Territorial Council which was a replica of a dyarchical form of government was converted into a Legislative Assembly of the Union Territory. The strength of the Assembly was fixed at 43 including 2 nominated members. The Assembly held its first sitting from 1 October 1963.

Again Yashwant Singh Parmar became the Chief Minister in 1963 and remained in power till 1977. In 1966 five more districts and parts of two others from Punjab were added to the territory. The state of Himachal Pradesh attained statehood in the year 1971, emerging as the eighteenth state of the Indian Union. It established its own High Court with headquarters at 'Revenswood' Shimla.

With the merger of new areas into Himachal Pradesh in 1966, the number of members in the House rose to 56 including 2 nominated members. The strength of the House was further raised to 63 (60 elected and 3 nominated) after section 24 (3) of Punjab Reorganization Act, 1966 (Act No. 31 of 1966) came into force in 1967. After delimitation of Assembly seats in the year 1971–72, the number of members in the Assembly now stands at 68. After Parmar, Ramlal Chauhan remained in the Chief Minister's office from 28 January to 22 June. Again he was the Chief Minister from 14 February 1980 to 8 April 1983. Virbhadra Singh, who had three tenures as Chief Minister, succeeded him. For the first time from 8 April 1983 to 5 March 1990 he was in the Chief Minister's post. Shanta Kumar of the BJP who previously served as the Chief Minister from 22 June 1977 to 14 February 1980 again came to power in 1990 and held the position of CM till 1993. He was succeeded by Virbhadra Singh. Prem Kumar Dhumal took over as the fifth Chief Minister of the state on 24 March 1998 and was the first non-Congressman to complete his term. Again Virbhadra Singh of the Congress party came to power in 2003.

Culture

Dances of Himachal include the Rakshasa (demon) dance, Kayang, Jataru Kayang, Chohara, Shand, Shabu, Lang-dar-ma, Jhanjhar and Rasa. These are accompanied by instruments like the Ranasingha, Karna, Turhi, Kindari, Jhanjh and Ghariyal. Popular weaving and handicrafts traditions include the Kullu and Kinnauri shawls, tweeds and blankets, carpets, traditional dresses, metal craft and pottery. Himachal is also famous for the Kangra Valley School of Painting.

Fairs and festivals: Prominent fairs and festivals of the state include Kullu Dussehra, Shimla's Summer Festival, Lohri or Maghi, Basant Panchami, Mandi Shivratri, Holi, Nalwari fair, Baisakhi, Phulech (Festival of Flowers), Minjar fair and Lahaul Festival.

Economy, Industry and Agriculture

Economy: The net state domestic product at current prices in 2002–03 (advance estimate) was Rs 14,202 crores. The per capita net state domestic product at current prices in 2002–03 (advance estimate) was Rs 22,576.

Minerals and industry: Major industries of Himachal Pradesh are chemicals and chemical products, textile, electronics, steel and steel products, paper and paper products, cement, beverages and plastic products. Minerals found in the state include limestone (light grade), quartzite, gold, pyrites, copper, rock salt, natural oil, gas, mica, barytes and gypsum.

Agriculture: Himachal Pradesh is predominantly an agricultural state with nearly 70% of the total population getting direct employment from agriculture. Important crops include maize, paddy, wheat, barley, vegetables, ginger and potato. Main fruits under cultivation are apple, pear, apricot, plum, peach, mango, litchi, guava and strawberry.

Power: Himachal has a huge identified hydroelectric potential in its five river basins. All of the state's power comes from hydroelectric plants.

Education

Educational institutes: Prominent educational institutions include
• Himachal Pradesh University, Shimla
• Dr Y.S. Parmar University of Horticulture and Forestry, Solan
• C.S.K. H.P. Krishi Vishva Vidyalaya, Palampur
• Jaypee University of Information Technology (JUIT), Solan
• Indian Institute of Advanced Studies, Shimla
• National Institute of Technology, Hamirpur
• Indira Gandhi Medical College, Shimla.

Tourism

Major tourist attractions:
1. Shimla: The Ridge, The Mall, Kali Bari Temple, State Museum, Chadwick Falls, Mashobra, Naldehra.
2. Chamba: Dalhousie, Laxmi Narayan Temple, Champavati Temple, Akhand Chandi Palace, Panchpula, Kalatop, Khajiar, Banikhet.
3. Kangra: Dharamshala, Kangra Fort, Palampur.
4. Solan: Kasauli, Chail.
5. Sirmaur: Nahan, Suketi Fossil Park, Paonta Sahib, Renuka.
6. Kullu: Manali, Bijli Mahadev Shrine, Raghunathji Temple, Camping Sight Raison, Hadimba Temple, Tibetan Monasteries, Rohtang Pass.
7. Kinnaur: Sangla Valley, Chitkul, Recong Peo, Rakchham.
8. Lahaul and Spiti: Gondla, Tandi, Shashur Monastery, Kardang Monastery, Thang. Yug Gompa.

Airports:
• Shimla
• Kullu
• Kangra (Gaggal).

National Parks:
• Great Himalayan National Park, Kullu (754 sq. km)
• Pin Valley National Park, Lahaul-Spiti (675 sq. km).

Administration

Legislature: The Himachal Pradesh Legislative Assembly has 68 seats, of which 16 are reserved for SCs and 3 for STs. The term of the current house expires on 9 March 2008. The current party position is as follows:

Name of Party	Seats
Indian National Congress	43
Bharatiya Janata Party	16
Himachal Vikas Congress	1
Lok Jan Shakti Party	1
Loktantrik Morcha Himachal Pradesh	1
Independents	6
Total	**68**

Judiciary: The seat of the Himachal Pradesh High Court is in Shimla. The current chief justice is Justice V.K. Gupta.

Districts:

District	Area (sq. km)	Population	Headquarters	Urban Agglomerations
Bilaspur	1,167	340,735	Bilaspur	
Chamba	6,528	460,499	Chamba	
Hamirpur	1,118	412,009	Hamirpur	
Kangra	5,739	1,338,536	Dharamshala	
Kinnaur	6,401	83,950	Recong Peo	
Kullu	5,503	379,865	Kullu	
Lahaul and Spiti	13,835	33,224	Keylong	
Mandi	3,950	900,987	Mandi	
Shimla	5,131	721,745	Shimla	Shimla
Sirmaur	2,825	458,351	Nahan	
Solan	1,936	499,380	Solan	
Una	1,540	447,967	Una	

Jammu and Kashmir

Key Statistics

Capital: Summer (May–October)—Srinagar; Winter (November–April)—Jammu.

Area: 222,236 sq. km.

Population: Total: 10,069,917
Male: 5,300,574
Female: 4,769,343

Population density: 99 per sq. km.

Sex ratio: 900 females per 1000 males.

Principal languages: Urdu, Kashmiri, Dogri.

Literacy rates: Total: 54.46%
Male: 65.75%
Female: 41.82%

Government

Governor: Lt Gen. (Retd) Sriniwas Kumar Sinha. He took over as governor on 4 June 2003.

Chief Minister: Mufti Mohammed Sayeed (PDP). He was sworn in on 2 November 2002.

Geography

Physical characteristics: The northern extremity of India, Jammu and Kashmir is bounded by Pakistan, Afghanistan and China from west to east. Himachal Pradesh and Punjab are on its south. The state has four geographical zones: (i) The submountainous and semi-mountainous plain known as Kandi; (ii) The Shivalik ranges; (iii) The high mountain zone constituting the Kashmir valley, the Pir Panjal range and its offshoots; (iv) The middle run of the Indus river comprising Leh and Kargil.

Neighbouring States and Union territories:
International border:
• Pakistan
• Afghanistan
• China.

States:
• Himachal Pradesh
• Punjab.

Major rivers:
• Indus
• Chenab
• Jhelum
• Ravi.

Climate: The climate varies from tropical in the plains of Jammu to semi-arctic cold in Ladakh. The mountainous tracts in Kashmir and Jammu have temperate climatic conditions. Annual rainfall varies from 92.6mm in Leh to 650.5mm in Srinagar and 1115.9mm in Jammu.

Flora and Fauna:
Flora: Flora in Jammu and Kashmir ranges from the thorn bush type in arid plains to the temperate and alpine flora in higher altitudes. Maple, horse chestnuts and silver fir are the common broad-leaf trees. Birch, rhododendron, berbers and a large number of herbs are found on higher altitudes. The state is also famous for its Chinar tree that is found all over the valley. Other trees found in the state include almond, walnut, willow and cedar. The mountain ranges have deodar, pine and fir.

Fauna: Wildlife in the state include leopard, hangul or Kashmir stag, wild sheep, bear, brown musk shrew, musk rat, varieties of snakes, chakor, snow partridge, pheasants and peacock. The fauna in Ladakh includes yak, Himalayan ibex, Tibetan antelope, snow leopard, wild ass, red bear and gazelle. Besides these, the state is known for its trout population.

History

Legend has it that Kashyapa Rishi reclaimed the land that now comprises Kashmir from a vast lake. It came to be known as Kashyapamar and, later, Kashmir. Emperor Asoka introduced Buddhism to the region in 3 BC. Subsequently, the valley became parts of the empires of Kanishka and Mihiragula. Around 7th century AD, a local dynasty, the Karkotas, believed to have been founded by Durlabhavardhana, came to power in the region. According to Kalhana, the famous historian of Kashmir, this dynasty spread its power under the reign of Lalitaditya. He is believed to have defeated Kanauj, the Tibetans and even the Turks in the Indus area. His grandson, Jayapada Vinyaditya, achieved victories over Gauda and Kanauj. This dynasty came to an end around 855. The house of Utpalas followed. Its founder was Avantivarman. His son, Sankaravarmana expanded the state's territorial limits and is believed to have even annexed a part of Punjab from the Gurjaras. A period of turmoil followed his death during which the widowed queen, Sugandha, attempted to rule. She faced fierce opposition from the Tantrins, a powerful military faction. They emerged as the virtual military dictators of the territory. But ultimately a group of Brahmanas elevated Yasaskara, a member of their order, to the throne of Kashmir. The lien started by Yasaskara was succeeded by the dynasty started by Parva Gupta.

The Hindu rule over Kashmir came to an end in the 14th century. In around 1339 or 1346, a Muslim adventurer named Shah Mirza seized power and assumed the title of Shams-ud-din Shah. The Sultanate of Kashmir thus established ruled till about 1540 when a relative of Humayun, Mirza Haidar, annexed Kashmir. He ruled Kashmir virtually as a sovereign although in theory he ruled on behalf of Humayun. In 1551, the local nobles ousted Mirza Haidar. In around 1555, the Chakks seized the throne. Kashmir ultimately became a part of the Mughal Empire in Akbar's reign.

In 1819, Kashmir was annexed to the Sikh kingdom of Punjab and later on to the Dogra kingdom of Jammu in 1846. In 1846, the treaties of Lahore and Amritsar that were signed at the conclusion of the First Sikh War made Raja Gulab Singh, the Dogra ruler of Jammu, the ruler of an extensive Himalayan kingdom. The state was under Dogra rule till 1947, when Maharaja Hari Singh signed the Instrument of Accession in favour of the Indian union.

Much drama surrounds Jammu and Kashmir's accession to the Indian Union. Jammu and Kashmir was one of the princely states of India on which British paramountcy lapsed at midnight on 15 August 1947. When power was transferred to the people in British India, the rulers of the princely states were given an option to join either India or Pakistan. The ruler of Jammu and Kashmir, Maharaja Hari Singh, did not exercise the option immediately. Instead, he offered a 'Standstill Agreement' to both India and Pakistan, pending a final decision. On 12 August 1947, the Prime Minister of Jammu and Kashmir sent identical communications to the governments of India and Pakistan, offering to enter into Standstill Agreements with both the countries. While Pakistan entered into a Standstill Agreement, India declined and instead asked the state to send its emissary for talks. Meanwhile, a 'Quit Kashmir' movement was active under the leadership of Sheikh Mohammad Abdullah. Sheikh Abdullah was against the Kashmir ruler's autocratic rule as well as an accession to Pakistan and enjoyed public support.

When Pakistani designs on acquiring the state failed, they sent in thousands of tribals along with regular Pakistani troops who entered the state on 22 October 1947. This finally caused the Maharaja to sign the Instrument of Accession in favour of India on 26 October 1947, agreeing to the prescribed terms and conditions. On 30 October 1947, an Emergency Government was formed in the state with Sheikh Mohammad Abdullah as its head. The Indian Army was sent in and it successfully flushed out the invaders. On 1 January 1948, India took up the issue of Pakistani aggression in Jammu and Kashmir at the United Nations. Consequently, a ceasefire came into operation on the midnight of 1 January 1949. At the time of ceasefire, Pakistan was in illegal possession of 78,114 sq. km. It remains in possession of this territory even today.

On 5 March 1948, the Maharaja announced the formation of an interim popular government with Sheikh Mohammad Abdullah as the Prime Minister. The Maharaja then signed a proclamation making Yuvraj Karan Singh the Regent. Pakistan waged two more wars, in 1965 and 1971, with the intention of annexing all of Jammu and Kashmir, but was beaten back.

In 1959, Chinese troops occupied the Aksai Chin part of Ladakh. In 1963, a Sino-Pakistani agreement defined the Chinese border with Pakistani Kashmir and ceded Indian-claimed territory to China.

Politics

Jammu and Kashmir was one of about 565 princely states of India on which the British paramountcy lapsed at the stroke of midnight on 15 August 1947. While the power was transferred to the people in British India, the rulers of the princely states were given an option to join either of the two Dominions – India or Pakistan. Moreover, in the Indian Independence Act, 1947, there was no provision for any conditional accession. The ruler of Jammu and Kashmir, Maharaja Hari Singh, did not exercise the option immediately and instead offered a proposal of Standstill Agreement to both the Dominions, pending final decision on the state's accession. India did not agree to the offer and advised the Maharaja to send his authorized representative to Delhi for discussion on the offer. The Maharaja was already facing a formidable challenge from the people who had launched the Quit Kashmir movement under the leadership of Sher-I-Kashmir Sheikh Mohammad Abdullah against the Maharaja's rule.

The Quit Kashmir movement ran parallel to the national movement with Sheikh Mohammad Abdullah having a close association with the leaders of the national movement against British rule. The national leaders like Mahatma Gandhi and Pandit Nehru too espoused the cause of the people of Kashmir seeking political freedom from auto-

cratic rule. To deal with the people's upsurge, the Maharaja had even detained Sheikh Abdullah on 20 May 1946 for spearheading the 'Quit-Kashmir' movement. Faced with a new alarming situation arising out of repeated violations of the Standstill Agreement by Pakistan and blocking of the Pindi-Srinagar road, the Maharaja set him free on 29 September 1947. Mohammad Abdullah deputed his close aide Kh.G.M.Sadiq to Pakistan to tell Pak leaders about the sentiments of the people who could not be taken for granted and coerced to join them. This plain speaking did not make Pakistan discontinue its intrusions into Kashmir. At last bowing before the wishes of the people as reflected by the Muslim dominated National Conference and to resist the invaders, the Maharaja signed the Instrument of Accession in favour of India on 26 October 1947 on the prescribed terms and conditions. This was accepted by the Governor General of India, Lord Mountbatten next day. The Instrument of Accession executed by Maharaja Hari Singh was the same which was signed by other rulers of the princely states. Similarly, the acceptance of the Instrument of Accession by the Governor General was also identical in respect of all such instruments.

With J&K becoming a legal and constitutional part of the Union of India, the Indian troops were rushed to the state to push back the invaders and vacate aggressors from the territory of the state. On 30 October 1947 an Emergency government was formed in the state with Sheikh Mohammad Abdullah as its head. The Army fought a sustained battle with the tribals and after several sacrifices pushed them out of the Valley and other areas in the Jammu region. On 1 January 1948 India took up the issue of Pak aggression in Jammu and Kashmir in the UNO under

Article 35 of its charter. The Government of India requested the Security Council to call upon Pakistan to put an end immediately to the giving of such assistance, which was an act of aggression against India. If Pakistan did not do so, India said, the Government of India may be compelled, in self defence, to enter into Pakistan territory to take military action against the invaders. After long debates, a cease-fire came into operation on the midnight of 1 January 1949. Presence of Pak regular troops in the Valley was attested even by UNCIP documents (UNCIP first report). At the time of cease-fire, Pakistan was holding 78,114 sq. kms illegally and this aggression on that territory continues even today. On 5 March 1948, the Maharaja announced the formation of an interim popular government with Sheikh Mohammad Abdullah as the Prime Minister. Subsequently, the Maharaja signed a proclamation making Yuvraj Karan Singh the Regent. So far India and Pakistan have been to war three times in Kashmir (1947-1948, 1965, 1971) and clashed there again during the Kargil Conflict of 1999.

J&K after attaining political freedom, marched ahead to strengthen its democratic structure. In 1951, the State Constituent Assembly was elected by the people. The Assembly met for the first time in Srinagar on 31 October 1951. Close on the heels of this, the Delhi Agreement was signed between the two Prime Ministers of India and Jammu and Kashmir giving special position to the state under the Indian Constitutional framework. The Constituent Assembly elected the Yuvraj as the Sadar-I-Riyasat on 15 November 1952, thus bringing to end the 106 year old hereditary rule in Jammu and Kashmir. The State Constituent Assembly ratified the accession of the state

to the Union of India on 6 February 1954 and the President of India subsequently issued the Constitution (Application to J&K) Order under Article 370 of the Indian Constitution extending the Union Constitution to the state with some exceptions and modifications. The state's own Constitution came into force on 26 January 1957 under which the elections to the state Legislative Assembly were held for the first time on the basis of adult franchise the same year. This Constitution ratified the state's accession to Union of India. Section 3 of the Constitution makes this historic fact a reality. This section 3 of the Constitution says that the state of Jammu and Kashmir is and shall be an integral part of the Union of India. Section 4 of the Constitution defined the territories which on the fifteenth day of August 1947, were under the sovereignty of the ruler of the state. Since then eight assembly elections have been held in the state besides Lok Sabha elections where the people exercised their franchise freely.

The first Legislature of Jammu and Kashmir, consisting of a Council of Ministers and an Assembly, was established in 1934. The Constitution of the state of Jammu and Kashmir framed by a separate Constituent Assembly came into force from 26 January 1957. Section 46 of the Jammu & Kashmir Constitution states that the Legislature shall consist of the Governor and the two Houses known as the Legislative Council (Upper House) and the Legislative Assembly (Lower House). The Legislative Assembly consisted of 100 members chosen by direct election from the territorial constituencies in the state. Subsequently, under the Constitution of Jammu and Kashmir (Twentieth Amendment) Act, 1988—this was raised to 111. However, as per section 48 of the state Constitution, twenty-four seats remain vacant in the Legislative Assembly for the area of the state presently under the occupation of Pakistan. The Jammu and Kashmir Legislative Assembly at present consists of 89 members out of which 87 are elected and 2 are nominated.

Bakshi Ghulam Mohammad held the reins of government in the wake of Sheikh Abdullah's deposition in 1953. Bakshi had to face unprecedented challenges from the forces of disintegration and secessionism, which got a new lease of life after the Sheikh's dismissal in 1953.He remained in power till 12 October 1963. He was succeeded by Khwaja Shams-ud-Din as Prime Minister who remained in power till 29 February 1964. Ghulam Mohammad Sadiq was the Prime Minister from 29 February 1964 to 30 March 1965. The state's Constitution was amended on 30 March 1965 to rename the Sadr-e-Riyasat (President) as Governor and the Prime Minister as the Chief Minister. Ghulam Mohammad Sadiq was the last Prime Minister and became the first Chief Minister of the state on 10 April 1965 and remained in office till December 1971. Syed Mir Qasim held the post between December 1971 and February 1975. The founder president of National Conference Shiekh Mohammad Abdullah held the post twice from 1975 to 1982. He was succeeded by Farroq Abdullah who held the post thrice heading a National Conference government from 1982-84, 1987-90 and 1996-2002. In between, Abdullah's brother-in-law Ghulam Mohammad Shah held the top office during 1984–86. A nine-member ministry headed by People's Democratic Party president Mufti Mohammad Sayeed as Chief Minister was sworn in in Jammu and Kashmir on 2 November 2002. Mufti Mohammad, who heads the PDP-Cong coalition government, is the sixth Chief Minister of the state. His government has the outside support of Peoples Democratic Front comprising independents and CPI(M) legislators.

Culture

Popular performing traditions of the Jammu region include Kud, a ritual dance performed in honour of local deities and the traditional theatre form Heren. Folk traditions in the Kashmir region include the theatre-style Bhand Pather and the Chakri form of music. There is also a rich tradition in Sufiana music. Jabro and Alley Yate are popular dance forms in the Ladakh region.

Fairs and festivals: Principal festivals of the state include Lohri, Baisakhi and Bahu Mela in the Jammu region; Id-ul-Fitr, Id-ul-Zuha and Miraj Alam in the Kashmir region; and Mela Losar and Hemis festival in the Ladakh region.

Economy, Industry and Agriculture

Economy: The net state domestic product at current prices for 2001–02 was Rs 13,697crore. The per capita net state domestic product at current prices for 2001–02 was Rs 13,320.

Minerals and industry: Handicrafts production and export, mainly papier mache, wood carving, carpets, shawls, copper and silverware have been the traditional industry of the state. Other important industries include plastic products, cricket bats and other sports items, chemicals and basic drugs, electronics and precision engineering. The state has small mineral and fossil fuel resources largely concentrated in the Jammu region. There are bauxite and gypsum deposits in Udhampur district.

Other minerals include limestone, coal, zinc, and copper.

Agriculture: Nearly 80 per cent of the state's population depends on agriculture. Major crops include paddy, wheat, maize, pulses, cotton and barley. Horticulture is also widespread. Large orchards in the Kashmir valley produce apples, pears, peaches, walnuts, almonds, cherries, apricots, strawberries and saffron.

Power: Nearly all of Jammu and Kashmir's power comes from hydroelectric plants.

Education

Educational institutes:
• Notable educational institutes include University of Jammu, Jammu
• University of Kashmir, Srinagar
• Sher-e-Kashmir University of Agricultural Sciences and Technology, Srinagar.

Tourism

Major tourist attractions:
1. Jammu: Bahu Fort, Mubarak Mandi Complex, Ziarat Baba Buddan Shah, Raghunath Temple, Vaishno Devi Shrine, Mansar Lake, Patnitop.
2. Kashmir: Dal Lake, Hazratbal Shrine, Shankarcharya Temple, Gulmarg, Pahalgam, Sonamarg, Charar-i-Sharief, Amarnath.
3. Ladakh: Buddhist Gompas or monasteries at Hemis, Alchi, Thikse, and Spituk; Shey Palace, Jama Masjid, Leh Palace.

Airports:
• Srinagar
Jammu
• Leh.

National Parks:
• Dachigam in Srinagar (141 sq. km)
• Hemis Leh (4100 sq. km)
• Kishtwar Doda (310 sq. km).

Administration

Legislature: Jammu and Kashmir has a special status within the Union government: the state has its own Constitution (adopted in 1956) that affirms its integrity within the Republic of India.

The state assembly has a total of 87 seats, with seven seats reserved for scheduled castes. As per Article 52 of the Constitution of J&K, the term of the state assembly is for six years. The term of the current house expires on 20 November 2008. The current party position is as follows:

Name of Party	Seats
Jammu and Kashmir National Conference	28
Indian National Congress	20
Peoples Democratic Party	16
J and K National Panthers Party	4
Communist Party of India (Marxist)	2
Jammu and Kashmir Awami League	1
Democratic Movement	1
Bahujan Samaj Party	1
Bharatiya Janata Party	1
Independent	13
Total	**87**

Judiciary: The headquarters of the Jammu and Kashmir High Court is at Srinagar from May to October, and at Jammu from November to April. However, court sections of both Jammu and Srinagar wings of the High Court function throughout the year. The current chief justice is Sachchidanand Jha.

Districts:

District	Area (sq. km)	Population	Headquarters	Urban Agglomerations
Anantanag	3,984	1,170,013	Anantanag	Anantnag
Badgam	1,371	593,768	Badgam	
Baramula	4,588	1,166,722	Baramula	Baramula, Sopore
Doda	11,691	690,474	Doda	
Jammu	3,097	1,571,911	Jammu	Jammu
Kargil	14,036	115,227	Kargil	
Kathua	2,651	544,206	Kathua	Kathua
Kupwara	2,379	640,013	Kupwara	
Leh	45,110	117,637	Leh	
Pulwama	1,398	632,295	Pulwama	
Punch	1,674	371,561	Punch	
Rajauri	2,630	478,595	Rajauri	
Srinagar	2,228	1,238,530	Srinagar	Srinagar
Udhampur	4,550	738,965	Udhampur	Udhampur

Jharkhand

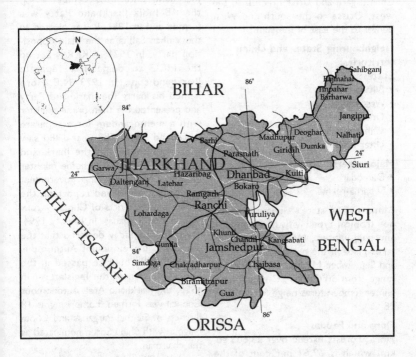

Key Statistics

Capital: Ranchi.
Area: 79,714 sq. km.
Population: Total: 26,945,829
Male: 13,885,037
Female: 13,060,792
Population density: 338 per sq. km.
Sex ratio: 941 females per 1000 males.
Principal languages: Local languages like Santhali, Hindi, Urdu.
Literacy rates: Total: 53.6%
Male: 67.3%
Female: 38.9%

Government

Governor: Syed Sibte Razi. He was sworn in on 10 June 2004.

Chief Minister: Arjun Munda (BJP). He was sworn in on 18 March 2003.

Geography

Physical characteristics: The Jharkhand region lies to the south of Bihar and encompasses Santhal Parganas and Chota Nagpur. It is a plateau region about 1000 metres above sea level, which features densely forested hill ranges. The highest part of the plateau is Netarhat (1100 metres). The Parasnath Hill is the highest point in the state (1500 metres). Bihar lies to the north, Chhattisgarh and Uttar Pradesh to the west, Orissa to the south and West Bengal to the east of the state.

Neighbouring States and Union territories:
States:
• Bihar
• West Bengal
• Orissa
• Chhattisgarh
• Uttar Pradesh.

Major rivers:
• Damodar
• Subarna-rekha.

Climate: The state's climate is of the hot tropical type, with hot summers and cold winters. Most of the rainfall takes place in the period between July and September. Maximum temperatures range from 30°C to 44°C in summer; winter temperatures range from 1°C to 28°C.

Flora and Fauna:
Flora: Forests extend over 23,605 sq. km, which is 29.61 per cent of the state's total geographical area. Of this, 82 per cent is categorized as 'Protected Forest' and 17.5 per cent as 'Reserve Forest'. A small portion (33.49 sq. km) is not categorized.

The state's forests consist largely of the tropical moist deciduous type. The state is home to a large number of threatened orchids. Sal and bamboo are the two key constituents of the state's forests.

Fauna: Important members of the state's animal population include gaur, chital, tiger, panther, wild boar, sambar, sloth bear, nilgai and deer.

History

In 1929 the Simon Commission was presented with a memorandum that demanded the formation of a separate Jharkhand state. In December 1947, the All India Jharkhand Party was formed and in 1951, it was elected to the Vidhan Sabha as the main opposition party. In 1971, A.K. Roy set up the MCC to demand a separate Jharkhand state. In 1973, N.E. Horo named his party the Jharkhand Party and presented the then prime minister with a memorandum for a separate Jharkhand state. The year 1980 saw the establishment of the Jharkhand Kranti Dal. In 1987, the home minister of India directed the Bihar government to prepare a detailed report on the profile of all districts of Chota Nagpur and Santhal Parganas. In January 1994, Laloo Prasad Yadav declared that the Jharkhand Development Autnomous Council Bill would be passed in the budget session of the legislature. In 1995, the Jharkhand Area Autonomous Council was formed, comprising as 18 districts of Santhal Parganas and Chota Nagpur, with Shibu Soren nominated as the chairman.

In July 1997, Shibu Soren offered his party's support to the minority government of Laloo Prasad Yadav, on the condition of a separate Jharkhand Bill in the assembly. In August 2000, the bill to create a separate state of Jharkhand out of the state of Bihar was passed in the Lok Sabha by a voice vote. Later that month, the Rajya Sabha cleared the formation of Jharkhand as well. On 25 August, the then President, K.R. Narayanan, approved the Bihar Reorganization Bill, 2000. The state of Jharkhand came into existence on 15 November 2000. The state's first Chief Minister was Babulal Marandi.

Politics

The Jharkhand movement started with the organizational activities of the Chhotanagpur Unnati Samaj (CUS), founded in 1921, and subsequently of the Adivasi Mahasabha, founded in 1939. Among those who spearheaded the Jharkhand movement was Jaipal Singh, an Oxford-returned tribal Christian who helped the regional aspiration gain national recognition. On 28 December 1947 All India Jharkhand Party came into being under the leadership of Jaipal Singh. It was with the emergence of this party that the Jharkhand movement became purely political. In 1951, the Jharkhand party became the largest opposition party in the Bihar Assembly winning all the 32 seats from south Bihar and giving fresh impetus to the movement for a separate state. As a leader of the Jharkhand Party, Jaipal Singh made the demand in Parliament in 1954 for a separate Jharkhand state. The movement's original demand was for the formation of a separate state with 16 districts of south Bihar's Chhotanagpur and Santhal Pargana regions. The Jharkhand Party also wanted three contiguous, tribal-dominated districts of adjoining West Bengal, four districts of Orissa and two districts of Madhya Pradesh to be included in the proposed state. West Bengal, Orissa and Madhya Pradesh have, however, refused to part with any territory. In 1955, the Jharkhand Party submitted a memorandum to the States Reorganisation Commission, reiterating the state demand. But it was turned down by the Commission.

Subsequently the Jharkhand Party suffered a series of splits. In 1970, Sibu Soren of Santhal Pargana quit the party to form the Jharkhand Mukti Morcha, with Benode Behari Mahato as its chairman. In 1971 A.K.Roy founded the Marxist M.C.C to demand the separate Jharkhand state. In 1973 N.E. Horo named his party as Jharkhand Party and on 12 March he presented the then Prime Minister a memorandum for a separate Jharkhand state. In 1977 Jharkhand Party proposed a separate Jharkhand state, which included not only Chhotanagpur and Santhal Pargana of Bihar but adjoining areas of Bengal. The year 1980 saw the establishment of the Jharkhand Kranti Dal. On 25 September 1986 All Jharkhand Students Union gave its first call for Jharkhand bandh, which was a huge success. In 1987 the home minister of India directed the Bihar government to prepare a report with detailed profiles of all districts of Chhotanagpur and Santhal Pargana. On 6 January 1994 Laloo Prasad Yadav declared in Ranchi that Jharkhand devlopment autnomous council bill would be passed in the budget session.

In 1995 Jharkhand Area Autonomous Council was formed which comprised of 18 districts of Santhal Pargana and Chhotanagpur and Shibu Soren was nominated the Chairman. In June 1997 Bihar government sanctioned 24 crores for conducting the elections of Jharkhand Autonomous Council. In July 1997, Shibu Soren offered support to the minority government of Laloo Prasad Yadav with a condition of a separate Jharkhand bill in the assembly. In the year 2000 the bill to create a separate state of Jharkhand to be carved out of Bihar was passed in Lok Sabha by voice with two key allies of ruling NDA strongly opposing the measure and the opposition Rashtriya Janta Dal and the CPI-M demanding it to be referred to a parliamentary committee. The long cherished demand of people of the region was fulfilled and the new state Jharkhand, formerly a part of

Bihar state, was formed on 15 November 2000. Jharkhand is the 28th state of the Indian Union. Babulal Marandi of the Bharatiya Janata Party was sworn in as the first Chief Minister of Jharkhand. On 18 March 2003 Arjun Munda was sworn in as the Chief Minister of Jharkhand state. On 2 March 2005 Sibu Soren was sworn in as the Chief Minister. But Sibu Soren failed to prove his majority in the assembly and resigned on 11 March 2005. On 12 March 2005 Arjun Munda was again sworn in as the Chief Minister of the state.

Culture

Folk music forms of Jharkhand include Akhariya Domkach, Dohari Domkach, Janani Jhumar, Mardana Jhumar and Faguwa. Folk dance forms include Paika, Chhau, Jadur and Karma. Santhali Bhittichitra, Oraon Bhittichitra, Jado Patiya are some local forms of painting.

Fairs and festivals: Sarhul, Karma, Sohrai, Badna and Tusu (or Makar) are notable among the local festivals.

Economy, Industry and Agriculture

Economy: The net state domestic product at current prices (new series) in 2002–03 (advance estimate) was Rs 27,358 crores. The per capita net state domestic product at current prices (new series) in 2002–03 (advance estimate) was Rs 9955.

Minerals and industry: Jharkhand has some of the richest deposits of minerals in the country. The steel plants at Bokaro and Jamshedpur are also in this state. Minerals mined in the state include iron ore, coal, copper ore, mica, bauxite as well as fireclay, graphite,

kyanite, sillimanite, limestone and uranium.

Agriculture: The main crops grown in the state are paddy, wheat, pulses and maize.

Power: The state gets its power from both thermal and hydroelectric sources.

Education

Educational institutes: Prominent institutes in the state include
• Ranchi University
• Siddhu Kanhu University (Dumka)
• Vinoba Bhave University (Hazaribagh)
• Birsa Agricultural University (Ranchi)
• Birla Institute of Technology and Science (Ranchi)
• Xavier Labour Relations Institute (Jamshedpur)
• National Metallurgical Laboratory (Jamshedpur)
• Central Mining Research Institute (Dhanbad)
• Research and Development Centre for Iron and Steel (Ranchi)

Tourism

Major tourist attractions: Dassam Falls, Netarhat, Hazaribagh National Park, Baidyanath Temple, Deoghar, Basakinath Temple, Deoghar, Topchanchi Lake, Dhanbad.

Airports: Ranchi.
National Parks:
• Palamau National Park (Betla) in Palamau dist. (226.32 sq. km)
• Hazaribagh National Park in Hazaribagh dist. (183.89 sq. km)

Administration

Legislature: Jharkhand has a unicameral legislature consisting of 81 seats, out of which 9 are reserved for SCs and 28 for STs. However, the tenure of the existing members of Legislative Council (MLCs) was carried over from Bihar at the time of the formation of the state, and were maintained.

The party position in the state assembly is as follows:

Name of Party	Seats
Bharatiya Janata Party	30
Indian National Congress	9
Nationalist Congress Party	1
Jharkhand Mukti Morcha	17
Rashtriya Janata Dal	7
Janata Dal (United)	6
United Goans Democratic Party	2
All India Forward Bloc	2
Communist Party of India (Marxist-Leninist) (Liberation)	1
All Jharkhand Students Union	2
Jharkhand Party	1
Independent	3
Total	**81**

Judiciary: The Jharkhand High Court is located at Ranchi. The chief justice is Altamas Kabir.

Districts:

District	Area (sq. km)	Population	Headquarters	Urban Agglomerations
Bokaro	2,861	1,775,961	Bokaro Steel City	Bokaro Steel City, Phusro
Chatra	3,706	790,680	Chatra	
Deoghar	2,479	1,161,370	Deoghar	Deoghar
Dhanbad	2,052	2,394,434	Dhanbad	Chirkunda, Dhanbad
Dumka	6,212	1,754,571	Dumka	
Garhwa	4,044	1,034,151	Garhwa	
Giridih	4,975	1,901,564	Giridih	Giridih
Godda	2,110	1,047,264	Godda	
Gumla	9,077	1,345,520	Gumla	
Hazaribagh	6,147	2,277,108	Hazaribagh	Hazaribag, Ramgarh
Kodarma	1,312	498,683	Kodarma	
Lohardaga	1,491	364,405	Lohardaga	
Pakur	1,806	701,616	Pakur	
Palamau	8,705	2,092,004	Daltonganj	
Pashchimi Singhbhum	9,907	2,080,265	Chaibasa	Chakradharpur, Jamshedpur
Purbi Singhbhum	3,533	1,978,671	Jamshedpur	Jamshedpur
Ranchi	7,698	2,783,577	Ranchi	Ranchi
Sahibganj	1,599	927,584	Sahibganj	

Karnataka

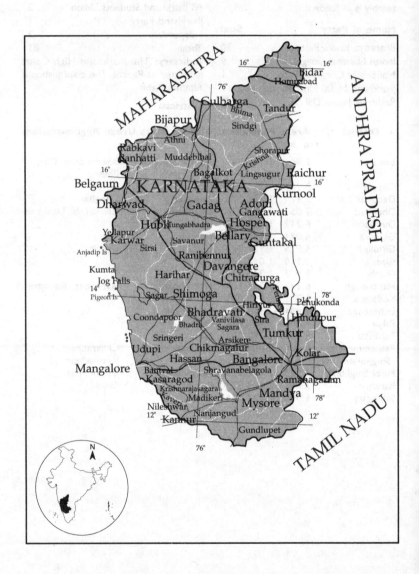

Key Statistics

Capital: Bangalore.
Area: 191,791 sq. km.
Population: Total: 52,850,562
Male: 26,898,918
Female: 25,951,644
Population density: 275 per sq. km.
Sex ratio: 965 females per 1000 males.
Principal languages: Kannada, Urdu, Telugu.
Literacy rates: Total: 66.6%
Male: 76.1%
Female: 56.9%

Government

Governor: T.N. Chaturvedi. He assumed office of the governor on 21 August 2002.

Chief Minister: N. Dharam Singh (INC), sworn in on 28 May 2004.

Geography

Physical characteristics: About 750 km from north to south and 400 km from east to west, Karnataka can be divided in four physiographic regions: (i) The Northern Plateau, with a general elevation of 300 to 600 metres from the mean sea level; (ii) The Central Plateau, with a general elevation of 450 to 700 metres; (iii) The Southern Plateau, with a general elevation of 600 to 900 metres; and (iv) The Coastal Region, comprising the plains and the Western Ghats.

Among the tallest peaks of the state are Mullayyana Giri, Bababudangiri and Kudremukh.

Neighbouring States and Union territories:
States:
• Goa
• Maharashtra
• Andhra Pradesh
• Tamil Nadu
• Kerala

Major rivers:
• Krishna
• Cauvery
• North Pennar
• South Pennar
• Palar
• Hemavati
• Kalinadi
• Gagavali
• Tungabhadra

Climate: The climate varies from hot with excessive rainfall in the coastal belt and adjoining areas to hot and seasonally dry tropical climate in the southern half, and to hot and semi-arid in the northern half. April and May are the hottest months with maximum temperatures going above 40°C. The period from October to March is generally pleasant over the entire state. The average annual rainfall for the state is 1390mm, with Bijapur, Raichur and Bellary receiving the minimum rainfall and Shimoga and Kodagu receiving the maximum.

Flora and Fauna:
Flora: Around 20 per cent of the state area is under forests, with teak, rosewood, honne, mathi, bamboo and sandal trees in abundance.

Fauna: Wildlife found in Karnataka include gaur, sambar, barking deer, elephant, tiger, leopard, wild dog, sloth bear, black buck, open-bill stork, white ibis, egret, heron, partridge, peafowl, quail and hornbill.

History

Around the mid-3rd century BC, the Mauryas ruled over major parts of present-day Karnataka. After the Mauryas up until the 11 century AD, the principal dynasties in the region were the Kadambas, the Gangas and the Pallavas. They were followed by the Chalukyas, the Hoysalas and the Rashtrakutas. After the 13th century, Mysore gradually came under the influence of the Vijayanagar empire.

Towards the end of the 16th century, the Vijayanagar empire declined, resulting in Mughal domination of the territory lying north of the Tungabhadra and the rajas of Mysore controlling the south. Hyder Ali rose to power in 1761and his invasions extended Mysore's dominion. After his son Tipu Sultan was killed in 1799, the area came under British control which continued until independence.

After independence, Mysore state went through two territorial reorganizations: in 1953 and in 1956. The state was renamed Karnataka on 1 November 1973. Arcot Ramaswami Mudaliar was the first Chief Minister of Karnataka.

Politics

After Indian independence, the Wodeyar Maharaja of Mysore acceded to India. In 1950, Mysore became an Indian state, and the former Maharaja became its Rajpramukh, or Governor. After accession to India, the Wodeyar family was given a pension by the Indian state until 1975, and members of the family still reside in part of their ancestral palace in Mysore. On 1 November 1956 or Rajyotsava Day (Formation Day), Mysore state was enlarged to its present boundaries, incorporating the state of Coorg and the Kannada-speaking portions of neighboring Madras, Hyderabad, and Bombay states, with an elected Chief Minister and state assembly. On 1 November 1973 the name of the state was changed to Karnataka.

The first Chief Minister was Arcot Ramaswami Mudaliar. Kysasambally Chengalaraya Reddy succeeded him and he was in power till 1952. Karnataka's first Assembly started functioning from18 June 1952 and was in force till 31 March 1957. During this period Karnataka had the highest dignitaries as its Chief Minister, including K.H. Hanumanthaiah (30-03-1952 to 19-08-1956), Kadidal Manjappa (19-08-1956 to 31-10-1956) and S. Nijalingappa (01-11-1956 to 16-05-1958). S. Nijalingappa was also the Chief Minister of Karnataka during the beginning of the second Assembly from 10 June 1957 to 1 March 1962. After Nijalingappa B.D. Jatti continued as the Chief Minister (16-05-1958 to 09-03-1962) of the state, until the beginning of third Assembly. The third Assembly was from 15 March 1962 to 28 February 1967. Karnataka had S.R. Kanthi from 14-03-1962 to 20-06-1962 and S. Nijalingappa as the Chief Minister from 21-06-1962 to 28-05-1968. The starting of the fourth Assembly saw for the first time in Karnataka politics the beginning of President's Rule. During this period the Chief Minister was Veerandra Patil (29 May 1968 to 18 March 1971) and President's Rule was declared from 19 March 1971 to 20 March 1972. The fifth Assembly also became important in Karnataka legislative history when term of the Assembly was extended by one year(to six years) by the 42nd Constitutional Amendment Act. D. Devaraj Urs was the Chief Minister during this period (20 March 1972 to 31 December1977) and President's Rule was imposed for the second time from 31 December 1977 to 28 February 1978.

The sixth Assembly started from 17 March 1978 and continued till 8 June 1983. Karnataka had two Chief Ministers during this period, Devaraj Urs from 28-02-1978 to 07-01-1980 and R. Gundu Rao from 12 January 1980 to 10 January 1983. The seventh Assembly was short lived (24 July 1983 to 2 January 1985). Ramakrishna Hegde started his first term as Chief Minister from 10 January 1983 to 29 December 1984. He dissolved the Assembly and went for fresh elections before the completion of his office. The eighth Assembly started from 18 March 1985 to 21 April 1989, when President's Rule was declared from 21 April 1989 to 30 November 1989. Ramakrishna Hegde and S.R. Bommai were the Chief Ministers during this period. The ninth Assembly started form 18 March 1985 and continued till 20 April 1989. Karnataka had three Chief Ministers, and a President's Rule during this period. Veerandra Patil started his term in office from 30 November 1989 to 10 October 1990, followed by President's Rule for seven days. After the short President's Rule in the state S. Bangarappa became the Chief Minister from 17 October 1990 to 19 November 1992. Later Bangarappa was succeeded by Veerappa Moily from 19 November 1992 to 11 December 1994. The tenth Assembly started from 25 December 1994 and lasted till 22 July 1999. During this period H.D. Deve Gowda (from 11 December 1994 to 31 May 1996) and J.H. Patel (from 31 May 1996 to 11 October 1999) were the Chief Ministers. The most important event during this period was the Chief Minister of Karnataka H.D. Deve Gowda becoming the Prime Minister of India. So J.H. Patel had to succeed Deve Gowda. The eleventh Assembly began on 25 October 1999. The Texas educated S. M. Krishna became the Chief Minister from 11 October 1999. On 28 May 2004 Dharam Singh of the Congress was sworn in as the Chief Minister of Karnataka.

Culture

Karnataka boasts a fascinating variety of folk theatre, called Bayalata. Dasarata, Sannata, Doddata, Parijata and Yakshagana are the most popular forms of Bayalata.

Fairs and festivals: Prominent festivals of the state include Ugadi, Dussehra, Kar Hunnive, Nagapanchami, Navaratri or Nadahabb, Yellu Amavasya, Ramzan and Deepavali. Major fairs are Sri Vithappa fair, Sri Shidlingappa's fair, the Godachi fair and Banashankari Devi fair.

Economy, Industry and Agriculture

Economy: The net state domestic product at current prices for 2002–03 (provisional) was Rs 100,406crores. The per capita net state domestic product at current prices for 2002–03 (provisional) was Rs 18,521.

Minerals and industry: Prominent industries in Karnataka are aeronautics, automobiles, biotechnology, electronics, textiles, sugar, iron and steel, information technology, pharmaceuticals, leather, cement and processed foods. Minerals found in the state include gold, silver, iron ore, manganese, chromite, limestone, bauxite, copper and china clay.

Agriculture: Important crops include paddy, jowar, bajra, ragi, maize, pulses, groundnut, sunflower, soyabean, cotton, sugarcane and tobacco. Principal plantation crops are coffee, cashew, coconut, arecanut and cardamom.

Power: With an installed capacity of 3066 MW, a large part of Karnataka's power comes from hydroelectric plants. The rest comes from thermal and nuclear power plants.

Education

Educational institutes: Prominent educational institutions of Karnataka include the

• Indian Institute of Management, Bangalore
• Indian Institute of Science, Bangalore
• National Law School of India University, Bangalore
• National Institute of Mental Health and Neuro Sciences, Bangalore
• University of Agricultural Sciences, Bangalore
• Bangalore University, Bangalore
• National Institute of Technology, Surathkal
• Indian Statistical Institute, Bangalore
• Central Institute of Indian Languages, Mysore
• Gulbarga University, Gulbarga
• Mangalore University, Mangalore
• Manipal Academy of Higher Education, Manipal
• University of Mysore, Mysore.

Tourism

Major tourist attractions:

1. Bangalore: Vidhana Soudha, Cubbon Park, Palace of Tipu Sultan, Ulsoor Lake.
2. Mysore: Mysore Palace, Srirangapatna, Gumbaz, St Philomena's Church, Brindavan Gardens.
3. Badami: The cave temples.
4. Aihole and Pattadakal.
5. Madikeri: Tipu's Fort, Omkareshwara Temple, Abbey Falls.
6. Hampi: Virupaksha Temple, Vittala Temple.
7. Belur and Halebid: Chennakeshava Temple, Shiva Temple.
8. Beaches: Karwar, Marwanthe, Malpe.
9. Jog falls.
10. Bijapur.
11. Sravanabelagola.
12. Sringeri.
13. Nandi Hills.

Airports:
International: Bangalore
Domestic:
• Belgaum
• Hubli
• Mangalore.

National Parks:
• Anshi (Uttarakanada) —250 sq. km.
• Bandipur Tiger Reserve (Mysore)—874.20 sq. km.
• Bannerghatta (Bangalore)—104.27 sq. km.
• Kudremukh (South Kanada and Chikmagalur)—600.32 sq. km.
• Nagarhole (Mysore Kodagu)—643.39 sq. km.

Administration

Legislature: The Karnataka legislature comprises two houses: the 75 member legislative council and the 225 member legislative assembly. Of the 225 assembly seats, 224 are for elected members (33 reserved for SCs, 2 for STs) and 1 for a nominated member. The current party position is:

Name of Party	Seats
Bharatiya Janata Party	79
Indian National Congress	65
Janata Dal (S)	58
Janata Dal (U)	5
Communist Party of India (Marxist)	1
Republican Party of India	1
Kannada Nadu Paksha	1
Kannada Chalarali Vatal Paksha	1
Independent	13
Nominated	1
Total	**225**

Judiciary: The seat of the Karnataka High Court is in Bangalore. The present chief justice is Nauvdip Kumar Sodhi.

Districts:

District	Area (sq. km)	Population	Headquarters	Urban Agglomerations
Bagalkot	6,575	1,652,232	Bagalkot	
Bangalore	2,190	6,523,110	Bangalore	Bangalore
Bangalore Rural	5,815	1,877,416	Bangalore	
Belgaum	13,415	4,207,264	Belgaum	Athni, Belgaum, Ramdurg
Bellary	8,450	2,025,242	Bellary	
Bidar	5,448	1,501,374	Bidar	Bidar
Bijapur	10,494	1,808,863	Bijapur	Bijapur
Chamarajanagar	5,101	964,275	Chamarajanagar	
Chikmagalur	7,201	1,139,104	Chikmagalur	
Chitradurga	8,440	1,510,227	Chitradurga	Chjtradurga
Dakshina Kannada	4,560	1,896,403	Mangalore	Mangalore
Davanagere	5,924	1,789,693	Davanagere	Harihar
Dharwad	4,260	1,603,794	Dharwad	
Gadag	4,656	971,955	Gadag	
Gulbarga	16,224	3,124,858	Gulbarga	Gulbarga, Shahabad, Wadi
Hassan	6,814	1,721,319	Hassan	Arsikere, Channarayapattana, Hassan
Haveri	4,823	1,437,860	Haveri	
Kodagu	4,102	545,322	Madikere	
Kolar	8,223	2,523,406	Kolar	Robertson Pet
Koppal	7,189	1,193,496	Koppal	Gangawati
Mandya	4,961	1,761,718	Mandya	
Mysore	6,854	2,624,911	Mysore	Mysore
Raichur	6,827	1,648,212	Raichur	
Shimoga	8,477	1,639,595	Shimoga	
Tumkur	10,597	2,579,516	Tumkur	
Udupi	3,880	1,109,494	Udupi	Udupi
Uttara Kannada	10,291	1,353,299	Karwar	Ankola, Bhatkal, Karwar, Kumta, Sirsi

Kerala

Key Statistics

Capital: Thiruvananthapuram.
Area: 38,863 sq. km.
Population: Total: 31,841,374
Male: 15,468,614
Female: 16,372,760
Population density: 819 per sq. km.
Sex ratio: 1058 females per 1000 males.
Principal languages: Malayalam, Tamil, Kannada.

Literacy rates: Total: 90.9%
Male: 94.2%
Female: 87.7%

Government

Governor: R.L. Bhatia. He was sworn on 23 June 2004.

Chief Minister: Oommen Chandy (INC). He was sworn in on 31 August 2004.

Geography

Physical characteristics: Kerala is a narrow strip of land on the south-west coast of India. The Lakshadweep Sea lies on the west, while the Western Ghats lie on the east. Karnataka is towards the north and northeast of the state while Tamil Nadu is to the east and the south. The Western Ghats are densely forested and have extensive ridges and ravines.

Anai Peak (2695 metres) is the highest peak of peninsular India. An interconnected chain of lagoons and backwaters is a feature of the coastline of Kerala.

Neighbouring states and Union territories:

States:
• Karnataka
• Tamil Nadu.

Union territories:
• Pondicherry.

Major rivers:
• Periyar
• Bharatapuzha
• Chalakudi
• Pamba.

Climate: Kerala has a tropical climate. The summer season is from February to May (24°C to 33°C). The monsoon season is from June to September (22°C to 28°C). The winter lasts between October and January (22°C to 32°C).

Kerala lies directly in the path of the south-west monsoon, but also receives rain from the north-east monsoon. Rainfall averages about 3000 mm annually, although some parts receive much more.

Flora and Fauna:

Flora: The state has 1,081,509 hectares of forest area. These are mostly rain forest, tropical deciduous forest and upland temperate grassland.

Fauna: The animal population of the state includes sambar, gaur, Nilgiri tahr, elephant, leopard, tiger, hanuman, Nilgiri langur, spectacled and king cobras, peafowl, bonnet monkey, lion-tailed macaque and hornbill.

History

Kerala has been mentioned in a rock inscription, dating back to the third century BC, of the Mauryan Emperor Asoka as 'Keralaputra'. Jewish immigrants arrived in the area in the first century AD, while Syrian Orthodox Christians believe that St Thomas the Apostle visited Kerala at around the same time. In the first five centuries AD, the region that is today Kerala was a part of Tamilakam and was at different times controlled by the eastern Pandya, Chola and the Chera dynasties.

Arab traders introduced Islam to the region in the latter part of the period between the sixth to eighth centuries AD. It was under the Kulasekhara dynasty that reigned between the years 800 and 1102 that Malayalam emerged as a distinct language.

In the early 14th century, Ravi Varma Kulasekhara of Venad established a short-lived domination over southern India. His death ushered in an era of confusion characterized by chieftains who constantly fought each other.

In 1498, the Portuguese explorer Vasco da Gama landed near Calicut (now Kozhikode). In the 16th century the Portuguese dominated trade and commerce in the Malabar region, successfully overtaking the Arab traders. Their attempts to establish political rule, however, were foiled by the hereditary rulers of Calicut, called 'zamorins'.

In the 17th century, the Dutch ousted the Portuguese. But even their ambition of imposing Dutch supremacy in the region was foiled by Marthanda Varma in 1741, in the Battle of Kolachel. Marthanda Varma adopted a system of martial discipline and expanded the new state of Travancore.

However, by 1806, Cochin, Travancore and Malabar had all become subject states under the British Madras Presidency. At the time of independence in 1947, the region that is today Kerala consisted of three separate territories: Cochin, Travancore and Malabar. On 1 July 1949, Cochin and Travancore were merged to form the Travancore–Cochin state. The present state of Kerala was formed on a linguistic basis, when Malabar along with the Kasargod taluka was added to the Cochin-Travancore state.

The new state was inaugurated on 1 November 1956. When Kerala was formed, the state was under President's rule. Elections were held for the first time in 1957 and E.M.S. Namboodiripad became the first Chief Minister.

Politics

The move towards democracy and social change started in Kerala towards the end of the 19th century. By the early 20th century, leaders like E.M.Sankaran Namboodiripad, A. K. Gopalan and T.M. Varghese used Communist ideologies to organize political mass movements both against British rule and the Travancore state. The Travancore state opened to include elected representatives in the political administration of the state. There were proposals to bring Travancore, Cochin and Malabar under one political administration. However, the political confrontations continued until 1947 when Travancore became free from the British. In 1949, the two separate states

of Travancore and Cochin were united. On 1 November 1956 the boundaries of the newly-united states were revised to include neighbouring Malayalam-speaking areas, and the whole territory was officially named Kerala. In the first elections that followed the Communists gained a majority and the first Kerala ministry was sworn in under the leadership of E.M. Sankaran Namboodiripad (known as EMS), head of the Communist Party of India-Marxist. On 16 March 1957 for the first time in the history of the world, the Communists had come to power through democratic means with the first legislative Assembly of Kerala, with E.M. Sankaran Namboodiripad as the Chief Minister.

The Assembly however, would last only until July 1959. The ministry was dismissed because the opposition parties launched an agitation called 'Vimochana Samaram' (Liberation Struggle) which led to clashes between the police and mass protesters. The state came under Presidential Rule. In February 1960 the second Assembly was formed with the coalition of the Congress party and the Praja Socialist Party, with Pattom Thanu Pillai as Chief Minister. The ministry lasted until September 1964. On 6 March 1967 E.M.S. Namboodiripad became the Chief Minister again with the Indian Communist Party (Marxist) getting an absolute majority. In October 1969 EMS resigned and C. Achutha Menon became the Chief Minister. In October 1970 the fourth legislative assembly was formed with Achutha Menon as the Chief Minister. This was the first ministry in the history of Kerala, which not only lasted five years, the full term, but also extended its term thrice. K. Karunakaran of the Congress party became the Chief Minister in March 1977.

In January 1980 seven political parties formed a coalition, the Left Democratic Front (LDF), under the leadership of the Communist Party of India-Marxist and won the election. E.K. Nayanar became the Chief Minister. After twenty-two months, the ministry lost its support and Nayanar resigned. A new ministry with K. Karunakaran of the Congress party as the Chief Minister came to power in December 1981 and lasted until March 1982. In May 1982, an election was held and a political coalition, the United Democratic Front (UDF), under the leadership of Congress got the majority. Again K.Karunakaran became the Chief Minister. In the election conducted in March 1987 the Left Democratic Front again came to power and E.K. Nayanar again became Chief Minister. In 1991 the UDF won the election and K. Karunakaran again became the Chief Minister in June 1991. In 1995 A.K. Antony became the Chief Minister, after resigning from the Central Cabinet and K. Karunakaran resigned from the Legislative Assembly and got elected to the Rajya Sabha, the Central Cabinet. In June 2001 A.K. Antony was sworn in again as Chief Minister. In 2004, Oommen Chandy was sworn in on 31 August as the 19th Chief Minister of Kerala.

Culture

The dance form of Kathakali, which is one of the six classical dance forms of India, is indigenous to the state of Kerala, as in Mohiniattam. There are also more than 50 well-known folk dances in Kerala. The most popular among these are the Kaliyattom, Kolam Thullal, Kolkli, Mudiettu. Poorakkali, Velakali, Kamapadavukali, Kanniyarkali, Parichmuttukali, Thappukali, Kuravarkali and Thiruvathirakali. Other folk dance forms include Arjuna Nritham, Thullal and Theyyam.

The state is also the birthplace of the Kalaripayuttu martial art form.

Aranmula is famous for its metal mirrors. The state is also famous for its brass lamps and Kathakali masks.

Fairs and festivals: Important festivals of the state are Onam, Vishu, Thiruvathira, Navarathri, Sivarathri, Oachira, Kettukazcha, Vallom Kali, Christmas, Easter, Bakrid, Idul Fitr, Miladi Sharif and Muharram.

Economy, Industry and Agriculture

Economy: The net state domestic product at current prices for 2002–03 (provisional) was Rs 71,064 crores. The per capita net state domestic product at current prices for 2002–03 (provisional) was Rs 21,853.

Minerals and industry: The state's industries are mostly based on its natural resources. It is noted for handloom, cashewnut processing, food processing, coir and handicrafts. Tourism is also a major industry. Other industries of the state include rubber, tea, ceramics, electronics, electronic appliances, engineering, bricks and tiles, tobacco products, precision engineering products, petroleum-based industries, drugs and chemicals, plywood and soaps and oils. The state's mineral resources include zircon, monazite, ilmenite, rutile, sillimanite, clay and quartz sand.

Agriculture: The agricultural pattern of Kerala is unique for the predominance of cash crops. The state is a major producer of coconut (the most important cash crop of the state), rubber, pepper, coffee, cardamom, ginger, cocoa, cashew, arecanut, nutmeg, cinnamon, cloves and tea. The state is also noted for the production of fruits like banana, plantain, mango, jackfruit and pineapple.

Power: Most of the state's power comes from hydroelectric sources, while the rest comes from thermal power plants.

Education

Educational institutes: The major institutes for higher education in the state include the
• Indian Institute of Management (Kozhikode)
• Kerala Institute of Tourism and Travel Studies (Thiruvananthapuram)
• Cochin University of Science and Technology (Kochi)
• Central Institute of Fisheries, Nautical and Engineering Training (Kochi)
• Central Marine Fisheries Research Institute (Kochi)
• Kerala Agricultural University (Trichur)
• University of Kerala (Thiruvananthapuram)
• University of Calicut (Kozhikode)
• Mahatma Gandhi University (Kottayam)
• Sree Chitra Tirunal Institute of Medical Sciences and Technology (Thiruvananthapuram)
• Sree Sankaracharya University of Sanskrit (Sree Sankarapuram)
• Kannur University (Kannur)
• Central Plantation Crops and Research Institute (Kudlu, near Kasargod).

Tourism

Major tourist attractions: Vembanad Lake; Kappad Beach, Kozhikode; Kottayam; Kovalam Beach, Trivandrum; Munnar; Ponmudi; Cheeyappara and Valara waterfalls; Thattekkad Bird Sanctuary, Idukki; Thekkady; Kasaragod; Periyar; Silent Valley.

Airports:
International:
• Thiruvananthapuram

• Nedumbassery (Kochi).
Domestic:
• Kozhikode.

National Parks:
• Periyar National Park (part of the Tiger Reserve) in Idukki dist. (Tiger Reserve Area—777 sq. km, National Park—350 sq. km)
• Eravikulam National Park in Idukki dist. (97 sq. km)
• Silent Valley National Park in Palakkad dist. (89.52 sq. km).

Administration

Legislature: Kerala has a unicameral legislature. There are 140 seats in the Kerala Legislative Assembly. This includes 13 seats reserved for SCs and one seat reserved for STs, and one member nominated by the Governor from the Anglo-Indian community. The term of the current assembly expires on 4 June 2006.

The current party position is as follows:

Name of Party	Seats
Indian National Congress	62
Communist Party of India (Marxist)	23
Muslim League Kerala State Committee	16
Kerala Congress (M)	9
Communist Party of India	7
Janadhipathiya Samrekshna Samiti	4
Janata Dal (Secular)	3
Kerala Congress	2
Revolutionary Socialist Party	2
Nationalist Congress Party	2
Kerala Congress (B)	2
Kerala Congress (J)	2
Revolutionary Socialist Party of Kerala (Bolshevik)	2
Communist Marxist Party Kerala State Committee	1
Independent	3
Total	**140**

Judiciary: The High Court of Kerala has its seat at Ernakulam. Its jurisdiction also includes the Union territory of Lakshadweep. The acting chief justice is K.S. Radhakrishnan.

Districts:

District	Area (sq. km)	Population	Headquarters	Urban Agglomerations
Alappuzha	1,414	2,105,349	Alappuzha	Alappuzha, Cherthala
Ernakulam	2,950	3,098,378	Ernakulam	Kochi
Idukki	4,476	1,128,605	Kuyilimala	
Kannur	2,966	2,412,365	Kannur	Kannur
Kasargod	1,992	1,203,342	Kasargod	Kanhangad, Kasargod
Kollam	2,491	2,584,118	Kollam	Kollam
Kottayam	2,208	19,52,901	Kottayam	Kottayam
Kozhikode	2,344	28,78,498	Kozhikode	Kozhikode, Vadakara
Malappuram	3,550	36,29,640	Malappuram	Malappuram
Palakkad	4,480	26,17,072	Palakkad	Chittur-Thathamangalam, Palakkad
Pathanamthitta	2,637	12,31,577	Pathanamthitta	
Thiruvananthapuram	2,192	32,34,707	Thiruvananthapuram	Thiruvananthapuram
Thrissur	3,032	29,75,440	Thrissur	Guruvayoor, Kodungallur, Thrissur
Wayanad	2,131	7,86,627	Kalpetta	

Madhya Pradesh

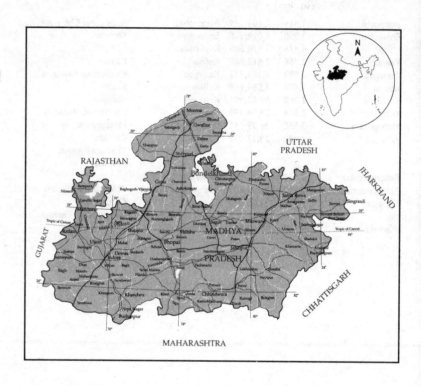

Key Statistics

Capital: Bhopal.
Area: 308,000 sq. km.
Population: Total: 60,348,023
Male: 31,443,652
Female: 28,904,371
Population density: 196 per sq. km.
Sex ratio: 919 females per 1000 males.
Principal languages: Hindi, Bhili/
   Bhilodi, Gondi.
Literacy rates: Total: 63.7%
Male: 76.1%
Female: 50.3%

Government

Governor: Balram Jakhar. He was
sworn in as the governor of Madhya
Pradesh on 30 June 2004.

Chief Minister: Babulal Gour (BJP). He
was sworn in on 23 August 2004.

Geography

Physical characteristics: Madhya
Pradesh is the second largest Indian
state covering 9.5 per cent of the
country's area. It lies between the

Indo-Gangetic Plain in the north and the Deccan Plateau in the south. Its landscape, which is largely made up of wide-ranging plateaus, low hills and river valleys, ranges from 100 to 1200 metres.

The land rises from south to north in the northern part of the state. In the southern part, its elevation increases towards the west. The Kaimur Hills and the Vindhya Range are situated in the north and the west respectively. To the northwest side of the Vindhya Range is the Malwa Plateau, which rises up to 100 metres. The Bundelkhand Plateau lies to the north of the Vindhya Range. There is also the Baghelkhand Plateau in the northeast, and Madhya Bharat Plateau in the extreme northeast. Various rivers originate from the state and flow into the adjoining states.

Neighbouring States and Union territories:
States:
• Gujarat
• Maharashtra
• Chhattis- garh
• Rajasthan
• Uttar Pradesh.

Major rivers:
• Narmada
• Chambal
• Betwa
• Tapti
• Wainganga are some of the major rivers.

Climate: The climate of Madhya Pradesh is mostly tropical, and largely governed by the monsoon. From March to May it experiences a hot, dry and windy summer, when the temperature can reach a maximum of about 48°C in some parts of the state. From June to September comes the southwest monsoon, when the rainfall fluctuates from region to region. The state

has been divided into five crop zones and seven agro-climatic zones due to this reason. The total annual rainfall varies from 600mm (in the extreme northwestern areas) to about 1200mm (southern areas). Winters (between October and February) are usually pleasant.

Flora and Fauna:
Flora: Madhya Pradesh is rich in forest resources. There are four important types of forest, namely the tropical dry forest, the tropical moist forest, the subtropical broadleaved hill forest, and the tropical thorn forest. Based on the composition of the forest and the terrain of the region, it is possible to classify forests into three types: teak forests, sal forests and miscellaneous forests. Bamboo, small timber, fodder and fuelwood also grow in many areas.

Fauna: Madhya Pradesh is famous for its tiger population and is known as the 'Tiger State'. It has 19 per cent of the tiger population in India, and 17 per cent of the tiger population in the world. Satpura, Bandhavgarh, Pench, Panna, and Kanha are the five Project Tiger areas in the state. Apart from these projects, there is the Ghatigaon Sanctuary, which is set up for the conservation of the great Indian bustard, also known as the Son Chiriya. The Ken-gharial and Son-gharial sanctuaries are home to the mugger and gharial, while the Sardarpur Sanctuary houses the kharmor or lesser florican. Other creatures found in the state include the bison, panthers, chital (spotted deer), wild buffalo, sambar, black buck, bears and many species of birds.

History

Madhya Pradesh was founded on 1 November 1956, and forty-four years later, on 1 November 2000, the new state of Chhattisgarh was carved out of it. Madhya Pradesh occupies some of the oldest inhabited parts of India. At Bhimbhetka, close to Bhopal, some fascinating paintings are preserved in pre-historic caves dating back to the Paleolithic times.

The whole state came under the territory of the Guptas during the ascendancy of the Gupta dynasty. It also constituted part of Harshavardhan's empire. During the decline of the imperial power, small principalities created out of the province began fighting each other to establish their superiority. The Chandel dynasty emerged out of this, and later constructed the great temples of Khajuraho, creating a prosperous kingdom after the fall of the imperial power.

The Pratihara and Gaharwar Rajput dynasties followed the Chandels, but lost out to the expanding Muslim power. Emperor Akbar finally subdued all the other contenders in the region, and with Aurangzeb, Mughal rule was established in the region.

With the decline of the Mughals the Marathas reigned supreme, but they were finally replaced by the British who entered into treaty relationships with the rulers of the princely states in the area and went on to gain power over them.

After independence, many such princely states were merged into the Union. With the reorganization of states, the boundaries were rationalized and the state of Madhya Pradesh came into existence. Pandit Ravishankar Shukla was the first Chief Minister of the state.

Politics

Madhya Pradesh was created in 1950 from the former British Central Provinces and Berar and the princely states of Makrai and Chhattisgarh, with Nagpur as the capital of the state. The state of Madhya Pradesh was formed on 1 November 1956, on the basis of the report of the States Reorganization Commission by merging the territories of the states of Madhya Bharat, a union of princely states in the Malwa plateau region; Vindhya Pradesh, a union of states in the Vindhya region; Bhopal, a centrally administered princely state; the Hindi-speaking areas, popularly known as Mahakoshal; and the Chhattisgarh region of the state of Central Provinces and Berar. The tenure of the first Legislative Assembly was very brief from 1 November 1956 to 5 March 1957. The first elections to the Madhya Pradesh Legislative Assembly, after the reorganization of the state, were held in 1957 and the Assembly was constituted on 1 April 1957. Bhopal became the new capital. Initially, the strength of the Legislative Assembly was 288, which was later raised to 321, including one nominated member. By an Act of Parliament titled the Madhya Pradesh Reorganisation Act 2000, the state was bifurcated into two states, viz. Madhya Pradesh and Chhattisgarh on 1 November 2000. Consequently, the strength of the state Legislature has come down to 231, including a nominated member. Elections were held in the state and the present House, the twelfth Legislative Assembly, was constituted on 5 December 2003.

Pandit Ravi Shankar Shukla was the Prime Minister of the Central Provinces and Berar (with the capital at Nagpur) before and after Independence. Pandit Ravi Shankar Shukla became Chief Minister of the renamed Madhya Pradesh (with its capital at Nagpur) on 26 January 1950 and remained so till 31 October 1956 and then took over again as the Chief Minister of Madhya Pradesh with its capital at Bhopal after the state was radically reorganized from 1 November 1956. He passed away on 31 December 1956. Bhagwantrao Mandloi succeeded him on 1 January 1957 and he remained in the post till 31 January 1957. Kailash Nathi Katju was in the office of Chief Minister from 31 January 1957 to 11 March 1962. Bhagwantrao Mandloi succeeded him. He became the Chief Minister for the second time and remained in power till 30 September 1963. Dwarka Prasad Mishra succeeded him and remained in the position till 30 July 1967. Govind Narayan Singh became Chief Minister after him and remained in the post till 13 March 1969. He was succeeded by Raja Naresh Chandra Singh who was Chief Minister just for 13 days. Shyama Charan Shukla of the Congress party became the Chief Minister for the first time on 26 March 1969. Prakash Chandra Sethi succeeded him on 29 January 1972 and he remained in the position till 23 December 1975. Again Shyama Charan Shukla came to power on 23 December 1975 and remained in power till 29 April 1977. Shukla headed the government in 1969, 1975 and 1989. Kailash Chandra Joshi was the Chief Minister from 26 June 1977 to 18 January 1978. On 20 January 1978 Virendra Kumar Saklecha became the Chief Minister of Madhya Pradesh and remained in office till 20 January 1980. Sunderlal Patwa of the Bharatiya Janata Party had two tenures as Chief Ministers; first from 20 January 1980 to 17 February 1980 and again from 5 March 1990 to 15 December 1992. From 9 June 1980 to 14 March 1985 Arjun Singh of the Congress party was the Chief Minister. Again he served as the Chief Minister of the state from 14 February 1988 to 25 January 1989.

Motilal Vora of the Congress party became the Chief Minister twice; first from 14 March 1985 to 14 February 1988 and again from 25 January 1989 to 9 December 1989.

On 7 December 1993, Digvijay Singh became Chief Minister of Madhya Pradesh. He was the longest serving Chief Minister in the history of Madhya Pradesh after winning the people's mandate for the second consecutive term in the year 1998. Victory of the ruling Congress party in the election in Madhya Pradesh was more significant because the political parties in power were losing elections in state after state in India in that year in the face of an anti-incumbency wave. Uma Bharti of the Bharatiya Janata Party was sworn in on 8 December 2003 as the first woman Chief Minister of Madhya Pradesh. She headed a 12-member ministry. Babulal Gaur of the Bharatiya Janata Party was sworn in as the Chief Minister of Madhya Pradesh on 23 August 2004.

Culture

In Madhya Pradesh, the Gwalior *gharana* is one of the most important propagators of style in Indian music. Madhya Pradesh is famous for the rivalry of Tansen and Baiju Bawra, and is also well known for the patronage of the Dhrupad singers by Raja Mansingh.

Other great musicians from Madhya Pradesh include the legendary Ustad Alauddin Khan, the guru of the famous sitarist Pandit Ravi Shankar; the sarod players Ali Akbar Khan and Ustad Hafiz Khan; and the *beenkar* Ustad Hussu Khan.

Madhya Pradesh is also famous for its craftsmen, including the sari weavers from Chanderi town, who are also regarded as true artists. Their silk and cotton saris, delicately woven with silver and gold threads, are extremely popular. Maheshwar in Madhya Pradesh is popular for sari making, while Bhopal is renowned for the bead work and embroidery, and Ujjain for its *chippa* work (block printing by hand). Other popular forms of craft include woodwork, terracotta display and metalware in the tribal areas of Bastar.

In the year 1980, the state government constituted a separate department for culture in Madhya Pradesh.

Fairs and festivals: Shivratri in Khajuraho, Ujjain, Pachmarhi and Bhojpur, the annual festival of dances at Khajuraho, Bhagoriya in Jhabua, Dussehra in Bastar, the Malwa Festival in Mandu, Ujjain and Indore, Ramnavami in Orchha and Chitrakoot, and the Pachmarhi Festival are some of the important cultural events in Madhya Pradesh. Some of the important cultural festivals held in the state include the All India Kalidasa Festival, Alauddin Khan Samaroh (Maihar), Tansen Sam-aroh (Gwalior), Lokranjan (Khajuraho), Miwar Utsav (Maheshwar), Khajuraho Dance Festival, Kumar Gandharva Samaroh (Dewas) and Shankara Samaroh.

Economy, Industry and Agriculture

Economy: The net state domestic product at current prices in 2002–03 (advance estimate) was Rs 71,387 crores. The per capita net state domestic product at current prices in 2002–09 (advance estimate) was Rs 11,438.

Minerals and industry: Madhya Pradesh is one of the largest producers of forest products, agricultural products, and minerals. Its important industries also include its modern biotech industries, horticulture, agro-industries,

and its eco-tourist and tourist industry, which are especially aided by the presence of world heritage sites like Khajuraho and Sanchi, and various tiger reserves in the state.

The state consists of 19 Industrial Growth Centres, and its infrastructure is an advantage, in terms of its railways and roads connecting all the important cities. The strongest optical fibre backbone is present in every district in Madhya Pradesh. Important minerals of Madhya Pradesh include limestone, bauxite, coal, manganese ore, diamond, base metals, dolomite, rock phosphate and granite.

Agriculture: In Madhya Pradesh, 49.5 per cent of its population depend on agriculture. The state produces about 2.19 million tonnes of sugar cane, 2.38 million tonnes of cotton, 3.969 million tonnes of oil seed, and nine million tonnes of food grain. Food grain production in Madhya Pradesh is about 260 kg per person, compared to the all-India production figure of about 200 kg per person per year. On the other hand, food grain yield in Madhya Pradesh, when compared to the all-India figure of 1.70 tonne per hectare (ha), is quite low at 1.14 tonnes per ha. Wheat, rice, a few varieties of coarse millets, and jowar (sorghum) are the main food crops in the state. Soyabean is produced on a large scale throughout the state.

Power: Thermal power is the main source of energy in the state. The rest of the energy is provided by hydroelectric sources.

Education

Educational institutes: Some of the important institutions of higher education are
• Awadhesh Pratap Singh University (Rewa)

- Barkatullah Vishwavidyalaya (Bhopal)
- Devi Ahilya Vishwavidyalaya (Indore)
- Dr Harisingh Gour Vishwa-vidyalaya (Sagar)
- Jawaharlal Nehru Krishi Vishwa-vidyalaya (Jabalpur)
- Jiwaji University (Gwalior)
- Lakshmibai National Institute of Physical Education (Gwalior)
- Madhya Pradesh Bhoj Open University (Bhopal)
- Maharishi Mahesh Yogi Vedic University (Jabalpur)
- Mahatma Gandhi Gramoday Vishwavidyalaya (Chitrakoot)
- Makhanlal Chaturvedi National University of Journalism (Bhopal)
- Rani Durgavati Vishwa-vidyalaya (Jabalpur)
- Vikram University (Ujjain)

Tourism

Major tourist attractions: Khajuraho; Amarkantak; The marble rocks at Bhedaghat, near Jabalpur; Bhimbhetka; Bhojpur; Chanderi; Chitrakoot; Mandu; Omkareshwar; Sanchi; Pachmarhi.

Airports:
- Gwalior
- Indore
- Jabalpur
- Bhopal
- Khajuraho

National Parks:
- Bandhavgarh National Park in Umaria and Jabalpur districts (448.85 sq. km)
- Fossil National Park in Mandla district (0.27 sq. km)
- Kanha National Park in Mandla and Balaghat districts (940 sq. km)
- Madhav National Park in Shivpuri district (375.22 sq. km)
- Panna National Park in Panna and Chhatarpur districts (542.67 sq. km)
- Pench (Priyadarshini) National Park in Seoni and Chhindwara districts (292.85 sq. km)
- Sanjay National Park in Sidhi district (466.88 sq. km)
- Satpura National Park in Hoshangabad district (585.17 sq. km)
- Van Vihar National Park in Bhopal district (4.45 sq. km).

Administration

Legislature: Madhya Pradesh has a unicameral legislature. There are 230 seats in the Madhya Pradesh assembly, of which 33 are reserved for SCs and 41 for STs.

The current party position is as follows:

Name of Party	Seats
Bharatiya Janata Party	173
Indian National Congress	38
Samajwadi Party	7
Gondvana Gantantra Party	3
Bahujan Samaj Party	2
Rashtriya Samanta Dal	2
Communist Party of India (Marxist)	1
Nationalist Congress Party	1
Janata Dal—United	1
Independent	2
Total	**230**

Judiciary: The High Court of Madhya Pradesh has its seat at Jabalpur. Justice Rajiv Gupta is the acting chief justice of the Madhya Pradesh High Court.

Districts:

District	Area (sq. km)	Population	Headquarters	Urban Agglomerations
Balaghat	9,229	1,445,760	Balaghat	Balaghat, Wara Seoni
Barwani	5,422	1,081,039	Barwani	
Betul	10,043	1,394,421	Betul	Betul
Bhind	4,459	1,426,951	Bhind	
Bhopal	2,772	1,836,784	Bhopal	Bhopal
Chhatarpur	8,687	1,474,633	Chhatarpur	Chhatarpur
Chhindwara	11,815	1,848,882	Chhindwara	Chhindwara,
				Chiklikalan Parasia Damoh 7,306
1,081,909	Damoh	Damoh	Damoh	
Datia	2,691	627,818	Datia	
Dewas	7,020	1,306,617	Dewas	
Dhar	8,153	1,740,577	Dhar	
Dindori	7,470	579,312	Dindori	
East Nimar (Khandwa)	10,776	1,708,170	Khandwa	
Guna	11,064	1,665,503	Guna	
Gwalior	4,560	1,629,881	Gwalior	Gwalior
Harda	3,330	474,174	Harda	Harda
Hoshangabad	6,707	1,085,011	Hoshangabad	Itarsi, Pipariya
Indore	3,898	2,585,321	Indore	Indore, Mhow Cantt
Jabalpur	5,211	2,167,469	Jabalpur	Jabalpur
Jhabua	6,778	1,396,677	Jhabua	
Katni	4,950	1,063,689	Katni	
Mandla	5,800	893,908	Mandla	Mandla
Mandsaur	5,535	1,183,369	Mandsaur	Mandsaur
Morena	4,989	1,587,264	Morena	Joura, Sabalgarh
Narsimhapur	5,133	957,399	Narsimhapur	Gadarwara, Narsimhapur Neemuch
4,256	725,457	Neemuch	Neemuch	
Panna	7,135	854,235	Panna	Panna
Raisen	8,466	1,120,159	Raisen	Baraily
Rajgarh	6,153	1,253,246	Rajgarh	
Ratlam	4,861	1,214,536	Ratlam	Jaora, Ratlam Rewa
6,314	1,972,333	Rewa		
Sagar	10,252	2,021,783	Sagar	Bina-Etawa, Garhakota, Khurai, Sagar
Satna	7,502	1,868,648	Satna	Satna
Sehore	6,578	1,078,769	Sehore	Ashta, Sehore
Seoni	8,758	1,165,893	Seoni	
Shahdol	9,952	1,572,748	Shahdol	Burhar-Dhanpuri,
Shajapur	6,195	1,290,230	Shajapur	Shajapur
Sheopur	6,606	559,715	Sheopur	Sheopur
Shivpuri	10,277	1,440,666	Shivpuri	
Sidhi	10,526	1,830,553	Sidhi	
Tikamgarh	5,048	1,203,160	Tikamgarh	
Ujjain	6,091	1,709,885	Ujjain	Badnagar, Mahidpur, Ujjain
Umaria	4,076	515,851	Umaria	
Vidisha	7,371	1,214,759	Vidisha	Basoda
West Nimar (Khargone)	8,030	1,529,954	Khargone	Barwaha, Khargone

Maharashtra

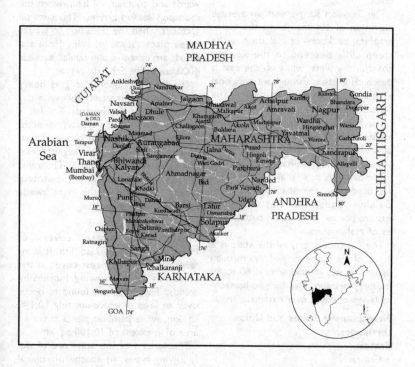

Key Statistics

Capital: Mumbai.

Area: 307,713 sq. km.

Population: Total: 96,878,627
Male: 50,400,596
Female: 46,478,031

Population density: 314 per sq. km.

Sex ratio: 922 females per 1000 males.

Principal languages: Marathi, Hindi, Urdu.

Literacy rates: Total: 76.9%
Male: 86.0%
Female: 67.0%

Government

Governor: S.M. Krishna. He was sworn in on 6 December 2004.

Chief Minister: Vilasrao Deshmukh (INC). He became the Chief Minister on 1 November 2004.

Geography

Physical characteristics: The dominant physical feature of the state is its plateau. The western upturned edges of this plateau rise to form the Sahyadri

Range. The major rivers and their main tributaries have eroded the plateau into alternating river valleys and intervening higher-level interfluves, such as the Ahmadnagar, Buldana and Yavatmal plateaus.

The Sahyadri Range, with an average elevation of 1000m, forms the topographical backbone of Maharashtra. Its steep cliffs descend to the Konkan coast in the west, while on the east it descends in steps through a transitional area called Mawal till it reaches the plateau level.

The Konkan area is a narrow coastal lowland that is hardly 50 km wide and 200m high. It lies between the Arabian Sea and the Sahyadri Range.

The Satpuras that lie along the northern border and the Bhamragad-Chiroli-Gaikhuri Range that lies along the eastern border serve as the natural limits of Maharashtra.

The flat topography of the state is a result of the outpouring of lava through fissures in the ground around 60 to 90 million years ago. This formed horizontal layers of basalt over extensive areas.

Neighbouring States and Union territories:
States:
- Gujarat
- Madhya Pradesh
- Karnataka
- Andhra Pradesh
- Goa
- Chhattisgarh

Union territories:
- Dadra
- Nagar Haveli

Major rivers:
- Godavari
- Tapi
- Wainganga
- Penganga
- Ulhas

- Wardha
- Bhima

Climate: Maharashtra has a tropical monsoon climate. The summers are hot and commence from March onwards and continue till June, when the monsoon season arrives. This lasts till October when the transition to winter takes place. Seasonal rains from sea clouds are intensive and rainfall exceeds 4000mm in the Sahyadri region.

The Konkan region also gets heavy rainfall, but the intensity follows a decreasing trend northwards. Rainfall is low east of the Sahyadris, around 700mm in the western plateau areas. The Solapur–Ahmadnagar region forms the heart of the dry zone. The rains increase marginally later in the season, mainly eastwards in the Marathwada and Vidarbha regions.

Flora and Fauna:
Flora: The forest cover of Maharashtra is 47,482 sq. km. It is interesting that the forest cover in the state has been showing increasing trends. Teak trees are found to occur over an area of approximately 10,180 sq. km, while bamboo plants cover an area of in excess of 10,100 sq. km.

The forests of the state are of the following types: (i) southern tropical semi-evergreen forests, (ii)) southern tropical moist deciduous forests, (iii) southern tropical dry deciduous forests, (iv) southern tropical thorn forests, and (v) littoral and swamp forests.

Fauna: Animals found in the state include tigers, bison, panthers, deer, antelopes, wild boar, blue bull, great Indian bustard, sloth bear, wild dog, jackal, hyena, chausingha, sambar, gaur, barking deer, ratel, pangolin, cheetal, mouse deer, flying squirrel and civet cat. Reptiles found in the state include monitor lizard, python, cobra, Russell's viper and pit viper.

A large variety of birds are found in the Sanjay Gandhi National Park. These include Tickell's flower pecker, sunbird, white-bellied sea eagle, paradise fly-catcher, trogon, various species of king-fisher, woodpeckers, and drongos. Besides these, the green barbet, the parakeet, the Malabar whistling thrush and spotted babbler are also found.

History

The name Maharashtra appeared in a seventh-century inscription and in the account of the Chinese traveller, Hiuen-Tsang.

During the early period, the territory that forms the modern state of Maharashtra was ruled over by several Hindu kingdoms. The Satavahanas, the Rashtrakutas, the Yadavas, the Vakatakas, the Kalachuris and the Chalukyas. After 1307 came the Muslim dynasties.

By the middle of the 16th century, Maharashtra was broken up into several smaller states and ruled by several inde-pendent, warring Muslim rulers. Shivaji was born in 1627. He set up a large Maratha empire that rivalled the Mughals in might and power. During the 18th century, almost the entire region of western and central India, as well as large parts of north and even eastern In-dia were brought under Maratha con-trol. Ultimately, even the mighty Marathas had to give way to the British in the 19th century.

At the time of independence in 1947, Bombay Presidency became the state of Bombay with B.G. Kher as its first Chief Minister. On 1 May 1960, the state was divided into two parts creat-ing Gujarat in the north and Maharashtra in the south, with Y.B. Chavan as its Chief Minister.

Politics

Bombay state was a former state of In-dia. During British rule, portions of the western coast of India under direct British rule were part of the Bombay Presidency. In 1937, the Bombay Presi-dency became a province of British In-dia. After Indian independence in 1947, many former princely states, including the Gujarat states and the Deccan states, were merged with the former Bombay province. Bombay state was significantly enlarged on 1 November 1956, expanding eastward to incorpo-rate the Marathi-speaking Marathwada region of Hyderabad state, the Marathi-speaking Vidarbha region of southern Madhya Pradesh, and Gujarati-speaking Saurashtra and Kutch. The southernmost, Kannada-speaking portion of Bombay state became part of the new linguistic state of Karnataka. Yashwantrao Chavan and later Morarji Desai were Bombay's only two Chief Ministers. Bombay state was parti-tioned into Gujarat and Maharashtra states on 1 May 1960, after an agita-tion for a separate Marathi state turned violent.

The Government of India Act 1935 which envisaged a federal type of gov-ernment, gave more powers to the Central and State Legislatures, and the control and interference of the Gover-nor-General and the Governors were to some extent reduced. In Maharashtra, the Legislative Council, understood today as an Upper Cham-ber, came to be established for the first time only after the Government of India Act, 1935, came into force. The Maharastra Legislature is bicameral consisting of a Legislative Council and a Legislative Assembly. The present strength of the Legislative Council is 78 members. It is a continuous House and not subject to dissolution. However, one-third of its members retire every second year and are replaced by new members.

Elected to the Bombay Legislative Assembly (1946), Yashwantrao Balwantrao Chavan of the Congress Party became the province's Chief Minister (1956) and was the first Chief Minister of the new state of Maharashtra (1960–62). He was succeeded by Marotrao Sambashio Kannamwar on 19 November 1962 and he remained in power till 25 November 1963. Vasantrao Phulsing Naik became the Chief Minister on 5 December 1963 and remained in power till 20 February 1975. Shankarrao Chavan succeeded him on 20 February 1975 and was in power till 1 April 1977. Shankarrao Bhaurao Chavan served two times as Chief Minister of Maharashtra and he was the Chief Minister for the second time from 13 March 1986 to 24 June 1988. Mr. Chavan was a staunch Congressman, except for a brief spell (1978–79) when he helped found and run the Maharashtra Samajwadi Congress, in association with Balasaheb Vikhe-Patil. On 1 April 1977 Vasantrao Patil of the Congress party became the Chief Minister. Again on 2 February 1983 Vasantrao Patil became the Chief Minister for the second time.

In 1978, Sharad Pawar toppled the Congress government in Maharashtra led by Vasantdada Patil and formed a government in coalition with the Janata Party under the banner of the Progressive Democratic Front. He became the Chief Minister for the second time on 25 June 1988. He remained in power till 25 June 1991. Again for the third time he was the Chief Minister from 3 March 1993 to 14 March 1994. Sharad Pawar is the president of the Nationalist Congress Party, which he formed in 1999. He is a former member of the Indian National Congress party. He has a prominent place in Indian national politics as well as regional politics of Maharashtra. After Sharad Pawar, Abdul Rahman Antulay of the Congress party became the Chief Minister on 9 June 1980. He was succeeded by Babasaheb Bhosale on 20 January 1982. The Shivajirao Patil Nilangekar government which took over in June 1985 lasted only a short time as he resigned on 13 March 1986. Sudhakarrao Naik was the Chief Minister from 25 June 1991 to 3 March 1993.

Shiv Sena, a political party, was founded on 19 June 1966 by Bal Thackeray who is the president of the party. It is a Hindu nationalist party, though it is strongly associated with Maratha identity. From 14 March 1995 to 1 February 1999 Manohar Joshi of the Shiv Sena Party was the Chief Minister. Narain Rane of Shiv Sena became the Chief Minister from 1 February to 18 October 1999. He was succeeded by Vilasrao Deshmukh of the Congress. He had been a minister in various governments in Maharashtra from 1982 to 1995 holding portfolios of revenue, co-operation, agriculture, home, industries and education. He had to step down as Chief Minister in January 2003 and make way for Sushilkumar Shinde, a prominent Dalit face of the Congress, following factionalism in the state unit of the party. Shinde was the first Dalit to have become the Chief Minister of Maharashtra. He served as Chief Minister from 18 January 2003 to 1 November 2004. Vilasrao Deshmukh again came back to the office of Chief Minister on 1 November 2004.

Culture

The tamasha form of folk drama is indigenous to this state. Marathi literature is also well known. Mumbai is also the most important centre of the Indian film industry.

Fairs and festivals: Ganesh Chaturthi is one of the most important festivals of the state. Modern festivals of the state include Pune Festival, Banganga Festival, Elephanta Festival, Ellora Festival (near Aurangabad), Kalidas Festival (Nagpur).

Economy, Industry and Agriculture

Economy: The net state domestic product at current prices for 2002–03 (provisional) was Rs 263,225 crores. The per capita net state domestic product at current prices for 2002–03 (provisional) was Rs 26,386.

Minerals and industry: Mumbai is regarded as the financial capital of India. The state is home to a wide range of manufacturing industries such as chemicals, textiles, automobiles, food products, machinery, electrical products, printing and publishing, paper and paper products, tobacco and related products. The film and tourism industries have an important place in the economic and social life of Maharashtra.

The districts of Chandrapur, Gadchiroli, Bhandara and Nagpur as constitute the main mineral-bearing areas of Maharashtra. Coal and manganese are the major minerals mined in the state. There are deposits of iron ore and limestone as well. Substantial deposits of ilmenite are found in the coastal area of Ratnagiri.

Agriculture: Major crops grown in the state are rice, jowar, bajra, wheat, pulses, oilseeds, cotton, sugar cane and turmeric. The main fruit crops are oranges, grapes, mangoes and bananas.

Power: The state gets most of its power from thermal power plants. Hydroelectric power plants are the second most important source while nuclear power plants are the third.

Education

Educational institutes: Prominent institutes of higher education in the state include the
* University of Mumbai
* University of Pune
* Nagpur University
* Indian Institute of Technology (Powai)
* Jamnalal Bajaj Institute of Management Studies (Mumbai)
* Narsee Monjee Institute of Management Studies (Mumbai)
* SNDT Women's University (Mumbai)
* Amravati University (Amravati)
* Bharati Vidyapeeth (Pune)
* Central Institute of Fisheries Education (Mumbai)
* Deccan College Post Graduate and Research Institute (Pune)
* Dr Babasaheb Ambedkar Marathwada University (Aurangabad)
* Dr Babasaheb Ambedkar Technological University (Raigad)
* Dr Panjabrao Deshmukh Krishi Vidyapeeth (Akola)
* Gokhale Institute of Politics and Economics (Pune)
* Indira Gandhi Institute of Development Research (Mumbai)
* International Institute for Population Sciences (Mumbai)
* Kavikulguru Kalidas Sanskrit Vishwavidyalaya (Ramtek)
* Konkan Krishi Vidyapeeth (Ratnagiri)
* Maharashtra University of Medical Sciences (Nashik)
* Mahatma Gandhi Antarrashtriya Hindi Vishwavidyalaya (Wardha)
* Mahatma Phule Krishi Vidyapeeth (Ahmadnagar)
* Marathwada Krishi Vidyapeeth (Parbhani)
* North Maharashtra University (Jaigaon)
* Shivaji University (Kolhapur)
* Swami Ramanand Teerth Marathwada University (Nanded)

- Tata Institute of Social Sciences (Mumbai)
- Tilak Maharshtra Vidyapeeth (Pune)
- Yahswantrao Chavan Maharasthra Open Univeristy (Nashik).

Tourism

Major tourist attractions: Mahabaleshwar, Lonavla, Elephanta Caves, Gateway of India, Ganapatiphule, Alibag, Raigad Fort, Sinhadurg Fort, Panchgani, Ajanta and Ellora.

Airports:
International:
- Mumbai.
Domestic:
- Pune
- Nagpur
- Akola
- Sholapur
- Kolhapur
- Aurangabad

National Parks:
- Sanjay Gandhi National Park in Thane dist. (86.96 sq. km).
- Gugamal National Park in Amaravati district. It is a part of Melghat Tiger Reserve. The Tiger Reserve covers an area of 1676.93 sq. km while the National Park has an area of 361.28 sq. km.
- Pench National Park in Nagpur dist. (257.26 sq. km).
- Navegaon National Park in Bhandara dist. (133.88 sq. km).
- Tadoba National Park in Chandrapur dist. (116.55 sq. km).

- The Andhari Wildlife Sanctuary (508.85 sq. km)
- Tadoba National Park together form the Tadoba-Andhari Tiger Reserve.

Administration

Legislature: Maharashtra has a bicameral legislature, which means that there is a legislative assembly as well as a legislative council. There are 288 seats in the assembly, of which 18 are reserved for SCs and 22 for STs. Elections were held in October 2004.

The current party position is as follows:

Name of Party	Seats
Nationalist Congress Party	71
Indian National Congress	69
Shiv Sena	62
Bharatiya Janata Party	54
Jan Surajya Sharti	4
Communist Party of India (Marxist)	3
Peasants and Workers Party of India	2
Akhil Bharatiya Sena	1
Bharipa Bahujan Mahasangha	1
Republican Party of India (A)	1
Swatantra Bharat Paksha	1
Independent	19
Total	**288**

Judiciary: The Bombay High Court has jurisdiction over Maharashtra, Goa, and Daman and Diu. Besides Mumbai, it has benches at Aurangabad, Nagpur and Panaji (Goa). Dalveer Bhandari is the chief justice.

Districts:

District	Area (sq. km)	Population	Headquarters	Urban Agglomerations
Ahmadnagar	17,048	4,088,077	Ahmadnagar	Ahmadnagar, Shrirampur
Akola	5,429	1,629,305	Akola	
Amravati	12,210	2,606,063	Amravati	
Aurangabad	10,107	2,920,548	Aurangabad	Aurangabad
Bhandara	3,895	1,135,835	Bhandara	
Beed	10,693	2,159,841	Beed	
Buldana	9,661	2,226,328	Buldana	
Chandrapur	11,443	2,077,909	Chandrapur	
Dhule	8,063	1,708,993	Dhule	
Gadchiroli	14,412	969,960	Gadchiroli	
Gondiya	5,425	1,200,151	Gondiya	
Hingoli	4,524	986,717	Hingoli	
Jalgaon	11,765	3,679,936	Jalgaon	Bhusawal
Jalna	7,718	1,612,357	Jalna	
Kolhapur	7,685	3,515,413	Kolhapur	Ichalkaranji, Kolhapur
Latur	7,157	2,078,237	Latur	
Mumbai	157	3,326,837	Mumbai	Greater Mumbai
Mumbai (Suburban)	446	8,587,561	Mumbai	Greater Mumbai
Nagpur	9,802	4,051,444	Nagpur	Kamptee, Nagpur
Nanded	10,528	2,868,158	Nanded	
Nandurbar	5,034	1,309,135	Nandurbar	
Nashik	15,530	4,987,923	Nashik	Nashik
Osmanabad	7,569	1,472,256	Osmanabad	
Parbhani	6,517	1,491,109	Parbhani	
Pune	15,643	7,224,224	Pune	Pune
Raigarh	7,152	2,205,972	Alibag	
Ratnagiri	8,208	1,696,482	Ratnagiri	
Sangli	8,572	2,581,835	Sangli	Sangli
Satara	10,480	2,796,906	Satara	
Sindhudurg	5,207	861,672	Oras	
Solapur	14,895	3,855,383	Solapur	
Thane	9,558	8,128,833	Thane	Bhiwandi, Greater Mumbai, Vasai
Wardha	6,309	1,230,640	Wardha	
Washim	5,153	1,019,725	Washim	
Yavatmal	13,582	2,460,482	Yavatmal	Yavatmal

Manipur

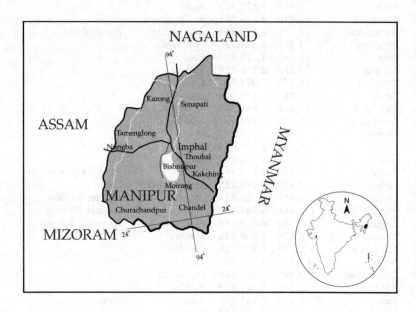

Key Statistics

Capital: Imphal.
Area: 22,327 sq. km.
Population: Total: 2,166,788
Male: 1,095,634
Female: 1,071,154
Population density: 107 per sq. km.
Sex ratio: 978 females per 1000 males.
Principal languages: Manipuri, Thado, Tangkhul.
Literacy rates: Total: 70.5%
Male: 80.3%
Female: 60.5%

Government

Governor: Shivender Singh Sidhu. He was sworn in on 6 August 2004.

Chief Minister: Okram Ibobi Singh (INC). He was sworn in on 7 March 2002.

Geography

Physical characteristics: Manipur can be divided into two distinct physical regions—the outlying area of rugged hills and narrow valleys, and the inner area of flat plains. The Loktak Lake is an important geographic feature of the central plain area. The total area occupied by all the lakes is about 600 sq. km. The highest point of the state is the Iso Peak near Mao (2,994m).

Neighbouring States and Union territories:
International border: Myanmar.

States:
- Assam
- Mizoram
- Nagaland

Major rivers:
- Manipur (also called Imphal)
- Barak

Climate: The average annual rainfall varies from 933mm at Imphal to 2593mm at Tamenglong. The temperature ranges from sub-zero to 36°C. Depending on the altitude, the climatic conditions vary from tropical to subalpine.

Flora and Fauna:

Flora: About 67 per cent of the geographical area of Manipur is hilly and covered with forests. The wet forests and the pine forests occur between 900–2700m above mean sea level. Manipur is home to 500 varieties of orchids. 'Siroi Lily', which is the only terrestrial lily in India, grows on the hilltops of the Siroi Hill.

Fauna: The rich fauna of Manipur includes the sangai (or dancing deer), slow loris, hornbill, hoolock gibbon, the clouded leopard, Mrs Hume's barbacked pheasant, spotted linshang, blyths tragopan, Burmese peafowl and salamander.

History

In 1762 the ruler of Manipur, Raja Jai Singh, made a treaty with the British to thwart a Myanmarese invasion. Again in 1824, the services of the British were sought to expel invaders from Myanmar. Political turmoil continued for some time until 1891, when Chura Chand, a five-year-old member of the ruling family, was nominated as the raja. The administration was henceforth conducted under British supervision for the next few years.

In 1907, the raja and the durbar regained control of the government. It is noteworthy that the vice-president of the durbar was a member of the Indian Civil Service. The administration was eventually transferred to the raja and the vice-president of the durbar became its president.

An uprising of the Kuki hill tribes in 1917 resulted in the adoption of a new system of government. The region was divided into three subdivisions. Each of these subdivisions was put under an officer from the government of the neighbouring state of Assam.

In 1947 Manipur joined the Indian Union and the political agency of Assam was abolished. In 1949 Manipur became a Union territory administered by a chief commissioner and an elected territorial council. In 1969, the office of the chief commissioner was replaced by a lieutenant governor. This in turn was converted to a governorship when Manipur became full-fledged state of the Indian Union on 21 January 1972. M. Koireng Singh as the first Chief Minister of Manipur.

Politics

The year 1934 marked a turning point in the political history of Manipur when a political organization called the Nikhil Manipuri Mahasabha under the presidentship of Maharaja Churchand Singh came into existence. The Mahasabha was initially a social organization, but in 1938 it became the first political party of Manipur, thus becoming a harbinger of regional parties in Manipur. On 15 August 1947, when India attained Independence from British rule, the supremacy of the British Crown over the native states also came to an end. Along with the lapse of suzerainty, all treaties and agreements in force ceased to operate. As a result, Manipur was free to accede to either Pakistan or India. However, in view of the wishes of the people and the pressures from social and political organizations, the Maharaja declared that he would introduce a fully democratic and constitutional form of government in Manipur and thereby announced the formation of a 'Constitution Making Committee' consisting of seventeen members. However, the Constitutional Monarchy established under the Manipur Constitution Act, 1947 did not last long. In the meanwhile, New Delhi evolved a plan to integrate all native states to counter a move for balkanization of the country. Under this scheme, the infamous Merger Agreement drive was brought out which was to be entered into with the rulers including the Raja of Manipur. The King of Manipur was one of the few rulers who refused to sign the agreement but was later reportedly coaxed and compelled to sign on 21 September 1949, which subsequently endorsed the formal merger of Manipur with the dominion of India on 15 October 1949.

As a matter of fact, the regional parties in India were born out of utter neglect by the Centre on the one hand and the people's strong desire to vindicate their rights and privileges as free men. This point could well be attributed to the rise of regional parties in Manipur particularly the Manipur People's Party (MPP). Among the existing and non-existing regional parties, the MPP is considered most important in Manipur. Defections, shifting of loyalties etc. have been an inherent character of political parties in Manipur. The MPP is no exception. It is in this backdrop the one must analyse the MPP, which was once a strong political force in the state. The Manipur People's Party, at the very outset, is an offshoot of the

defectors from Indian National Congress (INC). It was formed on 26 December 1968. The party built up its foundation on a very ambitious footing. The MPP initially stressed on the point of its being the real and the only alternative in the state. Emphasizing its regional character, the MPP claimed that it alone could bring prosperity to the people of Manipur. The MPP for the first time entered onto the arena of electoral tug-of-war in 1972. There was a tremendous excitement in the contest since it was also the first election after the conferment of statehood on Manipur. Almost all the parties, including the MPP, threw a challenge to the Congress and rallied around the banner of anti-Congressism. In the sixty member Assembly, the MPP won 15 out of 42 seats it contested. It polled 20% of the total votes but won 25% of the seats available for contest. The MPP utilized the fractured verdict and thus formed a coalition government with the help of Socialist Party, Congress (O), and the Independents. A ministry headed by Md Alimuddin under the name of United Legislature Party (ULP) was installed on 20 March 1972. However, dissensions soon cropped up in the government. As a result some members of the ULP ministry defected to the Opposition. Later on, the Opposition moved a no-confidence motion against the government and on 26 March 1973 Md Alimuddin submitted his resignation. Subsequently, the Assembly was adjourned sine-die and on 28 March 1973 it was dissolved and President's Rule was imposed. But, in the mid-term election held in 1974, MPP held the dominant position by winning 20 seats, leaving the Congress only with 13 seats. The MPP had improved its position by getting five more seats. But the fact remained that no party was able to secure an absolute majority in the house and political instability continued to plague Manipur politics as before. After the election, both the MPP and the Congress tried to win over different groups and the independents in order to form the government. Lastly, MPP with others' support formed the government under the name of United Legislature Party (ULP) headed by Md Alimuddin on 4 March 1974. But interestingly on 8 July 1974, in the course of the Budget session six ULP members crossed the floor. More defections followed on the same day resulting in the resignation of Alimuddin Ministry in the afternoon and thereby the Assembly was adjourned sine-die.

On 29 June 1977 a new Janata Ministry under Yangmaso Shaiza was installed. All the members of the Congress party and the MPP joined the Janata Legislature Party and the Janata Party's strength rose to 55 in the House. The above circumstances and the political behaviour of its leaders severely affected the prospects of one of the most promising regional parties of India. In the assembly election in 1980, MPP could win only four seats. In the Assembly elections of 1984, the MPP not only reduced in the number of seats it contested but also its electoral performance declined considerably; out of 34 seats it contested, it could gain only three seats. Again, after the 1990 Assembly election, on 23 February, a new Ministry was sworn in under the leadership of MPP stalwart R.K. Ranbir Singh making an event in the political history of Manipur of being the first non-Congress government in more than a decade despite the prevailing doubts on the question of 'stability', given the past experiences of coalition governments. The 22-months old Ranbir Ministry was finally closed on 7 January 1992 and President's Rule was imposed

thereafter keeping the option of restoring a popular ministry at an appropriate time. The President's Rule was short lived and lasted only till 8 April 1992, thanks to R.K. Dorendro and his political skills. He somehow convinced the former CM and his archrival R.K. Ranbir of MPP to support him. However, despite all these Dorendro's ministry fell on 31 December 1993 and subsequently President's Rule was implemented. After almost one year, another Congress ministry under Rishang Keishing was installed and reigned until the next elections held in February 1995. In this election, the Manipur People's Party (MPP) fielded 55 candidates but it could return only 18 members to the Assembly. Then came the 2000 elections in which the position of MPP declined considerably. In a sixty member Assembly it could win only four seats, that too from the valley constituencies only. Furthermore, to their utter disappointment and what could be termed as a downright betrayal, three of the four elected members left the party even before taking the oath as Member of the Legislative Assembly, thus making an irreparable dent in the party. In 2002, another Congress ministry headed by Okram Ibobi Singh was sworn in in Manipur.

Culture

The Manipuri dance form is indigenous to the state. For example, the Anal community have the Kamdom and the Ludem dance forms, while the Chote community has the Hucham Pulak. Different communities and tribes have varied art forms, folk dances, folk songs and folklore of their own.

Fairs and festivals: Important festivals of the state include Ningol Chakouba, Yaoshang (the most important festivals of Hindus of the state), Ramzan Id, Kut (a festival of Kuki-Chin-Mizo), Gang-Ngai (a festival of Kabui Nagas), Chumpha (festival of Tangkhul Nagas), Christmas, Cheiraoba (the Manipuri New Year), Kang (the Rathayatra of Manipur) and Heikru Hitongba.

Economy, Industry and Agriculture

Economy: The net state domestic product at current prices in 2002–03 (advance estimate) was Rs 3047 crores. The per capita net state domestic product at current prices (new series) in 2002–03 (advance estimate) was Rs 12,230.

Minerals and industry: Occurrences of asbestos, copper ore, coal, bog iron, lignite, chromite, limestone, nickel ore and petroleum are reported from the state. Iron and steel products, consumer products and cement are also produced in the state.

Agriculture: About 80 per cent of the state's population depends on agriculture for their livelihood. Rice and maize are the most important food crops. Besides this, the state is well known for its fruit production—orange, pineapple, jackfruit, peach, plum, pears and banana. Potato, turmeric, ginger, black pepper, tapioca, cotton, oilseeds, jute and mesta, cashew nut, tea, mushrooms, orchids and arecanut are also grown.

Power: The state mainly utilizes hydroelectric power, but thermal power is also used.

Education

Educational institutes: Prominent institutes of higher education are the
• Manipur University

• Central Agricultural University, both located at Imphal.

Tourism

Major tourist attractions: Ima Market, Imphal; Khomghampat Orchidarium, Imphal; Manipur Zoological Gardens, Imphal; Bishnupur; Moirang; Loktak Lake and Sendra Island; Waithou Lake; Kangchup; Ukhrul; Tamenglong.

Airport: Imphal.

National Parks:
• Keibul Lamjao National Park in Bishnupur district (40 sq. km). It is the world's only floating national park
• Shiroi Hill National Park in Ukhrul district (41 sq. km).

Administration

Legislature: Manipur has a unicameral legislature. There are 60 seats of which 1 is reserved for SCs and 19 are reserved for STs. The tenure of the present house ends on 11 March 2007. The current party position is as follows:

Name of Party	Seats
Indian National Congress	20
Federal Party of Manipur	13
Manipur State Congress Party	7
Communist Party of India	5
Bharatiya Janata Party	4
Nationalist Congress Party	3
Samata Party	3
Manipur Peoples Party	2
Democratic Revolutionary Peoples Party	2
Manipur National Conference	1
Total	**60**

Judiciary: The state comes under the Mizoram bench of the Guwahati High Court. Binod Kumar Roy is the chief justice.

Districts:

District	Area (sq. km)	Population	Headquarters	Urban Agglomerations
Bishnupur	496	205,907	Bishnupur	
Chandel	3,313	122,714	Chandel	
Churachandpur	4,570	228,707	Churachandpur	
Imphal East	709	393,780	Porompat	Imphal
Imphal West	519	439,532	Lamphel	Imphal
Senapati	3,271	379,214	Senapati	
Tamenglong	4,391	111,493	Tamenglong	
Thoubal	514	366,341	Thoubal	
Ukhrul	4,544	140,946	Ukhrul	

Meghalaya

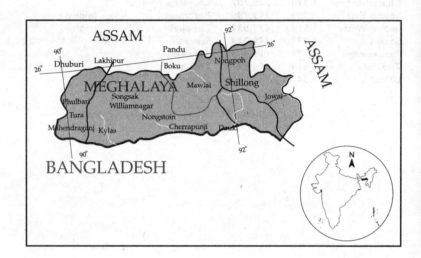

Key Statistics

Capital: Shillong.
Area: 22,429 sq. km.
Population: Total: 2,318,822
Male: 1,176,087
Female: 1,142,735
Population density: 103 per sq. km.
Sex ratio: 972 females per 1000 males.
Principal languages: Khasi, Garo, Bengali, Assamese.
Literacy rates: Total: 62.6%
Male: 65.4%
Female: 59.6%

Government

Governor: Mundakkal Matthew Jacob. He has been the governor of Meghalaya since 19 June 1995.

Chief Minister: D. Dethwelson Lapang (INC). He was sworn in on 4 March 2003.

Geography

Physical characteristics: The state of Meghalaya is a region of uplands that has been formed by a detached part of the Deccan Plateau. In the western part of Meghalaya, the Garo Hills rise abruptly from the Brahmaputra valley to about 300 metres. They merge with the Khasi Hills and Jaintia Hills. These adjacent highlands together form a single tableland region that is separated by a series of eastward-running ridges. The steep southern face of the plateau overlooks the lowlands of Bangladesh. A number of rivers and streams flow out of the plateau, to create deep, narrow valleys with steep sides. These include the Umiam–Barapani, a major source of hydroelectric power for Assam and Meghalaya.

Neighbouring States and Union territories:
International border: Bangladesh.

States: Assam

Major rivers: Although there are a number of rivers in Meghalaya, none of them are fit for navigation. In the Garo Hills, the Manda, the Janjiram and the Damring flow towards the north while the Ringge and the Ganol flow westwards. The south flowing rivers are the Simsang, the biggest river in Garo Hills, and the Bhogai.

Significant north-flowing rivers in the Khasi and Jaintia hills are the Khri, the Umkhem, the Umtrew and the Umiam. The Kulpi lies on the border between Jainita Hills and North Cachar Hills. The Kynshi, the Umiam Mawphlang and the Umngot flow south into Bangladesh.

Climate: This region experiences tropical monsoonal climate, that varies from the western to the eastern parts of the plateau. The Garo Hills district has a tropical climate characterized by high rainfall and humidity. Summers are generally warm while winters are moderately cold. The Khasi and Jaintia Hills have high rainfall, moderately warm summers and severely cold winters when temperature sometimes dips to below freezing point in the higher altitudes. The mean summer temperature in Meghalaya is 26°C and the mean winter temperature is 9°C.

A maximum rainfall of 12,000mm has been recorded on the southern slope of Khasi Hills along the Cherrapunjee–Mawsynram belt. The average annual rainfall is about 2600mm in western Meghalaya, between 2500 and 3000mm in northern Meghalaya and about 4000mm in south-eastern Meghalaya. There is substantial variation of rainfall in the central and southern parts of the state.

Flora and Fauna:
Flora: Meghalaya has a widely varied and unique flora. The vegetation of Meghalaya ranges from tropical and subtropical to temperate or near temperate. This is largely due to the diverse topography, abundant rainfall and climatic and soil conditions of the state.

The forest types found in the state are: (i) Tropical forests: tropical evergreen forests, tropical semi-evergreen forests, tropical moist and dry deciduous forests, and grasslands and savannas; and (ii) Temperate forests.

The different types of plants found in the state are: parasites and epiphytes, succulent plants, and trees and shrubs.

Meghalaya also produces timber, fuelwood, resin, fibre, latex, tannin, fodder, gums, shellac, essential oils, fats, edible fruits, honey and a large number of medicinal plants. Some of the important tree species that yield timber are Khasi pine, teak, sal, and bamboos. Meghalaya is also well known for a large variety of flowers, bay leaves, orchids and cinnamon.

Fauna: Meghalaya is home to a wide variety of animals. These include the elephant, serow, sambar, hoolock, leopard, golden cat, barking deer, pangolin, jungle cat, large Indian civet, binturong or bear cat and Himalayan black bear. Notable among the reptile population found in the state are Indian cobra, king cobra, coral snake, viper, green tree racer, red-necked kulback, copperhead, blind snake and python.

Some of the significant species of birds found in the state are hoopoe, black-breasted Kalij pheasant, jungle mynas, hill mynas, long-tailed broadbill, red jungle fowl, spotted forktail, Himalayan whistling thrush, Burmese roller, blue-throated barbet, and Himalayan black bulbul. Besides these, the great Indian hornbill, florican and black drongo are also found in the state. Meghalaya is also famous for its large butterfly population.

History

When the British came to Sylhet (now in Bangladesh) in 1765, the Khasis used to go to Pandua on the border of Sylhet to trade in various commodities in exchange for rice, salt and dried fish. At that time, limestone from the Khasi Hills was taken to Bengal. The British officials of the East India Company came in contact with the Khasis when they began trading in Khasi Hill limestone.

In 1824, the Burmese invaded Cachar and reached the border of the Jaintia Hills. The British sent a force to reinforce the Jaintia ruler's troops. This paved the way for a friendship treaty to be signed on 10 March 1824, whereby the Jaintia ruler accepted British protection. This led to other Khasi chiefs to allow the passage of the British troops through their territories. After the end of the Burmese invasion, the Khasi chiefs agreed to a British demand for a route through the Khasi and Jaintia Hills that would connect Assam Valley with Surma Valley. The road was completed in March 1929, but only after suppressing an uprising led by U Tirot Sing. This led to the signing of several treaties with different Khasi chiefs. These treaties let the British slowly take control of the mineral deposits and at the same time subjugate the chiefs and also gain control of the judiciary. In 1862 the Jaintias rose in revolt under U Kiang Nongbah.

Shillong, the present-day capital of Meghalaya was made the capital of Assam in 1874. It remained so till January 1972, when Meghalaya was created. At the time of independence in 1947, the rulers of the region acceded to India. The region was given special protection in the Indian constitution. It was included within the state of Assam but was granted a substantial amount of autonomy. On 2 April 1970, Meghalaya became an autonomous state within Assam and attained full statehood on 21 January 1972. Captain Williamson A. Sangma was the state's first Chief Minister.

Politics

With the partition of Bengal in 1905, Meghalaya became a part of the new province of Assam and Eastern Bengal. In 1912, when the partition of Bengal was reversed, Meghalaya became a part of the revived province of Assam. On 3 January 1921 following the Montagu-Chelmsford Report of 1917 and the Government of India Act of 1919, the Governor-General-in-Council declared the areas now in Meghalaya, excluding the Khasi states, as backward tracts. In the wake of the Government of India Act, 1935, the areas now in Meghalaya, excluding the Khasi states, became partially excluded areas. However, these areas were represented in the Assam Legislative Council since 1920 and later also in the pre-Independence Assam Legislative Assembly. On 2 April 1970 an Autonomous State of Meghalaya was created within the state of Assam by the Assam Reorganisation (Meghalaya) Act, 1969. In accordance with the Sixth schedule to the Constitution, a Legislature of the Autonomous State consisting of 37 members who were elected indirectly by the Autonomous District Councils was set up. The first sitting of the Assembly took place in Tura on 14 April 1970. In 1971, the Parliament passed the North-Eastern Areas (Reorganization) Act which conferred full statehood on the Autonomous State of Meghalaya. It attained statehood on 21 January 1972, with a Legislative Assembly. The Legislature of Meghalaya is unicameral. At present, the total membership of the Legislative Assembly is 60. Williamson A. Sangma, the first Chief Minister of Meghalaya, had three tenures as Chief Minister, from 1970 to 1978, from 1981 to 1983 and from 1988 to 1990. From 10 March 1978 to 7 May 1979 Darwin Diengdoh Pugh was the Chief Minister. Brinton Buhai Lyndoh who remained in office till 7 May 1981 succeeded him. Again he came to power on 2 March 1983 and remained in power till 2 April 1983. He took part in the movement that resulted in the creation of the autonomous state of Meghalaya in 1970, which was separated from Assam in 1972. In 1979, he entered into an agreement with Williamson A. Sangma, who was the Congress leader, and split the All-Party Hill Leaders' Conference (APHLC) to form a coalition government with the Congress. Lyngdoh and Sangma agreed to share the Chief Minister's post for two years each. Lyngdoh took over the reign of power as the Chief Minister for the first two years. As there was no formal agreement, it came to be known as a 'gentlemen's agreement' in political circles. In 1990, he was leader of the Hill Peoples Union and in 1998 of the United Democratic Party. Later he became a member of the Meghalaya Democratic Party.

From 6 February 1988 to 26 March 1990 P.A. Sangma was the Chief Minister. He was succeeded by Brington Buhai Lyngdoh on 26 March 1990; he remained in power till 11 October 1991. D.D. Lapang, the present Chief Minister of Meghalaya succeeded him on 5 February 1992 and remained in office till 19 February 1993. Salseng C. Marak held the office of Chief Minister from 19 February to 10 March 1998. B.B. Lyngdoh succeeded him on 10 March 1998 and became the Chief Minister for the fourth time. From 8 March 2000 to 8 December 2001 E.K. Mawlong was the Chief Minister. Flinder Anderson Khonglam was the Chief Minister from 8 December 2001 to 4 March 2003.

Culture

A common and unique cultural tradition of all the tribes of Meghalaya is the matriarchal law of inheritance, whereby custody of property and succession of family position runs through the female line. It passes from the mother to the youngest daughter. The traditional costume of the state is the 'Jainsem' and the 'Dhara', although Western clothes are gaining popularity amongst the younger generation.

The different tribes have their own set of traditions and art forms. Phawar is one of the basic forms of Khasi music. It is more of a 'chant' than a song and is often composed on the spot to suit the occasion. Other forms of songs include the exploits of legendary heroes, ballads and verses based on historical events and laments for martyrs. Khasi musical instruments include the tangmuri, shaw shaw, nakra, ksing padiah, besli, sharati, shyngwiang and duitara.

Fairs and festivals: The different Khasi festivals are Ka Shad Suk Mynsiem, Ka Pom-Blang Nongkrem, Ka-Shad Shyngwiang-Thangiap, Ka-Shad-Kynjoh Khaskain, Ka Bam Khana Shnong, Umsan Nongkharai and Shad Beh Sier. The key Jaintia festivals include

Behdienkhlam, Laho Dance and the sowing ritual ceremony. Other festivals commemorated by the Jaintias include the Tiger Festival, Bam Phalar/Bam Doh, Rong Belyngkan, Durga Puja, Seng Kut Snem and Christmas. The main festivals of the Garos are Wangala, Den Bilsia, Rongchu gala, Mangona, Grengdik BaA, Mi Amua, Jamang Sia, Ja Megapa, Sa Sat Ra Chaka, Ajeaor Ahaoea, Chambil Mesara, Dore Rata Dance, Saram Cha'A, Do'KruSua and A Se Mania.

Economy, Industry and Agriculture

Economy: The net state domestic product at current prices (new series) in 2002–03 (advance estimate) was Rs 3842 crores. The per capita net state domestic product at current prices (new series) in 2002–03 (advance estimate) was Rs 15,983.

Minerals and industry: The main industries of the state are tourism, iron and steel, consumer products, cement, handloom, silk production, lime and granite cutting and polishing. Small scale industries in the state include wooden furniture making, cane and bamboo works, tailoring, flour and rice mills, weaving and bakeries. There are six industrial estates, one designated industrial area and one export promotion industrial park in Meghalaya.

The significant mineral resources that are currently being exploited in the state are coal, limestone, clay and sillimanite. Other mineral resources found to occur in the state include phosphorite, glass sand, granite, quartz, feldspar, gypsum, gold, iron ore, uranium, base metal and gypsum.

Agriculture: Agriculture is the main occupation of the people of Meghalaya. Over 80 per cent of the total popula-

tion is dependent on agriculture for their livelihood. Rice and maize are the major food crops. Millets and pulses are also grown, but in lesser quantities. Potato is a major cash crop of Meghalaya. Oilseeds such as rapeseed, mustard, soyabean and sesame are also grown. Important fruits grown here are orange, pineapple, lemon, guava, litchi, plum, peach, pear, jackfruit and bananas. Jute, mesta and cotton are the main fibre crops grown in the state. Areca nut and betelvine are also grown. The most prominent spices of the state are ginger, chillies, turmeric, black pepper and bay leaf. Jhum or 'shifting system' of cultivation is now being replaced with scientific methods, thereby bringing more land under permanent cultivation.

Power: Hydroelectric power plants meet all of Meghalaya's power requirements. However, the state has a high thermal power generation potential.

Education

Educational institutes:
• North Eastern Hill University, Shillong
• Sacred Heart Theological College, Hawlai
• Jowai Polytechnic School
• North Eastern Indira Gandhi Regional Institute of Health and Medical Sciences

Tourism

Major tourist attractions:
1. Khasi Hills: Cherrapunjee (Sohra), Shillong Peak, Mawsynram, Ward's Lake, Sohpetbneng Peak, Botanical Garden, Lady Hydari Park, Umiam Water Sports Complex, Shillong Cathedral, Dwarksuid, Bishop and Beadon Falls, Elephant Falls, Sweet Falls, Nongkhnum Island, Crinoline Falls, Diengiei Peak, Spread Eagle Falls, Kyllang Rock, Noh Kalikai Falls, Ranikor.

2. Jaintia Hills: Megalithic Remnants at Nartiang, Syndai, Syntu Ksiar, Jowai, Thadlaskein Lake.

3. Garo Hills: Nokrek Peak, Imilchang Dare Waterfalls, Tura Peak, Naphak Lake.

Airport: Umroi.

National Parks:
• Balphakram National Park in South Garo Hills district (220 sq. km)
• Nokrek National Park in East, West and South Garo Hills districts (47.48 sq. km).

Administration

Legislature: Meghalaya has a 60-seat unicameral legislature of which 55 are reserved for STs. The term of the current house expires on 10 March 2008.

The present party position is as under:

Name of Party	Seats
Indian National Congress	22
Nationalist Congress Party	14
United Democratic Party	9
Meghalaya Democratic Party	4
Bharatiya Janata Party	2
Hill State People's Democratic Party	2
Khun Hynnieutrip National Awakening Movement	2
Independent	5
Total	**60**

Judiciary: Meghalaya is under the jurisdiction of the Gauhati High Court at Guwahati, Assam. The principal seat of the High Court is at Guwahati and there is a circuit bench at Shillong. Binod Kumar Roy is the chief justice.

Districts:

District	Area (sq. km)	Population	Headquarters	Urban Agglomerations
East Garo Hills	260	247,555	Williamnagar	
East Khasi Hills	2,748	660,994	Shillong	Shillong
Jaintia Hills	3,819	295,692	Jowai	
Ri Bhoi	2,448	192,795	Nongpoh	
South Garo Hills	1,887	99,105	Baghmara	
West Garo Hills	3,677	515,813	Tura	
West Khasi Hills	5,247	294,115	Nongstoin	

Mizoram

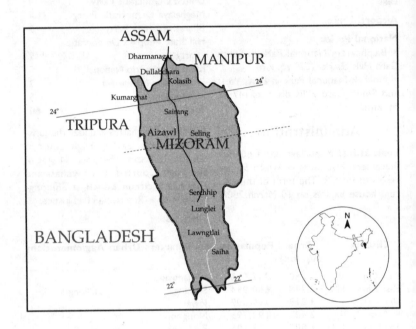

Key Statistics

Capital: Aizawl.
Area: 21,087 sq. km.
Population: Total: 888,573
Male: 459,109
Female: 429,464
Population density: 42 per sq. km.
Sex ratio: 935 females per 1000 males.
Principal languages: Lushai/Mizo,
Bengali, Lakher.
Literacy rates: Total: 88.49% (second
highest in the country)
Male: 90.69%
Female: 86.13%

Government

Governor: Amolak Rattan Kohli. He took over as governor on 18 May 2001.

Chief Minister: Pu Zoramthanga (MNF). He was sworn in on 4 December 2003.

Geography

Physical characteristics: Mizoram is bounded by Myanmar on the east and south and Bangladesh on the west. It is a mountainous region with steep hills separated by rivers that create deep gorges between them. Phawngpui or the Blue Mountain is the highest peak (2210m). The Tropic of Cancer runs through the state.

Neighbouring States and Union territories:
International borders:
• Myanmar
• Bangladesh

States:
• Assam
• Tripura
• Manipur

Major rivers:
• Tlawng is the longest river of the state.
• Tlau
• Chhimtuipui
• Tuichang
• Tuirial are other important rivers.

Climate: The hilly areas are cooler during summer, while the lower reaches are relatively warm and humid. The average maximum temperature in summer is 30°C. The average minimum temperature during winter is around 11°C. The months of May to September see heavy rains, with an average annual rainfall of 2500mm.

Flora and Fauna:
Flora: Three-fourths of the state's area is under forest cover. Prominent trees include the Himalayan maple, champak, ironwood, bamboo and gurjun. The region also abounds in various species of shrubs. About 150 species of orchids have also been identified.

Fauna: Wildlife found in the state include tiger, leopard, elephant, Malayan sun bear, Himalayan black bear, serow, wild boar, slow loris, Assamese macaque, capped langur, owl, pheasant, partridge, hawk, eagle, egret and heron.

History

Like many other northeast Indian tribes, the origin of the Mizos is shrouded in mystery. They are generally accepted as part of a great Mongoloid wave of migration from China. These include the Kuki, New Kuki and Lushai tribes. In 1895, the Mizo Hills were formally declared as a part of British India and subsequently marked as Lushai Hills district, with Aizawl as the headquarters.

At the time of India's independence, a subcommittee was formed under the chairmanship of Gopinath Bordoloi to advise the Constituent Assembly on the tribal affairs in the north-east. The region became a district of Assam.

In 1959, a great famine, known in Mizo history as the 'Mautam Famine', struck the Mizo Hills. The cause of the famine was the flowering of bamboos and the consequent manifold increase in the rat population which infested the villages and destroyed crops.

Movements for sovereignty for the region gained momentum in 1961, with the birth of the Mizo National Front (MNF). After a decade of insurgency, the region was declared a Union territory in 1972. Insurgency continued for another 14 years, and ended with MNF leader Laldenga signing an accord with the Union government. Mizoram became India's 23rd state on 20 February 1987. Laldenga was the state's first Chief Minister.

Politics

It was during the British regime that a political awakening among the Mizos in Lushai Hills started taking shape. The first political party, the Mizo Common People's Union, was formed on 9 April 1946. At the time of Independence a Sub-committee, under the chairmanship of Gopinath Bordoloi, was formed to advise the Constituent Assembly on the tribal affairs in the North East. The Mizo Union submitted a resolution of this Sub-committee demanding inclusion of all Mizo inhabited areas adjacent to Lushai Hills. However, a new party called the United Mizo Freedom (UMFO) came up to demand that Lushai Hills join Burma after Independence. After Independence of India, Mizoram continued to be part of Assam. Following the Bordoloi Subcommittee's suggestion, a certain amount of autonomy was accepted by the government and enshrined in the Sixth Schedule of the Constitution. The Lushai Hills Autonomous District Council came into being in 1952 leading to the abolition of chieftainship in the Mizo society. The autonomy however met the aspirations of the Mizos only partially. Representatives of the District Council and the Mizo Union pleaded with the States Reorganization Commission (SRC) in 1954 for integrating the Mizo-dominated areas of Tripura and Manipur with their District Council in Assam. The tribal leaders in the North East were laboriously unhappy with the SRC Recommendations. They met in Aizawl in 1955 and formed a new political party, Eastern India Union (EITU) and raised the demand for a separate state comprising of all the hill districts of Assam. The Mizo Union split and the breakaway faction joined the EITU. By this time, the UMFO also joined the EITU and the demand for a separate Hill state by EITU was kept in abeyance.

A new political organization, the Mizo National Front (MNF) was born on 22 October 1961 under the leadership of Laldenga with the specified goal of achieving sovereign independence of Greater Mizoram. While the MNF took to violence to secure its goal of estab-lishing a sovereign land, other political forces in the hills of Assam were striving for a separate state. The search for a political solution to the problems facing the hill regions in Assam continued. In 1966 the Mizos resorted to the use of armed struggle to put forth their demands to set up a homeland. The Mizo National Front was outlawed in 1967. A Mizo District Council delegation, which met Prime Minister Indira Gandhi in May 1971 demanded a full-fledged state for the Mizos. The Union government on its own offered the proposal of turning Mizo Hills into a Union Territory in July 1971. The Union Territory of Mizoram came into being on 21 January 1972. On 3 May 1972 L. Chal Chhunga was sworn in as the first Chief Minister of Mizoram. Thenphunga Sailo was the Chief Minister from 1978 to 1984. Mizoram has two seats in Parliament, one each in the Lok Sabha and in the Rajya Sabha.

In 1986 a peace agreement was signed between the government of India and MNF. Mizoram was created as a separate state within India, and Pu Laldenga became Chief Minister. The formalization of Mizoram state took place on 20 February 1987. Chief Secretary Lalkhama read out the proclamation of statehood at a public meeting organized at Aizawl's Parade Ground. Hiteshwar Saikia was appointed as Governor of Mizoram. However in 1989, MNF lost the first elections following the peace agreement. Former guerrilla leader Pu Zoramthanga became party leader following the death of Laldenga in 1990. In 1998 and 2003 MNF won the state assembly elections, and Pu Zoramthanga is currently Chief Minister. In the 2003 elections MNF won 21 out of 40 seats in the state assembly, and got 31.66% of the votes.

Culture

Popular dance forms of Mizoram are Khuallam, Cheraw or bamboo dance, Chailam and Tlanglam. These are accompanied by instruments like the gong and drum. Traditional crafts include exquisite cane and bamboo work and handloom weaving.

Fairs and festivals: Most Mizo festivals are connected with harvest or other agricultural operations. These include Mim Kut, Pawl Kut and Chapchar Kut.

Economy, Industry and Agriculture

Economy: The net state domestic product at current prices in 2001–02 was Rs 1777 crores. The per capita net state domestic product at current prices in 2001–02 was Rs 19,696.

Minerals and industry: Mizoram has no major industry. The small-scale sector comprises handloom, handicrafts, rice, oil and flour milling, mechanized bamboo workshops and sericulture. Major minerals include coal, limestone and natural gas.

Agriculture: Nearly 60 per cent of the population is engaged in agriculture. Shifting cultivation, or jhum, is the usual practice. Important crops include paddy, maize, soyabean, mustard, pulses, sugarcane, chilli, ginger, tobacco, turmeric, potato, banana and pineapple.

Power: The two main sources of power in the state are hydroelectric plants and diesel power plants.

Education

Educational institutes:
• The North Eastern Hill University, which is headquartered at Shillong, has a campus at Aizwal.

Tourism

Major tourist attractions: The Blue Mountain (Phawngpui); The famous caves: Pukzing Cave, Milu Puk, Lamsial Puk, and Kungawrhi Puk; Sibuta Lung; Thangliana Lung; Suangpuilawn Inscriptions; Mangkhai Lung; Buddha's Image near Mualcheng village.

Airport: Aizawl.

National Parks: Murlen (200 sq. km) and Phawngpui (50 sq. km).

Administration

Legislature: The Mizoram Legislative Assembly comprises 40 seats, of which 39 are reserved for STs. The term of the current assembly expires on 14 November 2008. Party position of the current house is as follows:

Name of Party	Seats
Mizo National Front	21
Indian National Congress	12
Mizoram People's Conference	3
Zoram Nationalist Party	2
Hmar Peoples Convention	1
Maraland Democratic Front	1
Total	**40**

Judiciary: Mizoram falls under the jurisdiction of the Gauhati High Court. There is a permanent bench located at Aizawl. Binod Kumar Roy is the chief justice.

Districts:

District	Area (sq. km)	Population	Headquarters	Urban Agglomerations
Aizawl	3,576.3	339,812	Aizawl	–
Champhai	3,185.8	101,389	Champhai	–
Kolasib	1,382.5	60,977	Kolasib	–
Lawngtlai	2,557.1	73,050	Lawngtlai	–
Lunglei	4,538.0	137,155	Lunglei	–
Mamit	3,025.8	62,313	Mamit	–
Chhimtuipui	1,399.9	60,823	Saiha	–
Serchhip	1,421.6	55,539	Serchhip	–

Nagaland

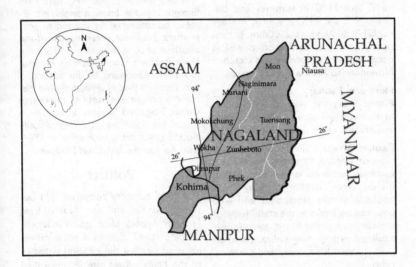

Key Statistics

Capital: Kohima.
Area: 16,579 sq. km.
Population: Total: 1,990,036
Male: 1,047,141
Female: 942,895
Population density: 120 per sq. km.
Sex ratio: 900 females per 1000 males.
Principal languages: Ao, Sema, Konyak.
Literacy rates: Total: 66.6%
Male: 71.2%
Female: 61.5%

Government

Governor: Shyamal Datta. He assumed the office of the governor of Nagaland on 28 January 2002.

Chief Minister: Neiphi-u Rio (NPF). He became Chief Minister on 6 March 2003.

Geography

Physical characteristics: Nagaland has state boundaries with Assam, Arunachal Pradesh and Manipur. On the east, it has an international boundary with Myanmar. The Naga Hills run through this state. Saramati (3840m) is the highest peak.

Neighbouring States and Union territories:
International border: Myanmar.

States:
• Arunachal Pradesh
• Assam
• Manipur

Major rivers:
• Dhansiri
• Doyang
• Dikhu
• Barak

• tributaries of the Chindwin of Myanmar. Others include
• Milak
• Zungki
• Tizu

Climate: Temperature varies between 16°C and 31°C in summer and between 4°C and 24°C in winter. Average rainfall is 2000mm to 2500mm. It rains heavily from May to August, as well as occasionally in September and October. November to April is the dry season.

Flora and Fauna:
Flora: Evergreen and coniferous forests, medicinal plants, bamboo, cane and orchids make up the state's flora.

Fauna: Animals like Asian elephant, clouded leopard, binturong, musk deer, macaque, common langur, gaur (Indian bison), tiger, sambar, barking deer, hoolock, serow, sloth bear and wild boar can be found in the state. Reptiles include the monitor lizard, tortoise, reticulated python, king cobra, common krait, banded krait, viper and common cobra.

The greyheaded fishing eagle, crested serpent eagle, forest eagle owl, tragopan and hornbill are notable among the birds found in Nagaland. Amongst the animals, the Asian elephant, spotted linsang, tiger civet, sloth bear, tiger and the tailed pig are endangered species. The gaur or Indian bison is also facing extinction in Nagaland. The diverse hornbills and tortoise are also endangered.

History

Medieval chronicles of the Ahom kingdom of Assam talk of the Naga tribes. The Myanmar invasion of Assam in 1816 was followed by the establishment of British rule in 1826. By 1892, British administration covered the entire Naga territory, with the exception of the Tuensang area.

After independence in 1947, Naga territory initially remained a part of Assam, after which there was a strong nationalist pressure for the political union of the Naga tribes. In 1957, an agreement was signed between the Naga leaders and the Indian government, following which the Naga Hill districts of Assam and the Tuensang division to the north-east were brought together under a single unit, directly administered by the Indian government. However, unrest continued and another accord was reached at the Naga People's Convention meeting of July 1960. According to this accord, it was decided that Nagaland should become a constituent state of the Indian Union. Nagaland became a state on 1 December 1963 and a democratically elected government took office in 1964. Shilu Ao was the first Chief Minister.

Politics

The Naga territory remained split between Assam and the North East Frontier Agency after Indian independence in 1947, despite a vocal movement advocating the political union of all the Naga tribes; one faction called for secession from India. The government of a newly independent India refused to accept such a demand, and some Nagas took to armed rebellion in an effort to gain independence. The area remained in a rebellious political condition for much of the 1950s. A voluntary plebiscite was held in May 1951 to determine whether Nagas would join the Indian Union, or live by themselves. The result was 99.9 in favour of independence. In persuance of their declared national decision, the Naga people launched a Civil Disobedience Movement and successfully boycotted the general elections of free India.

Nagaland was just a district in the state of Assam until 1957, known to others as 'The Naga Hills'. Not satisfied with such an obscure status, the leaders of various Naga tribes, in August 1957, formed the Naga People's Convention (NPC). In its first session held at Kohima on 21 August 1957, under the Presidentship of Dr Imkongliba Ao, the NPC proposed the formation of a separate administrative unit by merging the Tuensang division of NEFA with Naga Hills District. The Government of India agreed to the proposal and on 1 December 1957, the new administrative unit known as the Naga Hills and Tuensang Area (NHTA) was inaugurated. In July 1960, a delegation of the NPC met the then Prime Minister of India, the late Jawaharlal Nehru and a 16-point agreement was arrived at, which inter-alia provided for the formulation of a separate state for the Nagas within the Indian Union to be known as 'Nagaland' under the Ministry of External Affairs with a Governor and an Administrative Secretariat, a Council of Ministers and Legislative Assembly. (In 1972, the state was brought under the Ministry of Home Affairs). On 18 February 1961 an interim body of 42 members was constituted. This was to function as the de-facto legislature. It included a five-member Executive Council headed by a Chief Executive Councillor. This functioned as de-facto Council of Ministers. Dr Imkongliba Ao, who was the first Chairman of the Naga People's Convention, was appointed the first Chairman of the interim body. P. Shilo was appointed the Chief Executive Councillor and eventually became the first Chief Minister of Nagaland.

On 21 August 1962 the then Prime Minister Pandit Nehru introduced a Bill in the Parliament for the formation of Nagaland as a full-fledged state. The Act provided for the formulation of the state of Nagaland as the 16th state in the Indian Union, and on 1 December 1963, President Dr S. Radhakrishnan inaugurated the state of Nagaland. Vishnu Sahay became the first Governor of Nagaland. Pending the first general election, a caretaker government was formed with P. Shilo as the Chief Minister. The Naga National Organization (NNO) and Democratic Party, Nagaland had contested the election. The NNO won 34 seats (including the six members from Tuensang) while the Democratic Party claimed 12 seats. Fourteen members returned unopposed. The new Ministry headed by P. Shilu Ao was sworn in on 25 January 1964. On 8 December 1964 all the 12 MLAs of the Democratic Party including its leader Vizol resigned en-masse. By-elections were held in June 1965 in which the NNO captured all the 12 seats and an all NNO government was formed without opposition. On 11 August 1966, the Chief Minister, P. Shilu Ao was toppled following a no-confidence motion against him by his own party men. A new Ministry headed by T.N. Angami was sworn in on 14 August 1966. The second general election was held on 6 February 1969. A 17 member NNO Ministry, headed by Hokishe Sema was sworn in on 28 February 1969. In the third general election in February 1974 the two contesting parties in the state, the NNO and the UDF, secured 23 and 25 seats respectively. The United Democratic Front (UDF) formed the government with the help of the Independents. Vizol became the fourth Chief Minister of Nagaland. He was sworn in on 26 February 1974. However, following a grave political crisis in the state, President's Rule was imposed in Nagaland on 22 March 1975, the Assembly was suspended and subsequently dissolved on 22 May 1975. Just before President's Rule, a short-lived Ministry headed by J.B. Jasokie was sworn in on 10 March 1975 following the fall of Vizol's Ministry. Nagaland was under President's Rule for 32 months, so far the longest in the country.

In the fourth general election held on 18 November 1977, the UDF again won absolute majority. Vizol was elected Chief Minister for the second time and he was sworn in on 28 November 1977. S.C. Jamir became the first Deputy Chief Minister of Nagaland. Following yet another political crisis in April 1980, Vizol was replaced as the Chief Minister by S.C. Jamir. In the following June, a new Ministry headed by J.B. Jasokie had replaced the previous Ministry. The government headed by Jasokie had weathered till the next general election in 1982. After the fifth general election held on 10 November 1982, a new Congress government headed by S.C. Jamir was sworn in on 17 November 1982. However, Jamir had to step down from the Chief Ministership in favour of Hokishe Sema whose Ministry was sworn in on 29 October 1986. The Congress (I) had won absolute majority in the sixth general election held on 18 November 1987. The twenty-two member Ministry headed by Hokishe Sema took office on 22 November 1987. The Congress (I) government lasted for only eight months and on 7 August 1988, the Assembly was dissolved and President's Rule was imposed on Nagaland for the second time. In the seventh general election held on 21 January 1989, the Congress won absolute majority again. A new Congress government headed by S.C. Jamir was sworn in on 25 January 1989. In May1990 with the fall of S.C. Jamir's Ministry K.L. Chishi was installed as the new Chief Minister. The Ministry, however, came to an end when all the Congress (I) ministers re-

signed on 4 December 1990. Vamuzo formed another Ministry with the induction of twelve more Ministers on 6 December 1990. But on 27 March 1992, the state Governor Dr M.M. Thomas dissolved the state Legislative Assembly on the recommendation of the Chief Minister, Vamuzo. On 2 April, President's Rule was imposed in Nagaland. The eighth general election was conducted on 15 February 1993. The new Congress government was headed by S.C. Jamir. Once again, with a renewed mandate the Congress Ministry was installed on 5 March 1998, after winning absolute majority in the ninth general election. Neiphiu Rio, leader of the Democratic Alliance of Nagaland (DAN), was sworn in as the Chief Minister of the state on 6 March 2003. DAN, a conglomerate of five regional and non-Congress political parties, has 38 MLAs in the 60-member Nagaland Assembly.

Culture

Each of the several tribes and communities of Nagaland has its own unique folk dances, folk songs and folklore. They are skilful craftsmen specializing in woodcarving, weaving, spinning, metalwork and stonework. Pottery is considered a taboo among certain sections of the Ao community.

Fairs and festivals: The major festivals of the state are Sekrenyi of the Angamis, Moatsu of the Aos, Phom-Monyu of the Phom tribe and the Hornbill festival of Nagaland.

Economy, Industry and Agriculture

Economy: The net state domestic product at current prices in 2001–02 was Rs 3864 crores. The per capita net state domestic product at current prices in 2001–02 was Rs 18,911.

Minerals and industry: The process of industrialization of the state is in its infancy. There is a need for more industries in the state. There are several plans in the pipeline to increase industrial investment and activity in the state. Coal, limestone, petroleum and marble are the main minerals found in the state.

Agriculture: Agriculture is the most important occupation of the people. Rice, wheat, maize and pulses are the chief agricultural products of the state. Fruits like banana, orange, passion fruit, pears, plum and jackfruit are grown. Vegetables like ginger, cabbage, chilli, tomato, potato and garlic are also grown.

Power: The main sources of power in the state are diesel power plants and hydroelectric plants.

Education

Educational institutes: Nagaland University is at Kohima.

Tourism

Major tourist attractions: Shangnyu village; Longwa village; Veda peak; Naginimora; Dzukou Valley; Kohima village; War Cemetry, Kohima; Dzulekie; Ruins of medieval Kachari kingdom, Dimapur; Chumukedima.

Airport: Dimapur.

National Parks: Intanki National Park in Kohima district (202.02 sq. km).

Administration

Legislature: Nagaland has a unicameral legislature. The Nagaland Legislative Assembly has 60 seats out of which 59 are reserved for STs. The term of the present house runs out on 13 March 2008. The current party position is:

Name of Party	Seats
Indian National Congress	21
Nagaland Peoples Front	19
Bharatiya Janata Party	7
Nationalist Democratic Movement	5
Janata Dal (United)	3
Samata Party	1
Independent	4
Total	**60**

Judiciary: Nagaland falls under the jurisdiction of the Gauhati High Court with a bench at Kohima. Binod Kumar Roy is the chief justice.

Districts:

District	Area (sq. km)	Population	Headquarters	Urban Agglomerations
Dimapur	927	308,382	Dimapur	–
Kohima	3,114	314,366	Kohima	–
Mokokchung	1,615	227,230	Mokokchung	–
Mon	1,786	259,604	Mon	–
Phek	2,026	148,246	Phek	–
Tuensang	4,228	414,801	Tuensang	–
Wokha	1,628	161,098	Wokha	–
Zunheboto	1,255	154,909	Zunheboto	–

Orissa

Key Statistics

Capital: Bhubaneswar.
Area: 155,707 sq. km.
Population: Total: 36,804,660
Male: 18,660,570
Female: 18,144,090
Population density: 236 per sq. km.
Sex ratio: 972 females per 1000 males.
Principal languages: Oriya, Hindi, Telugu.

Literacy rates: Total: 63.1%
Male: 75.3%
Female: 50.5%

Government

Governor: Rameshwar Thakur. He was sworn in on 16 November 2004.

Chief Minister: Naveen Patnaik (BJD). He was sworn in on 16 May 2004.

Geography

Physical characteristics: The state is surrounded by the Bay of Bengal on the east, Chhattisgarh in the west, Jharkhand and West Bengal in the north and Andhra Pradesh in the south. It has a coastline of about 450 km. Orissa is divided into five major physiographic regions: the central plateaus, the coastal plain in the east, the western rolling uplands, the middle mountainous and highland regions, and the flood plains. The middle mountainous and highland region covers about three-fourths of the entire state and is a part of the Eastern Ghats.

Neighbouring States and Union territories:
States:
• West Bengal
• Chhattisgarh
• Jharkhand
• Andhra Pradesh

Major rivers:
• Subarnarekha
• Mahanadi
• Baitarani
• Burabalang
• Brahmani
• Rushi-kulya
• Vamsadhara

Climate: The coastal lowland receives substantial rainfall every year because it comes directly under the influence of tropical depressions originating in the Bay of Bengal in the monsoon season. This is a distinctive climatic feature of this region. The state is sometimes hit by tropical cyclones which cause a lot of damage to property and human life. Summers are extremely hot, with temperatures rising up to 45°C; winters are temperate.

Flora and Fauna:
Flora: The state has tropical semi-evergreen, tropical moist deciduous, tropical dry deciduous, littoral and swamp forests.

Fauna: Wildlife found in the state includes tiger, elephant, gaur, chital, leopard, mouse deer, flying squirrel, mugger, salt water crocodile, monitor lizards, snakes, fishing cat, hyena, wild pig, water birds and Ridley sea turtle.

History

At various points in ancient and medieval times, the land corresponding roughly with modern Orissa was known as Utkala, Kalinga, and Odra Desa. These names were initially associated with peoples. The Okkala or Utkala, the Kalinga, and the Odra or Oddaka were mentioned in literature as tribes. Later on these names became identified with territories. For many centuries preceding and following the birth of Christ, Kalinga was a very strong political power. Its territories extended from the Ganga to the Godavari. At some point of time between the 11th and the 16th centuries, the name fell into disuse. In its place came the name Odra Desa, which was gradually transformed into Uddisa, Udisa, or Odisa and ultimately, Orissa.

In 260 BC, Asoka fought the famed Kalinga War and this is now considered the turning point in Asoka's own life. The bloodshed and loss of life in this war led him to renounce warfare and violence. It was after this that he took up Buddhism and preached the gospel of peace and harmony.

In the 1st century BC, the Kalinga emperor Kharavela achieved great power by conquering vast tracts of land and setting up a Kalinga empire. In the eighth, ninth and 10th centuries AD, the area was ruled by the Bhuma-Kara dynasty and in the 10th and 11th centuries by the Soma dynasty.

Between 1028 and 1434–35, Kalinga was ruled by the Ganga dynasty followed by the Surya dynasty. After the fall of the Surya kings, Orissa passed into the hands of the Afghan rulers of Bengal.

In the 1590s, the Mughal emperor Akbar conquered Orissa from the Afghans. With the decline and fall of Mughal empire in the 1760s, a part of Orissa remained under the Bengal nawabs and the rest went to the Marathas. The Bengal region passed into British rule in 1757, after the Battle of Plassey. The British conquered the Maratha areas in 1803. After 1803, the British controlled the entire Oriya-speaking area and it was administered as two separate units, the Northern Division and the Southern Division. It was only in April 1936 that the British constituted Orissa as a separate province on a linguistic basis, with the exception of 26 princely states that stayed outside provincial administration. After independence in 1947, all these princely states (except Saraikela and Kharsawan that merged with Bihar) became parts of Orissa. The first Chief Minister of Orissa was Harekrushna Mahatab.

Politics

Orissa became a separate province on 1 April 1936 by the Government of India (Constitution of Orissa) Order 1936. It comprised certain portions of the Bihar and Orissa Province, Madras Presidency and the Central Provinces. Under the Government of India Act, 1935, the strength of the Legislative Assembly of the Orissa Province was fixed at 60, including four nominated members. On 1 January 1948, 24 princely states merged in the province of Orissa. After the final merger of princely states with Orissa in 1949, the total number of seats in the Orissa Legislative Assembly was revised to 91 to represent the people of the merged states or groups of states.

Harekrushna Mahtab became the first Chief Minister of Orissa on 5 August 1947 and he remained in power till 12 May 1950. On 12 May 1950 the second Ministry under the leadership of Nabakrushna Choudhury was formed. Dr H.K. Mahtab headed the third and the fourth ministry. He assumed office on 15 October 1956 and remained in office till 25 February 1961. On 28 January 1961 the Congress party formed the fifth Ministry under the leadership of Bijayandra Patnaik and remained in power till 2 October 1963. From 2 October 1963 to 21 February 1965 the sixth Ministry under the leadership of Biren Mitra of Congress was formed. On 21 February 1965 the seventh Ministry under the leadership of Sadashiv Tripathy assumed office. In 1967 a new party called Jana Congress was formed under the leadership of Harekrushna Mahtab. On 8 March 1967 the eighth Ministry by the Swatantra-Jana Congress coalition was formed. R.N. Singh Deo was the Chief Minister.

Utkal Congress was formed in 1969 when Biju Patnaik left Indian National Congress. After the 1971 Orissa elections UC took part in the Biswanath Das Ministry in the state. In 1977 Utkal Congress merged into Janata Party. As a result of an indecisive verdict in the mid-term poll held in March 1971, the Swatantra Party, the Jharkhand Party and the Utkal Congress Party formed a coalition government under the leadership of Biswanath Das. In the 1971 and 1974 state elections Jana Congress faired badly, and could only win a single seat. In 1977 Jana Congress merged into Janata Party.

On 14 June 1972 Nandini Satpathy took over as the Chief Minister of the tenth Ministry formed after large-scale defections from the ruling coalition. President's Rule was imposed on Orissa on 3 March 1973. On 6 March 1974 Nandini Satpathy formed the eleventh Ministry. On 29 December 1976 Binayak Acharya was sworn in as the Chief Minister of the twelfth Ministry. The Ministry remained in office only for 123 days. In a mid-term poll, the Janata Party led by Biju Patnaik secured 110 seats out of 147. Nilamani Routray was made the Chief Minister. The Ministry remained in office till 1980.

In 1981 the Congress party won a resounding victory to form the fourteenth Ministry in the state. Janaki Ballav Patnaik became the Chief Minister. Again the Congress won an imposing victory in the elections held in 1985. Janaki Ballav Patnaik became the Chief Minister of the fifteenth Ministry. Hemananda Biswal became the sixteenth Chief Minister after the resignation of J.B. Patnaik. Under the leadership of Biju Patnaik, the Janata Dal won an astounding victory in the elections held in 1990. J.B. Patnaik was the Chief Minister from 15 March 1995 to 15 February 1999. He was succeeded by Giridhar Gomango who remained in power till 6 December. Hemananda Biswal was Chief Minister from 6 December 1999 to 5 March 2000. On 5 March 2000 Naveen Patnaik of the Biju Janata Dal was elected the Chief Minister.

Orissa Gana Parishad (Orissa Popular Association), a political party in the state of Orissa, is a splinter group of Biju Janata Dal. The party was founded on 29 October 2000. The president of OGP is Bijoy Mahapatra. Mahapatra had been expelled from BJD in February 2000. Mahapatra had come into conflict with BJD leader Navin Patnaik over the election of Dilip Ray to the Rajya Sabha. In the 2004 Lok Sabha elections OGP was allied with Indian National Congress. OGP had four candidates to the Orissa state Legislative Assembly, out of whom two got elected.

Culture

The state is home to the Odissi and Chhau dance forms as well as the Patachitra art form. It is the home of renowned weaves of saris like Sambalpuri, Katki, Behrampuri, Bomkai and Baraghat.

Fairs and festivals: The major festivals of the state include Dola Purnima (Holi), Ratha Yatra, Chandan Yatra, Snana Yatra, Konark Dance Festival, Puri Beach Festival, Bali Yatra and Dhanu Yatra.

Economy, Industry and Agriculture

Economy: The net state domestic product at current prices for 2002–03 (provisional) was Rs 38,737 crores. The per capita net state domestic product at current prices for 2002–03 (provisional) was Rs 10,340.

Minerals and industry: Orissa has substantial mineral resources such as dolomite, chromite, limestone, high quality iron ore, coal and manganese. The state is home to steel mills, nonferrous smelting, paper mills, fertilizer industries, cement plants, foundries and glass works. The famous steel plant at Rourkela is in Orissa.

Agriculture: About 80 per cent of the area sown is under rice cultivation. Other important crops are oilseeds, pulses, jute, sugar cane, and coconut.

Adverse crop-growing conditions such as poor soil quality and low availability of sunlight combine to hamper agriculture in the state.

Power: Most of Orissa's power is generated by hydroelectric plants. The rest comes from thermal power plants.

Education

Educational institutes: Notable educational institutes in the state include
• Utkal University, Bhubaneswar
• Fakir Mohan University, Balasore
• Orissa University of Agriculture and Technology, Bhubaneswar
• Regional Engineering College (National Institute of Technology), Rourkela
• Xavier Institute of Management, Bhubaneswar

Tourism

Major tourist attractions: Bhitarkanika National Park; Simlipal National Park; Lingaraj Temple, Bhubaneswar; Mukteswar Temple, Bhubaneswar; Rajarani Temple, Bhubaneswar; Shanti Stupa, Bhubaneswar; Jagannath Temple, Puri; Sun Temple, Konark; Barabati Fort, Cuttack; Chilka Lake; Puri beach.

Airports:
• Bhubaneswar
• Jharsuguda.

National Parks:
• Simlipal (Mayurbhanj) —845.7 sq. km
• Bhitarkanika (Cuttack) —367 sq. km.

Administration

Legislature: The state has a unicameral legislature of 147 members. Out of this, 22 seats are reserved for SCs and 34 for STs. The tenure of the current house ends on 29 June 2009. The current party position is:

Name of Party	Seats
Biju Janata Dal	61
Indian National Congress	38
Bharatiya Janata Party	32
Jharkhand Mukti Morcha	4
Orissa Gana Parishad	2
Communist Party of India	1
Communist Party of India (Marxist)	1
Independent	8
Total	147

Judiciary: The Orissa High Court is situated at Cuttack. The chief justice is Sujit Burman Ray.

Districts:

District	Area (sq. km)	Population	Headquarters	Urban Agglomerations
Anugul	6,375	1,139,341	Anugul	
Balangir	6,575	1,335,760	Balangir	Titlagarh
Baleshwar	3,806	2,023,056	Baleshwar	Baleshwar
Bargarh	5,837	1,345,601	Bargarh	
Baudh	3,098	373,038	Baudh	
Bhadrak	2,505	1,332,249	Bhadrak	
Cuttack	3,932	2,340,686	Cuttack	Cuttack
Debagarh	2,940	274,095	Debagarh	
Dhenkanal	4,452	1,065,983	Dhenkanal	
Gajapati	4,325	518,448	Parlakhemundi	
Ganjam	8,206	3,136,937	Chatrapur	
Jagatsinghapur	1,668	1,056,556	Jagatsinghapur	
Jajapur	2,899	1,622,868	Panikoili	Byasanagar
Jharsuguda	2,081	509,056	Jharsuguda	
Kalahandi	7,920	1,334,372	Bhawanipatna	
Kandhamal	8,021	647,912	Phulbani	
Kendrapara	2,644	1,301,856	Kendrapara	
Kendujhar	8,303	1,561,521	Kendujhar	
Khordha	2,813	1,874,405	Khordha	Bhubaneswar, Jatani
Koraput	8,807	1,177,954	Koraput	
Malkangiri	5,791	480,232	Malkangiri	
Mayurbhanj	10,418	2,221,782	Baripada	Baripada
Nabarangapur	5,291	1,018,171	Nabarangapur	
Nayagarh	3,890	863,934	Nayagarh	
Nuapada	3,852	530,524	Nuapada	
Puri	3,479	1,498,604	Puri	
Rayagada	7,073	823,019	Rayagada	Gunupur
Sambalpur	6,657	928,889	Sambalpur	Sambalpur
Sonapur	2,337	540,659	Sonapur	
Sundargarh	9,712	1,829,412	Sundargarh	Raurkela

Punjab

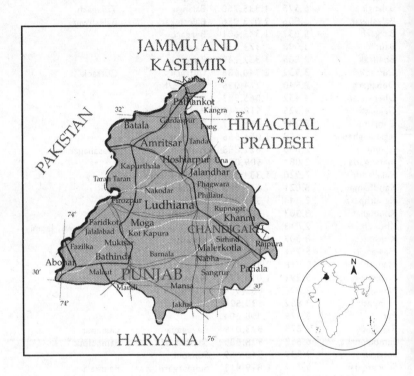

Key Statistics

Capital: Chandigarh.
Area: 50,362 sq. km.
Population: Total: 24,358,999
Male: 12,985,045
Female: 11,373,954
Population density: 482 per sq. km.
Sex ratio: 876 females per 1000 males.
Principal languages: Punjabi, Hindi, Urdu.
Literacy rates: Total: 69.7%
Male: 75.2%
Female: 63.4%

Government

Governor: Gen. S.F. Rodrigues. He was sworn in on 16 November 2004.

Chief Minister: Captain Amarinder Singh. He was sworn in on 27 February 2002.

Geography

Physical characteristics: Punjab is largely a flat plain that rises gently from about 150 metres in the southwest to about 300 metres in the northeast. Physiographically, it can be divided into three parts: (i) The Shiwalik Hills in the northeast rising from about 300 to 900 metres; (ii) The zone of narrow, undulating foothills dissected by seasonal rivers terminating in the plains and not flowing into bigger waterbodies and (iii) The flat tract with fertile alluvial soils. The low-lying floodplains lie along the rivers while the slightly elevated flat uplands lie between them. Sand dunes are found in the southwest and west of the Sutlej.

Neighbouring States and Union territories:
International border: Pakistan.

States:
• Haryana
• Himachal Pradesh
• Jammu and Kashmir
• Rajasthan.

Union territories: Chandigarh.

Major rivers:
• Ravi
• Beas
• Sutlej
• Ghaggar with their numerous small and seasonal tributaries.

Climate: Punjab has three major seasons. These are: (i) The hot weather from April to June with temperatures rising as high as 45°C; (ii) The rainy season from July to September with average annual rainfall in the state ranging between 960mm in the submontane region to 580mm in the plains and (iii) The cold weather from October to March with temperatures going down to 4°C.

Flora and Fauna:
Flora: The rapid growth of human settlement resulted in the clearing out of most of the forest cover of the state. Consequently, trees have been replaced by bush vegetation in the Shiwalik Hills. Attempts at aforestation have been made on the hills while eucalyptus trees have been planted along major roads.

Fauna: Wildlife faces intense competition from agriculture for its natural habitat. Many species of birds, some monkeys, rodents, and snakes have adapted to the farmland environment.

History

Punjab was the site of the Indus Valley Civilization. Archaeological excavations all over the state have revealed evidences of the cities belonging to the civilization that also included Harappa and Mohenjodaro, which are now in Pakistan. The *Mahabharata* contains rich descriptions of the land and people of Punjab. It is also believed that parts of the *Ramayana* were written around the Shri Ram Tirath Ashram near Amritsar and that it was in the forests of what is today Punjab that Lav and Kush, the sons of Rama, grew up.

Other important historical centres are at Ropar, Kiratpur, Dholbaha, Rohira and Ghuram. Sanghol, in Fatehgarh Sahib district near Ludhiana, is home to sites associated with Mauryan Dynasty. Relics found here record the presence of Buddhism in the region.

The Vedic and the later epic periods of the Punjab are of great significance. The Rig Veda was composed here. Numerous cultural and educational centres were established in the region during the period.

A few years before the birth of Buddha (556 BC), the armies of Darius I, King of Persia, had arrived in Punjab and made the area a protectorate of the Persian empire. The Buddhists referred to Punjab as 'Uttar Path' or the way to the north, namely the valleys of Afghanistan, Central Asia and China. In 327 BC Alexander invaded Punjab, defeating Raja Paurava. In subsequent centuries, there were more invasions from the north. This happened during the rules of the Mauryas, the Sungas, the Guptas and the Pushpabhuti.

Modern-day Punjab owes its origin to Banda Singh Bahadur who led a group of Sikhs to free parts of the region from Mughal rule in 1709–10. In 1716, however, the Mughals defeated and killed Banda Singh. This sparked off a prolonged struggle between the Sikhs and the Mughals and Afghans.

By 1764–65, the Sikhs established their dominance in the region. Ranjit Singh led Punjab into a powerful kingdom and also added the provinces of Multan, Kashmir, and Peshawar. In 1849, Punjab had passed into the hands of the British East India Company. It later became a province of the British empire in India.

Many Punjabis played significant roles during India's freedom struggle. These included Baba Ram Singh (of the Kuka or Namdhari movement fame), Lala Lajpat Rai, Madan Lal Dhingra, Bhagat Singh and Bhai Parmanand. The nationalist fervour was kept alive by several movements, such as the Singh Sabha, Arya Samaj and the Akali movements and by organizations like Bharat Mata Society, Naujawan Bharat Sabha and Kirti Kisan Sabha.

It was in Punjab that the infamous Jallianwala Bagh massacre took place at Amritsar on 13 April 1919. Hundreds of peaceful demonstrators were killed and over a thousand were injured when General Reginald Dwyer ordered his troops to open fire on civilians who had gathered in a peaceful protest meeting. This incident proved to be a turning point in the history of India.

At the time of independence in 1947, the province was divided between India and Pakistan. The smaller eastern portion was allocated to India. Gopichand Bhargava was the first Chief Minister of the state. In November 1956 the Indian state of Punjab was enlarged by the addition of the Patiala and East Punjab States Union (PEPSU). Pepsu was a collection of the erstwhile princely states of Faridkot, Jind, Kalsia, Kapurthala, Malerkotla, Nabha, Nalagarh and Patiala.

The present-day state of Punjab came into existence on 1 November 1966 when Punjab was divided on a linguistic basis. The Hindi-speaking parts were formed into a new state, Haryana. The northernmost districts were transferred to Himachal Pradesh.

Politics

With the partition of India in 1947, the East Punjab Legislative Assembly came into existence. It consisted of 72 members of the undivided Punjab Legislative Assembly representing the constituencies falling in East Punjab (India). On 15 July 1948, eight princely states of East Punjab grouped together to form a single state called PEPSU—Patiala and the East Punjab States Union—which, merged with Punjab on the Reorganization of States on 1 November 1956. Later, the state of Punjab was reorganized on 1 November 1966 when Haryana was carved out of it and some of its areas were transferred to Himachal Pradesh also.

The government and administration in Punjab are organized on the same lines as in other states of India. The Punjab state Legislature in independent India became bicameral for the first time in April 1952. On reorganization of the states, the strength of the Legislative Council of the new state of Punjab was raised from the earlier 40 seats to 46 seats. On 21 March 1957, the Punjab Legislative Assembly passed a resolution to the effect that in view of the increase in the area and population, the strength of the Punjab Legislative Council be increased to 51. Accordingly, under the Legislative Councils Act, 1957, the number of seats in the Punjab Legislative Council was raised to 51. With the further reorganization of the Punjab state in 1966, the number of members of the Punjab Legislative Assembly was reduced from 154 to 104. Consequently, the number of members on the Council was also reduced to 40. On 1 January 1970, the Legislative Council was abolished. At present, the state Legislature is a unicameral body with a Legislative Assembly, consisting of 117 members.

Following the partition of India in 1947, the Sikhs were concentrated in India in east Punjab. Sikh leaders demanded a Punjabi language majority state, which would have included most Sikhs. Fearing that a Punjabi state might lead to a separatist Sikh movement, the government opposed the demand. In 1966 a compromise was reached when two new states of Punjab and Haryana were created. Punjabi became the official language of Punjab, and Chandigarh became the shared capital of the two states. However the agreement did not resolve the Sikh question.

Gopichand Bhargava of the Congress party was the first Chief Minister of Punjab. He came to power on 15 August 1947 and remained in the position till 13 April 1949. For the second time he served as the Chief Minister from 18 October 1949 to 20 June 1951. Bhim Sen Sachar became the Chief Minister of Punjab on 13 April 1949 and remained in power till 18 October 1949. In 1951 President's Rule was imposed on Punjab. In the 1952 general election Sachar was elected member of

Punjab Assembly from Ludhiana city constituency. He again became the Chief Minister of Punjab from 1952 to 1956. From 23 January 1956 to 21 June 1964 Sardar Pratap Singh Kairon was the Chief Minister. Gopichand Bhargava succeeded him and became the Chief Minister for the third time and remained in power till 6 July 1964. Ram Kishan of the Congress party became the next Chief Minister and remained in the post till 5 July 1966. President's Rule was imposed in August 1966. From 1 November 1966 to 8 March 1967 Gurumukh Singh Musafir of the Congress was the Chief Minister.

From the late '60s the Akali Dal won power in the state. Sardar Gurnam Singh succeeded Gurumukh Singh Musafir and remained in power till 25 November 1967. Again he came to power on 17 February and remained in power till 27 March 1970. In between Gurnam Singh's two tenures from 25 November 1967 to 23 August 1968 Sardar Lachhman Singh Gill was the Chief Minister. In 1970, Prakash Singh Badal formed an Akali government in Punjab. He replaced Gurnam Singh as Chief Minister of Punjab. From 17 March 1972 to 30 April 1977 Zail Singh of the Congress party served as the Chief Minister. He later became the President of India. Prakash Singh Badal became the Chief Minister for the second time on 20 June 1977 and remained in the post till 17 February 1880. From 6 June 1980 to 6 October 1983 Darbara Singh was the Chief Minister. Surjit Singh Barnala served as the Chief Minister of Punjab from 29 September 1985 to 11 May 1987.

In the '70s there was a strong secular democratic movement led in Punjab by the revolutionary democratic forces represented by groups of Communist revolutionaries. The Communist revolutionaries in Punjab were divided into different sects. There was the Charu Mazumdar trend (upheld by Jagjit Singh Johal), the trend following Chandra Pulla Reddy and Satya Narayan Singh (referred to as the Punjab Himachal Committee) and the proletarian revolutionary trend following Nagi Reddy. From the early '80s to the early part of the '90s the state of Punjab was ravaged by Khalistani terrorism. Communal fascists were a great threat to the people's democratic movement.

In 1977, Sant Jarnail Singh Bhindranwale, an obscure but charismatic religious leader, made his appearance. He preached strict fundamentalism and armed struggle for national liberation. His speeches inflamed both young students and small farmers dissatisfied with their economic lot. Tensions between Punjabi Sikhs and New Delhi heightened during the 1980s. Over the years that followed, Punjab was faced with escalating confrontations and increased terrorist incidents. The Akali Dal only achieved limited concessions from the government and Sikh separatists prepared for battle. In the Golden Temple enclosure 10,000 Sikhs took an oath to lay down their lives if necessary in the struggle. Renewed confrontations in October 1983 resulted in Punjab being placed under central government authority. The violence continued and hundreds of Sikhs were detained in the first part of 1984. Followers of Jarnail Singh Bhindranwale established a terrorist stronghold inside the Golden Temple. The Prime Minister, Indira Gandhi, initiated Operation Blue Star, which took place on 5-6 June 1984. The Golden Temple was shelled and besieged by the army to dislodge the terrorists. The fighting continued for five days. Bhindranwale was killed and there was serious damage to sacred buildings. The intervention had disastrous consequences for the Sikh community and the whole country. Sikh-Hindu communalism was aggravated, Sikh extremism was reinforced, and political assassinations increased. On 31 October 1984 Indira Gandhi was assassinated in New Delhi by two Sikh bodyguards.

A peace agreement was concluded between the Indian government and moderate Akali Dal Sikhs led by Harchand Singh Longowal in July 1985, which granted many of the Sikh community's longstanding demands. However the extremists regarded Longowal as a traitor to the Sikh cause and he was assassinated in August 1985. In 1987 the state government was dismissed and Punjab was placed under President's Rule. Extremists spread terror throughout Punjab and the Indian government mounted a campaign of anti-terrorist measures designed to restore the situation in Punjab to normal. In May 1988 the Punjab police and Indian paramilitary forces launched Operation Black Thunder against armed extremists who had again created a fortified stronghold within the Golden Temple. At least 40 extremists and several police officers were killed during the battle.

President's Rule was finally brought to an end following elections in February 1992, which were won by Congress (I). However the elections were boycotted by the leading factions of Akali Dal and attracted an extremely low turnout (only about 22% of the electorate). Beant Singh of the Congress (I) was sworn in as Chief Minister. Despite the continuing violence between the separatists and the security forces, the large turnout in the municipal elections in September 1992, the first in thirteen years, afforded some hope that normalcy was returning to Punjab. The local council elections in January 1993, the first for ten years, also attracted a large turnout. On 31 August 1995 Beant Singh was killed by a car bomb, which exploded close to his car outside the Punjab Secretariat in Chandigarh. Fifteen security men and aides were also killed. The Babbar Khalsa claimed responsibility and three suspects were later arrested. Harcharan Singh Brar took over as Chief Minister. Virtually all of the militant groups in Punjab pursued their campaign for a separate state of Khalistan through acts of violence directed not only at members of the police and security forces but also specifically at Hindu and Sikh civilians.

Rajinder Kaur Bhattal who became Chief Minister on 21 November 1996 was the first woman Chief Minister of Punjab. After the February 1997 state election, Prakash Singh Badal became Chief Minister a third time, being chosen by the Akali Dal. He remained in power till 27 February 2002. In state elections in Punjab in 2002, the Congress party won 64 of 117 seats and the Shiromani Akali Dal 43. Amarinder Singh was sworn in as Chief Minister on 27 February 2003.

Culture

Patiala and Muktsar are famous for *juttis*, the traditional shoes worn by Punjabis. Punjab's most famous example of handicraft, phulkari, is a shawl that is completely covered in silk embroidery, with folk motifs in jewel tones on an ochre background.

Punjabi ornaments include the sagi, which is a central head stud. There are many varieties of sagi. These include the sagi uchhi, sagi motianwali, sagi phul, sagi chandiari, sagi meenawali. The state is famous for its gold and silver ornaments and objects made out of these metals.

Punjab is also noted for its weaving of durries which are cotton bedspreads or floor spreads in a variety of motifs and designs. The state's needlework is also unique. These include baghs, phulkaris, handkerchiefs and scarfs. In Punjab, needlework is done on a wide variety of objects. Punjabi hand fans are also well known. Punjab is famous for its woodwork. These include elaborate decorated beds called pawas, low seats called peeras. Besides furniture, the state's woodwork is also noted for boxes, toys and decorative pieces.

The state's many dance forms include Bhangra, Gidda, Jhumar, Luddi, Julli, Dankara, Dhamal, Sammi, Jaago, Kikli and Gatka.

In the 18th and 19th centuries a new school of classical music grew up around Patiala. This is known today as the Patiala Gharana. The founders of this gharana were Ustaad Ali Bux and Ustaad Fateh Ali, singers at the Patiala Darbar. Notable amongst their disciples were Ustaad Bade Ghulam Ali and his brother Barkat Ali. The gharana of tabla playing which is known as the Punjab style also developed in the state. Ustaad Alla Rakha was its best-known exponent.

Various songs are associated with Punjabi weddings. These include suhag, sehra, ghodi, sithaniya and patal kaavya. The instruments used in Punjabi folk art forms include the toombi, algoza, chheka, chimta, kaanto, daphali, dhad and manjira.

Fairs and festivals: Lohri, Baisakhi and Maaghi Da Mela are the most significant among the Punjabi festivals.

Economy, Industry and Agriculture

Economy: The net state domestic product at current prices for 2002–03 (provisional) was Rs 64,621 crores. The per capita net state domestic product at current prices for 2002–03 (provisional) was Rs 25,855.

Minerals and industry: The main industrial products of the state include engineering goods, pharmaceuticals, leather goods, food products, textiles, electronic goods, sugar, machine tools, hand tools, agricultural implements, sports goods, paper and paper packaging.

Agriculture: Agriculture is the most important component of Punjab's economy. As much as 97 per cent of the total cultivable area is under the plough. The main crops grown in the state are wheat, rice and cotton. Sugar cane and oilseeds are also grown. In recent times, impetus is being given to horticulture and forestry. The state has recorded highest yield per hectare of wheat, rice, cotton and bajra. It also has the highest per capita milk and egg production in the country.

Power: Punjab gets its power requirements both from thermal and from hydroelectric sources.

Education

Educational institutes: Well-known institutions of higher education in Punjab include
• Baba Farid University of Health Sciences (Faridkot)
• Guru Nanak Dev University (Amritsar)
• Punjab Agricultural University (Ludhiana)
• Punjab Technical University (Jalandhar)
• Punjabi University (Patiala)
• Thapar Institute of Engineering and Technology (Patiala).

Tourism

Major tourist attractions:
Religious centres: Golden Temple, Amritsar; Ram Tirth, Amritsar; Durgiana Mandir, Amritsar; Bhagwathi Mandir, Maisar Khanna, Bathinda City; Shiv Mandhir, Gur-mandi, Jalandhar; Sodal Mandir, Jalandhar City; Panch Mandir, Kapurthala Town; Kali Devi Temple, Patiala; Mazaar, Pir Baba Haji Rattan, Bathinda City; Rauza Sharif, Sirhind; Qadian; The Moorish Mosque, Kapurthala City; Imam Nasir Mausoleum and Jamma Masjid, Jalandhar City; Chilla Baba Seikh Farid, Faridkot City; Gurudwaras at Kiratpur Sahib; Gurudwaras at Anandpur Sahib; Bhaini Sahib; Radha Soami Dera Baba Jaimal Singh; Swetamber Jain Temple, Zira, Ferozpur District; Budhist Caves, Doong, Gurdaspur; Catholic Cathedral, Jalandhar Cantt.

Archaeological centres: Ghuram, Patiala Dist.; Sanghol, Fatehgarh Sahib Dist.; Ropar; Dholbaha.

Forts: Govindgarh Fort, Amritsar; Bathinda Fort; Faridkot Fort; Qila Mubark, Patiala; Bhadurgarh Fort; Anandpur Sahib Fort, Ropar; Phillaur Fort, Ludhiana; Shahpur Kandi Fort, near Pathankot.

Palaces: Summer Palace of Maharaja Ranjit Singh, Amritsar; Sheesh Mahal, Patiala.

Museums: Maharaja Ranjit Singh Museum, Amritsar; Sanghol Museum; Angol Sikh War Memorial, Ferozeshah; Government Museum, Hoshiarpur; Rural Museum, Punjab Agricultural University, Ludhiana; Qila Mubarak Patiala, Museum of Armoury and Chandeliers; Art Gallery at Sheesh Mahal, Patiala; Sports Museum, National Institute of Sports, Patiala; Guru Teg Bahadur Museum, Anandpur Sahib, Ropar.

Others: Jallianwala Bagh Martyr's Memorial, Amritsar; Bhagat Singh, Sukhdev and Rajguru Memorial, Ferozepur; The Sargarhi Memorial at Ferozepur; Desh Bhagat Hall, Jalandhar.

Airports:
International: Amritsar.
Domestic:
- Chandigarh
- Ludhiana

National Parks: None.

Administration

Legislature: The state has a 117-seat legislative assembly of which 29 are reserved for SCs. The term of the current house expires on 20 March 2007.

The party position is as under:

Name of Party	Seats
Indian National Congress	62
Shiromani Akali Dal (Badal)	41
Bharatiya Janata Party	3
Communist Party of India	2
Independent	9
Total	**117**

Judiciary: The High Court of Punjab and Haryana is at Chandigarh. The chief justice is D.K. Jain.

Districts:

District	Area (sq. km)	Population	Headquarters	Urban Agglomerations
Amritsar	5,094	3,074,207	Amritsar	Amritsar
Bhatinda	3,382	1,181,236	Bhatinda	Rampur Phul
Faridkot	1,469	552,466	Faridkot	Faridkot, Jaitu
Fatehgarh Sahib	1,180	539,751	Fatehgarh Sahib	Gobindgarh
Firozpur	5,300	1,744,753	Firozpur	Jalalabad, Zira
Gurdaspur	3,569	2,096,889	Gurdaspur	Batala, Gurdaspur, Pathankot, Qadian
Hoshiarpur	3,364	1,478,045	Hoshiarpur	
Jalandhar	2,634	1,953,508	Jalandhar	Jalandhar
Kapurthala	1,633	752,287	Kapurthala	Phagwara
Ludhiana	3,767	3,030,352	Ludhiana	
Mansa	2,169	688,630	Mansa	
Moga	2,216	886,313	Moga	Moga
Muktsar	2,615	776,702	Muktsar	
Nawanshahr	1,266	586,637	Nawanshahr	Nawanshahr
Patiala	3,627	1,839,056	Patiala	Patiala
Rupnagar	2,056	1,110,000	Rupnagar	Kharar, Nangal
Sangrur	5,021	1,998,464	Sangrur	Sunam

Rajasthan

Key Statistics

Capital: Jaipur.
Area: 342,239 sq. km.
Population: Total: 56,507,188
Male: 29,420,011
Female: 27,087,177
Population density: 165 per sq. km.
Sex ratio: 921 females per 1000 males.

Principal languages: Hindi, Bhili/ Bhilodi, Urdu.
Literacy rates: Total: 60.4%
Male: 75.7%
Female: 43.9%

Government

Governor: Pratibha Patil. She was sworn in on 8 November 2004.

Chief Minister: Vasundhara Raje Scindia (BJP). She is the first woman Chief Minister of the state, and was sworn in on 8 December 2003.

Geography

Physical characteristics: Rajasthan shares an international boundary with Pakistan in the west. On the Indian side there is a border with Punjab and Haryana in the north, Uttar Pradesh and Madhya Pradesh in the east and Gujarat in the south. The southern part of the state is about 225km from the Gulf of Kutch and about 400km from the Arabian Sea. The Aravalli mountain range divides the state into two regions. The north-west region mostly consists of a series of sand dunes and covers two-thirds of the state, while the eastern region has large fertile areas. The state includes The Great Indian (Thar) Desert.

Neighbouring States and Union territories:
International border: Pakistan.

States:
• Punjab
• Haryana
• Uttar Pradesh
• Madhya Pradesh
• Gujarat

Major rivers:
• Chambal is the only river that flows throughout the year.
• Banas, the only river that has its entire course in Rajasthan, is one of its main tributaries.
Other important rivers of the state are
• Banganga
• Gambhiri
• Luni
• Mahi
• Sabarmati
• Ghaghar

Climate: The climate of Rajasthan is warm and dry, with peak summer temperatures in the west reaching 49°C. In June, the arid zone of the west and the semi-arid zone of the mid-west have an average maximum temperature of 45°C. January is the coldest month of the year, with minimum temperatures as low as minus 2°C.

The annual rainfall west of the Aravallis ranges from less than 100mm in the Jaisalmer region to more than 400mm in Sikar, Jhunjhunu and Pali regions. On the eastern side, rainfall ranges from 550mm in Ajmer to 1020mm in Jhalawar. Mount Abu in the southwest usually receives the highest rainfall. Notably, Rajasthan's climate and parched landscape are undergoing significant changes because of developmental efforts like the Indira Gandhi Nahar. As a result, Rajasthan is today a major producer of a number of agricultural crops.

Flora and Fauna:
Flora: The flora of Rajasthan includes the semi-green forests of Mount Abu, dry grasslands of the desert, the dry deciduous thorn forest of the Aravallis and the wetlands of Bharatpur. 16,367 sq. km of area is under forest cover.

Fauna: Notable among the fauna of Rajasthan are black buck, chinkara, tigers, the rare desert fox, the endangered caracal, gharial, monitor lizard, wild boars, porcupine and the great Indian bustard.

In the winter months, migratory birds like the common crane, coots, pelicans, ducks, the rare Siberian cranes, imperial sand grouse, falcons and buzzards flock to this state.

History

Before AD 700, the region corresponding with present-day Rajasthan was a part of several republics including the

Mauryan empire, the Malavas, Kushans, Saka satraps, Guptas and Huns. The Rajput clans, primarily the Pratihars, Chalukyas, Parmars and Chauhans, rose to ascendancy from the eighth to the 12th century AD.

A part of the region came under Muslim rule around AD 1200, Nagaur and Ajmer being the centres of power. Mughal dominance reached its peak at the time of Emperor Akbar, who created a unified province comprising different princely states. The decline of Mughal power after 1707 was followed by political disintegration and invasions by the Marathas and Pindaris.

From 1817–18, almost all the princely states of Rajputana, as the state was then called, entered treaties of alliance with the British, who controlled their affairs till the time of independence. The erstwhile Rajputana, comprising 19 princely states and the British administered territory of Ajmer–Merwara, became the state of Rajasthan after a long process of integration that began on 17 March 1948 and ended on 1 November 1956. Rajasthan's first Chief Minister was Gokul Lal Asawa.

Politics

After Independence Sardar Vallabhbhai Patel, Deputy Prime Minister, persuaded the ruling princes of the Indian states to merge their principalities into the Indian Union. The merger of the states was considered a major triumph towards the establishment of a democratic nation. Though the 22 princely states of Rajputana region were declared to have been annexed to the Union of India on 15 August 1947, the process of merger and their unification became complete only in April 1949, in five phases. In the first phase of merger four princely states of Alwar, Bharatpur,

Dholpur and Karauli formed the Matsya Union and it was inaugurated on 18 March 1948. The Cabinet of this Union was formed under the leadership of Shobha Ram. The Union of Rajasthan, consisting of Banswara, Bundi, Dungarpur, Jhalawar, Kishangarh, Pratapgarh, Shahapura, Tonk and Kota, was inaugurated on 25 March 1948. The Kota state got the honour of being the capital of this Union. The Kota Naresh was appointed as the Rajpramukh and Gokul Lal Asawa was appointed as the Chief Minister. He was the first Chief Minister of the state. But only three days after its inauguration the Maharana of Udaipur decided to join this Union, which was accepted by the Government of India. The Maharana of Udaipur was appointed as Rajpramukh and the Kota Naresh was appointed as Up-Rajpramukh of this Union and the Cabinet was formed under the leadership of Manikya Lal Verma. This Union was inaugurated by Pt. Jawaharlal Nehru on 18 April 1948.

The formation of the Union of Rajasthan paved the way for the merger of big states like Bikaner, Jaisalmer, Jaipur and Jodhpur with the Union and formation of Greater Rajasthan. It was formally inaugurated on 30 March 1949 by Sardar Vallabhbhai Patel. The Maharana Bhupal Singh of Udaipur was appointed as the Maha-Rajpramukh and the Kota Naresh was appointed as the Up-Rajpramukh and the Cabinet was formed under the leadership of Hira Lala Shastri. Matsya Union was merged with Greater Rajasthan on 15 May 1949. Rajasthan attained its current dimensions in November 1956 with the additions of Ajmer-Merwara, Abu Rd and a part of Dilwara, originally part of the princely kingdom of Sirohi, which had been divided between Gujarat and Rajasthan. The princes of the former kingdoms were constitutionally granted handsome remuneration in the form of privy purses to assist them in the discharge of their financial obligations. In 1970, Indira Gandhi, who had come to power in 1966, commenced undertakings to discontinue the privy purses, which were abolished in 1971.

The Rajasthan Legislative Assembly is a unicameral legislative chamber. As per the provisions of Article 168 of the newly framed Constitution of India, every state had to establish a legislature consisting of one or two Houses. Rajasthan opted for unicameral character and its legislature is known as the Rajasthan Legislative Assembly. The legislature, which is running its twelfth term, was first elected by adult franchise in 1952 and this process is continuing with the exceptions of 1980 and 1992 when Presidential Rule was in force. The strength of the Rajasthan Legislative Assembly, which is determined by delimitation Commission, was 160 in1952 and presently stands as 200 of which 57 seats are reserved for Scheduled Castes and Scheduled Tribes after many more recommendations of the same Commission.

An Indian Civil Service officer, Cadambi Seshachar Ventachari, took over charge as Chief Minister on 5 January 1951, but relinquished charge a few months later, on 26 April 1951. Jai Narain Vyas then took over. He remained in office till 3 March 1952, when he quit following his defeat in the first general election. In the 1952 elections held for 20 constituencies in the state, the Congress won nine seats, the Ram Raj Parishad three, the Swantantra Party and the Bharatiya Jan Sangh took one seat each, while Independents won six. Tikaram Paliwal be-

came Chief Minister on 3 March 1952. He handed the charge back to Vyas on 10 October 1952, after Vyas entered the assembly by winning a by-election from Kishangarh in Ajmer district. But trouble again confronted Vyas. He faced a tough challenge from within his legislature party. In the first-ever trial of strength in the state, Mohanlal Sukhadia was elected leader of the Congress Legislature Party. Sukhadia was sworn in on 13 November 1954, for the first time. He again took the Chief Minister's oath in 1957, 1962, and 1967, and ruled the state for a total of 17 years. His first and fourth terms were incomplete. Sukhadia held the post of Chief Minister for the longest duration, from 1954 to 1971. Another Congressman, Heeralal Deopura, had the shortest tenure of 16 days, from 23 February to 10 March 1985. Barkatullah Khan succeeded Sukhadia from 9 July 1971 to 15 March 1972 and from 16 March 1972 to 11 November 1972. After Khan's death in office, Harideo Joshi was sworn in and held the post thrice, from 11 October 1973 to 29 April 1977, from 10 March 1985 to 20 January 1988, and from 4 December 1989 to 20 January 1990. Bhairon Singh Shekhawat became the state's first non-Congress Chief Minister on 22 June 1977, and remained in office till 16 February 1980, when he was dismissed. He became Chief Minister again on 4 March 1990, only to be dismissed again on 15 December 1992, in the aftermath of the demolition of the Babri Masjid at Ayodhya. He was sworn in for the third time on 4 December 1993. From 6 June 1980 to 14 July 1981 Jagannath Pahadia was the Chief Minister. Shiv Charan Mathur of Congress (I) succeeded him and remained in power till 23 February 1985. Again he came to power on 20 January 1988 and remained in power till 4 December 1989. The Congress (I) Legislature Party elected state party president Ashok Gehlot to be the Chief Minister on 1 December. Gehlot, at 47, was the youngest Chief Minister Rajasthan has had. A five-time Member of Parliament from Jodhpur, he took over as the Pradesh Congress(I) Committee president in 1985. He remained in power till 8 December 2003. BJP leader Vasundhara Raje Scindia was sworn in on 8 December 2003 as the first woman Chief Minister of Rajasthan, along with a small team of nine ministers.

Culture

Communities of musicians like the Mirasis, Manganiyars and Langas have preserved the rich traditions that exist in folk music and dance, like the Maand style of singing. The state is also home to different schools of painting like the Mewar school, the Bundi–Kota *kalam*, and the Jaipur school. The Kishengarh school is best known for its Bani Thani paintings.

Fairs and festivals: The major festivals of the state include Holi, Diwali, the Desert Festival (Jaisalmer), Gangaur and Teej (Jaipur), Urs Ajmer Sharif (Ajmer) and the Pushkar Fair.

Economy, Industry and Agriculture

Economy: The net state domestic product at current prices for 2002–03 (provisional) was Rs 75,048 crores. The per capita net state domestic product at current prices for 2002–03 (provisional) was Rs 12,753.

Minerals and industry: Textiles are the major industry in the large and me-

dium category of industries, followed by agro-food and allied products, as well as cement. Other important industries are chemical gases, lubricants and plastics, heavy machinery and metal and allied products. Tourism is also a major industry. More than half the heritage hotels in India are located in Rajasthan.

Major minerals include zinc, gypsum, silver ore, asbestos, mica, rock phosphate, limestone and marble. Recently, oil reserves have been discovered around Barmer. Rajasthan holds a share of about 24 per cent in the total national production of non-metallic minerals.

Agriculture: Rajasthan produces a wide variety of cereals, oilseeds, pulses, cash crop like cotton, vegetables and fruits. The state accounts for a large proportion of the seed spices grown in the country, mainly coriander, cumin, fennel, chillies and garlic. The state produces jowar, maize, wheat, rice and millet and it is amongst the largest producers of bajra in the country.

Power: The majority of the state's power requirements are met by thermal power plants. Besides these, nuclear and hydroelectric power plants also contribute to the state's power needs.

Education

Educational institutes: Notable educational institutes include
- Rajasthan University (Jaipur)
- Jai Narayan Vyas University (Jodhpur)
- Birla Institute of Technology and Science (Pilani)
- Vanasthali Vidyapeeth (Tonk)
- Kota Open University
- Maharshi Dayanand Saraswati University (Ajmer)
- Mohanlal Sukhadia University (Udaipur)

- Rajasthan Agricultural University (Bikaner)
- Rajasthan Vidyapeeth (Udaipur).

Tourism

Major tourist attractions:

1. Ajmer: The Dargah of Khawaja Moinuddin Chisti, Adhai-din-ka-jhonpra, Taragarh Fort, Pushkar.
2. Alwar: City Palace, Government Museum, Vijai Mandir Palace, Sariska Wildlife Reserve, Ranthambore National Park, Keoladeo Ghana National Park.
3. Bharatpur: Lohagarh Fort, Deeg Palace, Jawahar Burj and Fateh Burj.
4. Chittorgarh: Vijay Stambh, Rana Khumbha's Palace, Saas–Bahu Temple, Meerabai Temple.
5. Jaipur: The City Palace, Jantar Mantar, Hawa Mahal, Amer Palace, Jaigarh and Nahargarh.
6. Jaisalmer: The Fort, Manak Chowk and Havelis, Sam Sand Dunes.
7. Jodhpur: Mehrangarh Fort, Umaid Bhawan Palace, Mandore.
8. Kota: Chambal Garden, Maharao Madho Singh Museum, Jag Mandir.
9. Mount Abu: Gaumukh Temple, Delwara Jain Temple, Guru Shikhar.
10. Udaipur: City Palace, Haldighati, Eklingji, Nathdwara, Kumbhalgarh Fort, Ranakpur Jain Temples.

Airports:

- Jaipur
- Udaipur
- Jodhpur
- Jaisalmer.

National Parks:

- Keoladeo Ghana National Park in Bharatpur dist. (29 sq. km)
- Ranthambhor National Park in Sawai Madhopur dist. (392 sq. km)
- Sariska Tiger Reserve in Alwar dist. (866 sq. km)
- Desert National Park in Jaisalmer dist. (3162 sq. km).

Administration

Legislature: The state has a unicameral legislature. The legislative assembly consists of 200 members, of which 57 seats are reserved for SCs (33) and STs (24).

The party position of the current assembly is as follows:

Name of Party	Seats
Bharatiya Janata Party	120
Indian National Congress	56
Indian National Lok Dal	4
Bahujan Samaj Party	2
Janata Dal (United)	2
Communist Party of India (Marxist)	1
Lok Jan Shakti Party	1
Rajasthan Samajik Nyaya Manch	1
Independent	13
Total	**200**

Judiciary: The seat of the Rajasthan High Court is at Jodhpur, with a bench at Jaipur. The acting chief justice is Y.R. Meena.

Districts:

District	Area (sq. km)	Population	Headquarters	Urban Agglomerations
Ajmer	8,481.0	2,180,526	Ajmer	Ajmer, Beawar
Alwar	8,380.0	2,990,862	Alwar	Alwar
Banswara	5,037.0	1,500,420	Banswara	Banswara
Baran	6,992.0	1,022,568	Baran	
Barmer	28,387.0	1,963,758	Barmer	
Bharatpur	5,066.0	2,098,323	Bharatpur	Bharatpur
Bhilwara	10,455.0	2,009,516	Bhilwara	
Bikaner	27,284.0	1,673,562	Bikaner	
Bundi	5,550.0	961,269	Bundi	Lakheri
Chittaurgarh	10,856.0	1,802,656	Chittaurgarh	
Churu	16,830.0	1,922,908	Churu	Churu, Rajgarh
Dausa	3,432.0	1,316,790	Dausa	
Dhaulpur	3,033.0	982,815	Dhaulpur	Dhaulpur
Dungarpur	3,770.0	1,107,037	Dungarpur	
Ganganagar	7,984.0	1,788,487	Ganganagar	Ganganagar
Hanumangarh	12,650.0	1,517,390	Hanumangarh	
Jaipur	11,143.0	5,252,388	Jaipur	
Jaisalmer	38,428.0	507,999	Jaisalmer	
Jalor	10,640.0	1,448,486	Jalor	
Jhalawar	6,219.0	1,180,342	Jhalawar	
Jhunjhunu	5,928.0	1,913,099	Jhunjhunu	Khetri, Pilani
Jodhpur	22,783.0	2,880,777	Jodhpur	Jodhpur, Phalodi
Karauli	5,524.0	1,205,631	Karauli	
Kota	5,443.0	1,568,580	Kota	Kota
Nagaur	17,718.0	2,773,894	Nagaur	Nagaur, Makrana
Pali	12,387.0	1,819,201	Pali	
Rajsamand	3,860.0	986,269	Rajsamand	
Sawai Madhopur	4,498.0	1,116,031	Sawai Madhopur	Sawai Madhopur, Gangapur City
Sikar	7,732.0	2,287,229	Sikar	Sikar, Khandela
Sirohi	5,136.0	850,756	Sirohi	Abu Road
Tonk	7,194.0	1,211,343	Tonk	Malpura
Udaipur	13,419.0	2,632,210	Udaipur	

Sikkim

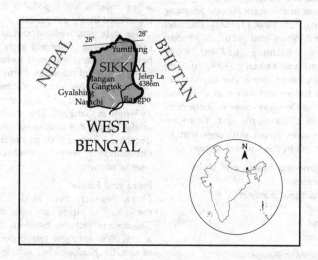

Key Statistics

Capital: Gangtok.
Area: 7096 sq. km.
Population: Total: 540,851
Male: 288,484
Female: 252,367
Population density: 76 per sq. km.
Sex ratio: 875 females per 1000 males.
Principal languages: Nepali, Bhutia, Lepcha.
Literacy rates: Total: 68.8%
Male: 76.0%
Female: 60.4%

Government

Governor: V. Rama Rao. He was appointed on 23 September 2002.

Chief Minister: Pawan Kumar Chamling (SDF). He was sworn in on 21 May 2004.

Geography

Physical characteristics: Sikkim is a small hilly state situated in the Eastern Himalayas. It is a basin surrounded on three sides by steep mountain walls. It extends for approximately 114km from north to south and 64km from east to west. The state is surrounded by the Tibetan Plateau towards the north, the Chumbi Valley of China and Bhutan towards the east, Darjeeling district of West Bengal in the south and Nepal towards the west. The state is a part of the inner ranges of the Himalayas and as such it has no open valley or plains.

Within a distance of 80 km, the elevation rises from 200 metres in the Teesta river valley to 8598 metres at Kanchenjunga, India's highest peak and the world's third highest. The 31-km long Zemu glacier lies on the western side of the peak.

Besides the Kanchenjunga, other major peaks in the state include Jongsang (7459m), Tent Peak (7365m), Pauhunri (7125m), Sinioulchu (6887m), Pandim (6691m), Rathong (6679m), Talung (6147m) and Koktang (6147m). The Singalila range forms the barrier between Sikkim and Nepal in the west, while the Dongkya range is at the border with China on the east. There are many passes across this range that allow access to the Chumbi Valley.

Neighbouring States and Union territories:
International borders:
• China
• Nepal
• Bhutan

States: West Bengal

Major rivers:
• Teesta
• Rangit are the two most important rivers of the state. Other significant rivers include
• Rongni Chu
• Talung
• Lachung
Sikkim is also home to many hot water springs like
• Ralang Sachu
• Phur-Cha
• Yumthang
• Momay.

Climate: The climate of Sikkim can be divided into tropical, temperate and alpine zones. For most of the year, the climate is cold and humid as rainfall occurs in each month.

In Sikkim, temperatures tend to vary with altitude and slope. The maximum temperature is usually recorded in July and August, while the minimum is usually registered during December and January. Fog is a common feature, mainly between May and September. Intense cold is experienced at high altitudes in the winter months and snowfall is also not uncommon during this period.

The state gets well-distributed heavy rainfall between May and early October. The wettest month is usually July in most parts of the state. Mean annual rainfall varies between a minimum of 82mm at Thangu and a maximum of 3494mm at Gangtok. The intensity of rainfall during the southwest monsoon decreases from south to north. The distribution of winter rainfall is in the reverse pattern.

Flora and Fauna:
Flora: Forests cover 36 per cent of the land. The plants vary with altitude. The flora at altitudes between 1500 m and 4000 m is largely temperate forest of oak, birch, alder, chestnut, magnolia maple, and silver fir. The alpine zone lies above 4000 m with plants like juniper, cypress and rhododendron. The perpetual snowline lies at 5000 m. More than 4000 species of plants have been recorded in Sikkim. Sikkim is also home to over 600 species of orchids.

Fauna: Notable among the animals found in Sikkim are the snow leopard, the red panda, the musk deer, the Himalayan black bear, the tahr, the yak, the wild ass and the blue sheep. The state is also home to many species of birds like vulture, eagle, whistling thrush, giant lammergeier, minivets, bulbuls and pheasants.

History

In pre-historic times, land that is today Sikkim was inhabited by three tribes—

the Naongs, the Changs and the Mons. The Lepchas who entered Sikkim later absorbed them completely. The Lepchas were organized into a society by a person named Tur Ve Pa No who was eventually elected the leader or the king 'Punu', in 1400. After his death in battle three kings succeeded him—Tur Song Pa No, Tur Aeng Pa No and Tur Alu Pa No. After the death of Tur Alu Pa No, the monarchy came to an end. From then on, the Lepchas resorted to an elected leader. The area witnessed a major migration from Tibet later on.

In 1642, a young man named Phuntsok was crowned the king. He was named Namgyal and also endowed with the title of Chogyal or religious king. The Namgyal dynasty ruled over Sikkim as hereditary rulers for about 332 years. Phuntsok Namgyal ruled over a vast territory, much larger than present-day Sikkim. In his times, the kingdom extended till Thang La in Tibet in the north, Tagong La near Paro in Bhutan in the east, Titalia on the West Bengal–Bihar border in the south and Timar Chorten on the Timar river in Nepal in the west. Even the Dalai Lama recognized Phuntsok Namgyal as the ruler of the southern slopes of the Himalayas and sent ceremonial gifts to him. At the time the capital city was at Yoksom.

In 1670, Phuntsok Namgyal's son, Tensung Namgyal, succeeded his father. He moved the capital to Rabdentse. Chador Namgyal, a minor son from Tensung's second of three wives, succeeded to the throne upon the death of his father. This led to much conflict as Pedi, the daughter from the first wife, challenged the succession and secretly invited Bhutan, her mother's homeland, to intervene. A loyal minister named Yungthing Yeshe ferreted away the minor king to Lhasa. In Tibet, Chador Namgyal made his mark as a scholar of Buddhist learning and Tibetan literature. He even became a state astrologer to the sixth Dalai Lama. When Bhutanese forces imprisoned Yugthing Yeshe's son, Tibet intervened and forced Bhutan to withdraw.

Chador Namgyal evicted the rest of the invading Bhutanese forces on his return. Although the Bhutanese made a second attempt to capture Sikkim territory, Chador Namgyal put up a worthy resistance but certain areas were lost forever. However, the old family feud returned to cost Chador Namgyal his life. He was killed in 1716 as a result of a conspiracy hatched by Pedi.

The next few years saw rebellions, internal conflicts and border disputes. Gurkhas encroached into Sikkimese territory under the leadership of Raja Prithvi Narayan Shah of Nepal. They also incited the rebellious factions within Sikkim. But they were repelled 17 times. In 1775, a peace treaty was signed, whereby Gurkhas promised to refrain from attacks and also stay away from collaborating with the Bhutanese. Nevertheless, they violated the treaty when they took land in western Sikkim. The period also saw a Bhutanese invasion. They captured all areas east of the Teesta river, but later retreated following negotiations.

In the 19th century, the British struck up a friendship with Sikkim. This was largely due to the fact that they had a common enemy—the Gorkhas. The British defeated Nepalese forces in the Anglo-Nepalese War (1814–16). In 1817, British India signed the Treaty of Titalia with Sikkim. Consequently, territories that the Nepalis had taken away were restored to Sikkim. By the treaty, British India gained a position of great power and influence in the state and Sikkim almost became a British protectorate.

Sikkim even gifted Darjeeling to British India in return for an annual payment and Chogyal Tsudphud Namgyal signed the gift deed in 1835. The British however, did not pay the compensation. This led to a deterioration in relations between the two countries. There were also differences between the British government and Sikkim over the status of the people of Sikkim. The relations deteriorated to the extent that in 1849, when the Superintendent of Darjeeling visited Sikkim along with a scientist on a research trip, they were taken prisoner. They were later freed after the British issued an ultimatum. In 1850, British India stopped the annual grant of Rs 6000 to the Maharaja of Sikkim and also annexed part of Darjeeling and a large portion of Sikkim.

When India became independent, the then Chogyal, Tashi Namgyal, obtained the status of a protectorate for Sikkim. However, local parties like the Sikkim State Congress wanted a democratic set-up and the accession of Sikkim to the Union of India. After Tashi Namgyal died in 1963, demands for the removal of the monarchy and the establishment of a democratic set-up intensified. By 1973, the agitation against the Sikkim Durbar had taken a serious turn and resulted in a collapse of the administration. This led the Indian government to intervene, and Sikkim was transformed from a protectorate to an associate state.

In 1975, a referendum was held. More than 97 per cent of the electorate voted for the merger of Sikkim with India. Sikkim became the 22nd state of the Indian Union on 15 May 1975. Kazi Lhendup Dorji was the first Chief Minister.

Politics

In 1947, after the British withdrew from India, Tashi Namgyal of the Chogyal dynasty was successful in getting a special status of protectorate for Sikkim. On 4 September 1947, the leader of Sikkim Congress, Kazi Lendup Dorji, was elected as the Chief Minister of the state. The Chogyal however still remained as the constitutional figurehead monarch in the new setup. In 1955, democratic progress brought about the institution of the Sikkim Council as a legislative body, under the 1955 Constitution, consisting of a President nominated and appointed by the ruler and councillors. The old ruler Tashi Namgyal died in 1963 and the crown prince Chogyal Palden Thondup Namgyal ascended the throne in 1964. Troubles arose in 1973, when the Sikkim National Congress demanded fresh elections and establishment of a democratic set up. The Kazi was elected by the Council of Ministers, which was unanimous in its opposition to the retention of the monarchy. After a period of unrest in 1972-73, matters came to a head in 1975, when Kazi appealed to the Indian parliament for representation and change of status to statehood.

A referendum was held in which 97.5% of the people voted to join the Indian Union. Kazi was elected the Chief Minister, ruling with the aid of cabinet. Sikkim became a full-fledged state of the Indian Union on 16 May 1975. It was the twenty-second state. On 13 August 1979, the Assembly was dissolved and the government resigned a few days later. On 8 August, Sikkim came under President's Rule. Fresh elections were held on 12 October 1979. A popular ministry headed by Nar Bahadur Bhandari, leader of the Sikkim Parishad Party, came into power from 18 October 1979. The Assembly comprised of 32 members of which 17 were general seats, 12 seats were reserved for Scheduled Tribes including mainly Sherpas, Lepchas and Bhutias, two for Scheduled Castes and one for Sanghas (Monasteries). Bhandari held on to power in the 1984 and 1989 elections. In the 1994 elections Pawan Kumar Chamling from the Sikkim Democratic Front became the Chief Minister of the state. The party has since held on to power by winning the 1999 and 2004 elections. In 2003, China officially recognized Indian sovereignty over Sikkim as the two nations moved toward resolving their border disputes. Sikkim no longer figures as an 'independent nation' in the world map and index of the annual yearbook published by the Chinese Foreign Ministry.

Culture

Sikkim is famous for its mask dance that is performed by lamas in gompas. The state is also known for its handicrafts and handloom objects. The Kagyat dance is performed every 28th and 29th day of the Tibetan calendar. The dance is one of solemnity interspersed with comic relief provided by jesters.

Fairs and festivals: Different communities in the state have different festivals. Saga Dawa is an auspicious day for the Mahayana Buddhists and they go to monasteries to offer butter lamps and worship. Monks take out a procession that goes around Gangtok with holy scriptures.

Phang Lhabsol is a unique festival that is celebrated to offer thanks to Mount Kanchenjunga. The biggest and most important festival of the Hindu–Nepali population is Dasain. It is celebrated in September/October and symbolizes the victory of good over evil. Tyohar or Dipavali is the festival of lights and is celebrated 10 days after Dasain. Other festivals include Drupka Tseshi that is celebrated around August. Losoong is

the Sikkimese New Year which is celebrated in the last week of December, while Losar is the Tibetan New Year and is celebrated around February.

Economy, Industry and Agriculture

Economy: The net state domestic product at current prices for 2002–03 (provisional) was Rs 1139 crores. The per capita net state domestic product at current prices for 2002–03 (provisional) was Rs 20,456.

Minerals and industry: Sikkim is an industrially underdeveloped state. There are public–sector undertakings for the manufacture of precision instruments and watches. Besides these, there are handicrafts, handlooms, liquor, and pisciculture ventures in the state.

Agriculture: Maize, rice, wheat, barley, pulses, potato and cardamom are the most important crops grown in the state. The economy is based largely on agriculture and animal husbandry.

Power: The state mainly utilizes hydroelectric power.

Education

Educational institutions:
• The Sikkim Manipal University of Health, Medical and Technology Sciences is at Gangtok.
• Other institutes of learning in the state include the Directorate of Handicraft and Handloom and the Sikkim Research Institute of Tibetology (SRIT).

Tourism

Major tourist attractions:
1. North Sikkim: Singba Rhododendron Sanctuary, Yumthang, Chungthang, Singiek, Kabi Lungtsok.
2. South Sikkim: Namtse, Varsey Rhododendron Sanctuary, Borong Tsa-

Chu hot spring, Maenam Hill, Ravangla.

3. East Sikkim: White Hall, Ridge Garden, Do-Drul Chorten, Rumtek Dharma Chakra Centre, Kyongnosla Alpine Sanctuary, Fambong La Wildlife Sanctuary.

4. West Sikkim: Pelling, Ruins of Rabdentse, Yuksom.

Airports: None.

National Parks: Kanchenjunga National Park in North Sikkim dist. (850 sq. km).

Administration

Legislature: There are 32 seats in the legislative assembly, out of which two are reserved for SCs and 12 for STs (for the Bhutia and Lepcha community). One general seat is reserved for the Sangha community. The term of the current house expires on 14 October 2004. The current party position is:

Name of Party	Seats
Sikkim Democratic Front	31
Indian National Congress	1
Total	**32**

Judiciary: The High Court of Sikkim is at Gangtok. N. Surjawani Singh is the acting chief justice.

Districts:

District	Area (sq. km)	Population	Headquarters	Urban Agglomerations
East	954.0	244,790	Gangtok	–
North	4,226.0	41,023	Mangan	–
South	750.0	131,506	Namchi	–
West	1,166.0	123,174	Gyalshing	–

Tamil Nadu

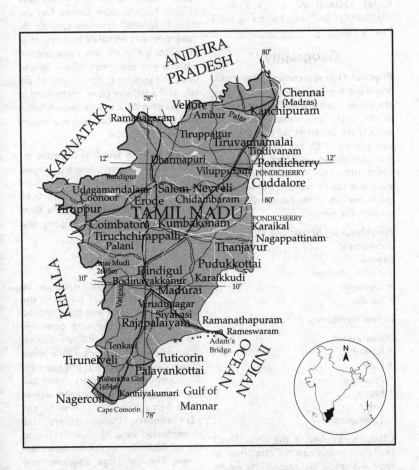

Key Statistics

Capital: Chennai.
Area: 1,30,058 sq. km.
Population: Total: 62,405,679
Male: 31,400,909
Female: 31,004,770
Population density: 478 per sq. km.

Sex ratio: 987 females per 1000 males.
Principal languages: Tamil, Telugu, Kannada.
Literacy rates: Total: 73.5%
Male: 82.4%
Female: 64.4%

Government

Governor: Surjeet Singh Barnala. He assumed the office on 1 November 2004.

Chief Minister: J. Jayalalithaa (AIADMK). She was sworn in on 2 March 2002.

Geography

Physical characteristics: Tamil Nadu is divided between the flat areas along the eastern coast and the hilly regions in the north and west. The Kavery delta is the broadest part of the eastern plains, with the arid plains of Ramanathapuram and Madurai towards the south. The Western Ghats run along the state's western border, while the lower hills of the Eastern Ghats run through the centre.

Neighbouring States and Union territories:

States:
• Andhra Pradesh
• Karnataka
• Kerala.

Union territories: Pondicherry.

Major rivers:
• Kavery
• Palar
• Ponnaiyar
• Pennar
• Vaigai
• Tamiraparani.

Climate: Excepting the hills, Tamil Nadu's climate can be classified as semi-arid tropic monsoonal. Maximum temperatures in the plains go up to 45°C in summer, with minimum temperatures in the winter hovering around 10°C. The average annual rainfall ranges between 650mm and 1900mm. The hill areas have maximum temperatures around 30°C in the summer and minimum temperatures as low as 3°C in the winter and also receive substantially higher rainfall.

Flora and Fauna:

Flora: Nearly 18 per cent of the area of Tamil Nadu is under forests. Dry deciduous forests, thorn forests, scrub, mangroves and wetlands cover most of the plains and lower hills. Moist deciduous and wet evergreen forests as also shoal and grassland occupy most of the hills in the moister parts, particularly in the Western Ghats. Sandalwood, pulpwood, rubber and bamboo are important forest products.

Fauna: Wildlife found in the state includes elephant, tiger, leopard, striped hyena, jackals, Indian pangolin, slender loris, lion-tailed macaque, sloth bear, bison or gaur, black buck, Nilgiris tatur, grizzled giant squirrel, dugong and mouse deer.

History

The early history of the region can be traced to a trinity of powers: the Cheras, the Cholas and the Pandyas. From the sixth to the ninth centuries, the Chalukyas and the Pallavas also established their dominance with a series of wars in the region. From the mid-ninth century, Chola rulers dominated the region, the most prominent among them being Rajendra I. Around the 12th century, Muslim rulers also strengthened their position, leading to the establishment of the Bahamani sultanate. The Vijayanagar kingdom came into prominence in the mid-14 century and ruled for nearly 300 years. The British control over the region began from the mid-17th century and continued until independence.

After independence, the areas of present-day Tamil Nadu, Andhra Pradesh and some territorial areas of

Kerala came under the governance of Madras state. In 1953, the Telugu-speaking areas of Madras state were carved out into the state of Andhra Pradesh. In 1956, the Madras state was further divided into the states of Kerala, Mysore and Madras. In August 1968, Madras state was renamed Tamil Nadu. O.P. Ramaswamy Reddyar was the first Chief Minister.

Politics

Modern Tamil Nadu has emerged from Madras Presidency of the British administration. At the time of Indian Independence on 15 August 1947, Madras state comprised of Tamil Nadu, Andhra Pradesh and some territorial areas of present Kerala. In 1953, however, the Madras state bifurcated into two states, viz. Andhra state, comprising of Telugu speaking areas and Madras state, comprising of Tamil speaking areas. The old capital city of Madras was retained in the Madras state. Under the States Reorganisation Act, 1956, the Madras state was further divided into the states of Kerala, Mysore and Madras. Later, on 1 April 1960, territories comprising of Chittoor district in Andhra Pradesh was transferred to Madras state in exchange of territories from the Chingleput and Salem districts. In 1968, Madras state was renamed as Tamil Nadu.

Amandur Ramaswami Reddiar of the Indian National Congress was the first Chief Minister who remained in office from 15 August 1947 to 6 April 1949. He was succeeded by Poosapati S. Kumaraswamy Reddiar and he served as the Chief Minister till 10 April 1952. The first Legislature of the erstwhile Madras state under the Constitution of India was constituted on 1 March 1952, after the first general elections held in January 1952 on the basis of adult suffrage. From 1967 onwards, the strength of the Assembly continued to remain at 234 besides a nominated member. During the term of the fourth Legislative Assembly on 18 July 1967, the House by a resolution unanimously adopted and recommended that steps be taken by the state government to secure necessary amendment to the Constitution of India to change the name of Madras state to 'Tamil Nadu'. During the term of the eighth Assembly, a government resolution seeking to abolish the Legislative Council was moved and adopted by the House on 14 May 1986. The Tamil Nadu Legislative Council was thus abolished with effect from the 1 November 1986. Thus the bicameral Legislature established in 1937 under the Government of India Act, 1935 has become a unicameral Legislature in Tamil Nadu.

Regional political parties have been strongest in Tamil Nadu, where they have dominated state politics since 1967. Regional parties in the state trace their roots to the establishment of the Justice Party by non-Brahman social elites in 1916 and the development of the non-Brahman Self-respect Movement, founded in 1925 by E.V. Ramaswamy Naicker. As leader of the Justice Party, in 1944 Ramaswamy renamed the party the Dravida Kazhagam (DK—Dravidian Federation) and demanded the establishment of an independent state called Dravidasthan. In 1949, charismatic film script writer C.N. Annadurai, who was chafing under Ramaswamy's authoritarian leadership, split from the DK to found the DMK (Dravida Munetra Kazhagam) in an attempt to achieve the goals of Tamil nationalism through the electoral process.

During the fifties and sixties, however, there were several developments which gradually led to a change in the basic political thrust of DMK. Naicker gave up his opposition to Congress when in 1954, Kamraj, a non-Brahmin, displaced C. Rajagopalachari, the dominant leader of the Congress party in Tamil Nadu who was the Chief Minister from 10 April 1952 to 13 April 1954, and became the Chief Minister. He remained in power till 2 October 1963. DMK participated in the 1957 and 1962 elections. That a change was coming became visible when, in the 1962 elections, it entered into an alliance with Swatantra Party and CPI and did not make a separate Dravidnadu a campaign issue, though it was still a part of its manifesto. Although the DMK dropped its demand for Dravidasthan in 1963 it played a prominent role in the agitations that successfully defeated attempts to impose the northern Indian language of Hindi as the official national language in the mid-1960s.

With each election the DMK kept expanding its social base and increasing its electoral strength. In 1962 it had 50 seats in the state Assembly and 7 for the Lok Sabha. From 2 October 1963 to 4 March 1967 M. Bhaktavatsalam was the Chief Minister. The DMK routed the Congress in the 1967 elections in Tamil Nadu and took control of the state government. DMK formed the government in the state with Annadurai as Chief Minister. With the deterioration of Annadurai's health, M. Karunanidhi became Chief Minister in 1969 and took control of the party after Annadurai's death in 1969. Kalaignar Muthuvel Karunanidhi remained in power till 31 January 1976.

Karunanidhi's control over the party was soon challenged by M.G. Ramachandran (best known by his initials, M.G.R.), one of South India's most popular film stars. In the 1971 elections to the Lok Sabha and the state assembly, DMK teamed up with the Indira Gandhi-led Congress (R), which surrendered all claims to Assembly seats in return for DMK's support to it in 9 parliamentary seats which it won. DMK won 183 out of the 234 Assembly seats and 23 Lok Sabha seats. In 1972 M.G.R. split from the DMK to form the All-India Anna Dravida Munnetra Kazhagam (AIADMK). Under his leadership, the AIADMK dominated Tamil politics at the state level from 1977 through 1989.

The importance of personal charisma in Tamil politics was dramatized by the struggle for control over the AIADMK after M.G.R's death in 1988. Janaki Ramachandran succeeded him on 7 January 1988 and remained in power till 30 January 1988. M.G.R's widow, Janaki, herself a former film star, vied for control with Jayalalitha, an actress who had played M.G.R.'s leading lady in several films. The rivalry allowed the DMK to gain control over the state government in 1989. Kalaignar Muthuvel Karunanidhi was the Chief Minister from 27 January 1989 to 30 January 1991. The ninth Tamil Nadu Legislative Assembly was constituted on 27 January 1989 after the general elections held on 21 January 1989. Before the expiry of the term of the ninth Assembly, the President by a proclamation issued on 30 January 1991, under Article 356 of the Constitution of India dissolved the Tamil Nadu Legislative Assembly and imposed President's Rule in Tamil Nadu. Karunanidhi came to power on 13 May 1996 and remained in power till 14 May 2001.

The AIADMK, securely under the control of Jayalalitha, recaptured the state government in 1991. However, since 1980, the Congress (I), usually in alliance with the AIADMK, has won a majority of Tamil Nadu's seats in Parliament. On May 27 1991 while campaigning at Shreeperampudur in Tamil Nadu on behalf of Congress (I), Rajiv Gandhi was assassinated by a human bomb. From 21 September 2001 to 2 March 2002 O. Paneerselvam of the AIADMK was the Chief Minister. On 2 March Jayalalitha, head of the state's ruling All India Anna Dravida Munnetra Kazhagam (AIADMK) party began her third term in office after winning a by-election in Andipatti.

Culture

Tamil Nadu has more than 30,000 temples, for which reason the state is sometimes called 'A Land of Temples'. The festivals held in many of them attract large congregations of devotees throughout the year.

The Bharatnatyam form of classical dancing has its origin in the temples of Tamil Nadu and continues to be followed with a lot of fervour. Another reputed art form that has flourished over the ages is Carnatic music.

Fairs and festivals: Prominent festivals and fairs include Pongal, Chithirai Festival, Navarathri, Saral Vizha, Kanthuri Festival, Mahamagam Festival, Thyagaraja Festival and Mamallapuram Dance Festival.

Economy, Industry and Agriculture

Economy: The net state domestic product at current prices for 2002–03 (provisional) was Rs 135,252 crores. The per capita net state domestic product at current prices for 2002–03 (provisional) was Rs 21,433.

Minerals and industry: Important industries of Tamil Nadu include cement, automobiles and auto components, railway coaches, leather, cotton textiles, sugar, software, biotechnology, agro-based industries and paper. Major minerals found in the state include garnet, lignite, magnesite, monazite, quartz/silica sand, gypsum, ilmenite, rutile, vermiculite, zircon, graphite.

Agriculture: Paddy, millets and other cereals, pulses, sugar cane, groundnut, gingelly, tea, rubber, cashew and cotton are the principal crops of the state.

Power: A large part of Tamil Nadu's power comes from thermal power plants and hydroelectric plants.

Education

Educational institutes: Prominent educational institutions of the state include
• Alagappa University, Karaikudi
• Annamalai University, Annamalainagar
• Bharathiar University, Coimbatore
• Bharthidasan University, Tiruchirapalli
• Chennai Medical College and Research Institute, Chennai
• Indian Institute of Technology Madras, Chennai
• University of Madras, Chennai
• Madurai Kamraj University, Madurai
• Periyar University, Salem
• Sri Ramachandra Medical College and Research Institute, Chennai
• Tamil Nadu Dr Ambedkar Law University, Chennai
• Tamil Nadu Dr MGR Medical University, Chennai.

Tourism

Major tourist attractions:
1. Chennai: Planetorium, Vandalur zoo, Art gallery, Snake park, Marina beach.
2. Chidambaram: Poompuhar, Tarangambadi, The Church of Zion, Masilaminathar Temple.

3. Coimbatore: Indira Gandhi National Park, Maruthamalai Temple.

4. Kancheepuram: Tiruttani, Vellore, Vedanthangal, Elagiri Hills.

5. Kanniyakumari: Suchindram, Nagercoil, Pechipara Dam, Padmanabhapuram, Valluvar Statue, Udayagiri Fort, Vivekananda Rock.

6. Kodaikkanal: Palani, Hill range.

7. Madurai: Alagarkoil, Pazhamudircholai, Thiruparankunram, Thiruvadavur, Tiruvedagam.

8. Mamallapuram: Tirukkalukunram, Crocodile bank.

9. Pondicherry: Auroville, Cuddalore, Tiruvannamalai, Sathanur, Gingee Fort.

10. Rameswaram: Kurusadai islands.

11. Thanjavur: Thiruvaiyaru, Swamimalai, Tirubuvanam, Kumbakonam, Kodikkarai.

12. Tiruchirappally: Srirangam, Thiruvanaikkaval, Gangaikondancholapuram.

13. Udagamandalam (Ooty): Mudumalai, Coonoor.

Airports:

International: Chennai.

Domestic:

- Tiruchirappally
- Madurai
- Coimbatore
- Tuticorin.

National Parks:

- Guindy (Chennai)—2.82 sq. km
- Indira Gandhi National Park (Coimbatore)—117.10 sq. km
- Gulf of Mannar Biosphere Reserve and National Park—6.23 sq. km
- Mudumalai (Nilgiris)—103.23 sq. km
- Mukurthi (Nilgiris)—78.46 sq. km.

Administration

Legislature: The unicameral Tamil Nadu state assembly comprises 234 elected members and one nominated member (Anglo-Indian). Of the 234 seats 42 are reserved for SCs and three for STs. The term of the current house expires on 21 May 2006.

The current party position is as follows:

Name of Party	Seats
All India Anna Dravida Munnetra Kazhagam	132
Dravida Munnetra Kazhagam	31
Tamil Maanila Congress (Moopanar)	23
Pattali Makkal Katchi	20
Indian National Congress	7
Communist Party of India (Marxist)	6
Communist Party of India	5
Bharatiya Janata Party	4
M.G.R. Anna D.M. Kazhagam	2
All India Forward Bloc	1
Independent	3
Total	**234**

Judiciary: Madras High Court, with its seat in Chennai, has jurisdiction over Tamil Nadu and Pondicherry. The present chief justice is Markandey Katju.

Districts:

District	Area (sq. km)	Population	Headquarters	Urban Agglomerations
Chennai	178.2	4,216,268	Chennai	Chennai
Coimbatore	7,470.8	4,224,107	Coimbatore	Coimbatore, Pollachi, Tiruppur
Cuddalore	3,645.0	2,280,530	Cuddalore	Chidambaram, Neyveli
Dharmapuri	4,497.8	1,286,552	Dharmapuri	
Dindigul	6,058.0	1,918,960	Dindigul	
Erode	8,209.0	2,574,067	Erode	Erode, Bhavani
Kancheepuram	4,433.0	2,869,920	Kancheepuram	Kancheepuram
Kanniyakumari	1,684.0	1,669,763	Nagercoil	
Krishnagiri	5,143.0	1,546,700	Krishnagiri	
Karur	3,003.5	933,791	Karur	Karur
Madurai	3,497.8	2,562,279	Madurai	Madurai
Nagapattinam	2,715.8	1,487,055	Nagapattinam	
Namakkal	3,363	1,495,661	Namakkal	Erode, Bhavani, Mallasamudram
Perambalur	3,690	1,181,029	Perambalur	
Pudukkottai	4,651.0	1,452,269	Pudukkottai	
Ramanathapuram	4,129.0	1,183,321	Ramanathapuram	
Salem	5,219.6	2,992,754	Salem	Mallasamudram, Salem
Sivaganga	4,189.0	1,150,753	Sivaganga	Karaikkudi
Thanjavur	3,396.6	2,205,375	Thanjavur	Kumbakonam
The Nilgiris	2,549.0	764,826	Udhagamandalam	Coonoor, Devarshola
Theni	3,243.6	1,094,724	Theni	
Thiruvallur	3,424.0	2,738,866	Thiruvallur	Thiruvallur
Thiruvarur	2,167.6	1,165,213	Thiruvarur	
Tiruchirappalli	4,403.8	2,388,831	Tiruchirappalli	Tiruchirappalli
Tirunelveli	6,810.0	2,801,194	Tirunelveli	Ambasamudram, Tirunelveli
Tiruvanamalai	6,191.0	21,81,853	Tiruvanamalai	
Toothukudi	4,621.0	1,565,743	Toothukudi	Toothukudi, Tiruchendur
Vellore	6,077.0	3,482,970	Vellore	Arcot, Gudiyatham, Vaniyambadi, Vellore
Viluppuram	7,250.0	2,943,917	Viluppuram	
Virudhunagar	4,283.0	1,751,548	Virudhunagar	Sivakasi

Tripura

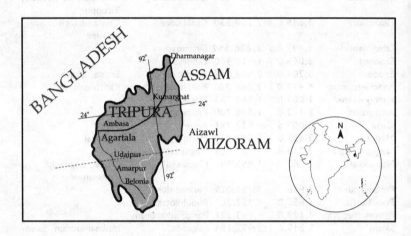

Key Statistics

Capital: Agartala.

Area: 10,491.69 sq. km.

Population: Total: 3,199,203

Male: 1,642,225

Female: 1,556,978

Population density: 304 per sq. km.

Sex ratio: 948 females per 1000 males.

Principal languages: Bengali, Tripuri, Hindi.

Literacy rates: Total: 73.2%

Male: 81.0%

Female: 64.9%

Government

Governor: Dinesh Nandan Sahaya. He assumed office on 2 June 2003.

Chief Minister: Manik Sarkar (CPIM). He was sworn in on 7 March 2003.

Geography

Physical characteristics: Tripura is a land of hills, plains and valleys. The central and northern part of the state is a hilly region that is intersected by four major valleys. These are the Dharmanagar, Kailashahar, Kamalpur and Khowai valleys. These valleys are formations resulting from northward-flowing rivers. The valleys in the western and southern part of the state are marshy. The terrain is densely forested and highly dissected in southern Tripura. Ranges running north–south cross the valleys. These hills are a series of parallel north–south ranges that decrease in elevation southwards and finally merge into the eastern plains. These are the Deotamura range, followed by the Atharamura, Langtarai, and Sakhan Tlang ranges. Of these peaks, Deotamura is the lowest and the height of each successive range increases eastwards. The 74-km-long Jamrai Tlang mountains have the highest peak, Betalongchhip (1097m).

The Tripura plains are also called the Agartala plains. The plains lie in the south-western part of the state and extend over approximately 4,150 sq. km. The Tripura plains are situated on a part of the bigger Ganga–Brahmaputra lowlands to the west of the Tripura Hills. The plains have extensive forest cover and have numerous lakes and marshes.

Neighbouring States and Union territories:
International border: Bangladesh.

States:
- Assam
- Mizoram

Major rivers:
- Gomti
- Muhuri
- Howrah
- Juri
- Manu
- Deo
- Dhalai
- Khowai
- Feni
- Longai

Climate: Summer temperatures range between 20°C and 36°C. In winter, the range is between 7°C and 27°C. Average annual rainfall in 2000 was 2500mm.

Flora and Fauna:
Flora: In 2000–01, Tripura had a forest area of 6,292.68 sq. km or around 60 per cent of the total land area. Sal is found extensively in the state. There are rubber, tea and coffee plantations as well.

Fauna: Tiger, elephant, jackal, leopard, wild dog, boar, wild buffalo and gaur are the most notable members of the state's animal population.

History

The early history of Tripura is described in the *Rajamala*, an account of people who are supposed to be the early rulers of Tripura. The *Rajamala*, written in Bengali verse, was compiled by the courtiers of Dharma Manikya, one of the greatest rulers of Tripura.

During the reign of Dharma Manikya and his successor, Dhanya Manikya, in the 15th and 16th centuries, rule of Tripura was extended over large portions of Bengal, Assam, and what is today Myanmar as a consequence of a string of military conquests.

It was only in the 17th century that the Mughal empire extended its rule over Tripura. The British East India Company gained control of parts of Tripura when it obtained the diwani of Bengal in 1765. But this was limited to the parts that were under Mughal control. From 1808 onwards, the rulers of Tripura had to be approved by the British government. In 1905, Tripura was attached to the new province of Eastern Bengal and Assam. It came to be known as Hill Tippera.

After independence, the Regent Maharani signed an agreement of merger with the Indian Union on 9 September 1947. Consequently, the administration of the state was taken over by the Government of India on 15 October 1949. On 1 November 1956, Tripura became a Union territory without legislature. A popular ministry took power on 1 July 1963. Tripura attained statehood on 21 January 1972. Sachindra Lal Singh was the first Chief Minister.

Politics

The princely state of Tripura was ruled by Maharajas of the Manikya dynasty.

It was an independent administrative unit under the Maharaja even during the British rule in India though this independence was qualified, being subject to the recognition of the British, as the paramount power, of each successive ruler. After independence of India, an agreement of merger of Tripura with the Indian Union was signed by the Regent Maharani on 9 September 1947 and the administration of the state was actually taken over by the Government of India on 15 October 1949. Tripura was merged with the Indian Union as a part 'C' state, administered by the Chief Commissioner. Tripura became a Union Territory without legislature with effect from 1 November 1956. A Territorial Council was formed on 15 August 1957 with 30 members to be elected on the basis of adult franchise and two to be nominated by the Government of India. On 1 July 1963, the Tripura Territorial Council was dissolved after forming a Council of Ministers and a Legislative Assembly with the existing members of the Territorial Council. On 21 January 1972, Tripura became a full-fledged state through an Act of Parliament titled as the North Eastern Areas (Reorganisation) Act, 1971.

The state Legislature is a unicameral body with a Legislative Assembly consisting of 60 members. The present House is the ninth Legislative Assembly. After annexation with India the Tripuri people became a microscopic minority because of the huge Hindu Bengali influx from East Pakistan (present Bangladesh). Therefore Tripura Peoples Democratic Front (TPDF) and National Liberation Front of Tripura (NLFT) started an armed national liberation struggle against Indian colonialism. They also wanted to reestablish Tripura as an independent country. On 1 July 1963 Sachindra Lal Singh became the first Chief Minister. Until 1977 the state was governed by Indian National Congress. Left Front governed from 1978 to 1988 and then returned to power in 1993. Comrade Nripen Chakraborty became the Chief Minister of the state's first Left Front government in 1978 and also of the second one in 1983. In Tripura CPI(M), CPI, RSP and AIFB are members of the Left Front. From 1988 to 1993 the state was governed by a coalition of Indian National Congress and Tripura Upajati Juba Samiti. An 18-member Left Front ministry was sworn-in in Tripura on 7 March 2003 headed by Manik Sarkar, who assumed the office of Chief Minister for the second consecutive term.

Culture

Tripura has a rich heritage of folk dances of the different communities of the state. The main folk dances of Tripura are Garia, Maimita, Masak Sumani, Jhum and Lebang Boomani dances of the Tripuri community, Hozagiri dance of the Reang community, Cheraw and Welcome dances of the Lusai community, Bizu dance of the Chakma community, Sangraiaka, Chimithang, Padisha and Abhangma dances of the Mog community, Hai-Hak dance of the Malsum community, Wangala dance of the Garo community, Basanta Rash and Pung Chalam dances of Manipuri community, Garia dances of Kalai and Jamatia communities, Gajan, Sari, Dhamail, and Rabindra dances of the Bengali community. The state is also well known for its cane and bamboo handicrafts and household items such as furniture, baskets and ornaments.

Fairs and festivals: In Tripura, Garia and Gajan festivals, Manasa Mangal, Durga Puja, Rabindra Jayanti and Nazrul Jayanti are celebrated all over the state. Events of specific places include

Ashokastami Festival of Unakoti, Kharchi Festival of Old Agartala, Dewali Festival of Mata Tripureswari Temple in Udaipur, Rasha Festival of Kamalpur, Kailashahar, Khowai and Agartala, Orange and Tourism Festival of Jampui Hill range and the Pous Sankranti Mela of Tirthamukh.

Economy, Industry and Agriculture

Economy: The net state domestic product at current prices (new series) in 2001–02 (quick estimates) was Rs 5660 crores. The per capita net state domestic product at current prices (new series) in 2001–02 (quick estimates) was Rs 17,459.

Minerals and industry: Jute, tourism, handicrafts, handloom and food products are the most notable among the existing industrial ventures of the state. There are five industrial estates and two industrial growth centres in Tripura. Both the state and the Central governments offer various incentives for the setting up of new industrial ventures in Tripura. It is also being promoted as the international gateway to the northeast region of India, given its proximity to Bangladesh, mainly the latter's port at Chittagong.

The two most important mineral resources of Tripura are oil and natural gas. Other significant minerals are glass sand, shale, plastic clay and sand.

Agriculture: The main crops grown in the state are rice, sugar cane, cotton, jute and mesta. Key plantation crops are tea, rubber and coffee. Besides these, banana, pineapple, cashew nuts, orange, mango, guava, litchi, potato, papaya and tomato are also grown.

Power: Thermal power plants contribute the biggest share of the energy produced in the state. Hydroelectric power plants are the second most important source.

Education

Educational institutions: Tripura University is at Agartala.

Tourism

Major tourist attractions: Sephahijala Wildlife Sanctuary, Trishna Wildlife Sanctuary, Gumti Wildlife Sanctuary, Roa Wildlife Sanctuary, Rudra Sagar (Neer Mahal), Kamala Sagar, Brahmakund, Udaipur, Deotamura, Dumbur, Pilak, Jampui Hills, Unakoti, Tripura Sundari Temple, Ujjayanta Palace.

Airports:
- Agartala
- Kailashahar
- Khowai
- Kamalpur

National Parks: None.

Administration

Legislature: The legislative assembly of Tripura has 60 seats, out of which 20 seats are reserved for STs and seven reserved for SCs. The term of the current house expires on 19 March 2008.

The current party position is as follows:

Name of Party	Seats
Communist Party of India (Marxist)	38
Indian National Congress	13
Indigenous Nationalist Party of Tripura	6
Revolutionary Socialist Party	2
Communist Party of India	1
Total	**60**

Judiciary: The jurisdiction is of the Agartala Bench of the Gauhati High Court. Binod Kumar Roy is the chief justice.

Districts:

District	Area (sq. km)	Population	Headquarters	Urban Agglomerations
Dhalai	2,212.3	307,417	Ambassa	–
North Tripura	2,100.7	590,655	Kailashahar	–
South Tripura	3,140.0	762,565	Udaipur	–
West Tripura	3,033.0	1,530,531	Agartala	–

Uttaranchal

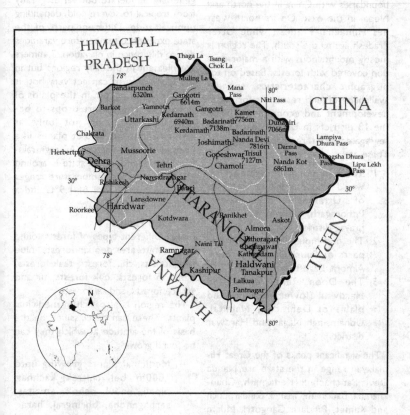

Key Statistics

Capital: Dehradun (provisional).
Area: 53,483 sq. km.
Population: Total: 8,489,349
Male: 4,325,924
Female: 4,163,425
Population density: 159 per sq. km.
Sex ratio: 962 females per 1000 males.
Principal languages: Hindi, Garhwali, Kumaoni.

Literacy rates: Total: 71.6%
Male: 83.3%
Female: 59.6%

Government

Governor: Sudarshan Agarwal. He was appointed on 8 January 2003.

Chief Minister: N.D. Tiwari. He was sworn in on 2 March 2002.

Geography

Physical characteristics: Uttaranchal is located in the foothills of the Himalayas. The state has international boundaries with China in the north and Nepal in the east. On its north-west lies Himachal Pradesh while Uttar Pradesh lies to the south. The region is mostly mountainous with a major portion covered with forests. Based on topographic characteristics, specific availability of land resources for urban development and economic mobility, the 13 districts in Uttaranchal can be segregated into three broad categories. These are:

1. The high mountain region (these would include significant port- ions of Uttarkashi, Champawat, Pithoragarh, Chamoli and Rudraprayag districts).

2. The mid-mountain region (major parts of Pauri Garhwal, Tehri, Almora, Bageshwar districts).

3. The Doon, Terai region and Hardwar (lower foothills and plains of Dehradun, Nainital, Udhamsingh Nagar and Hardwar districts).

The significant peaks of the Great Himalayan range in the state are Nanda Devi, Panchachuli, Kedarnath, Chaukhamba, Badrinath, Trishul, Bandarpunch and Kamet. Pindari, Gangotri, Milam and Khatling are the important glaciers.

Neighbouring States and Union territories:
International borders:
• China
• Nepal

States:
• Himachal Pradesh
• Uttar Pradesh

Major rivers:
• Ganga
• Yamuna
• Ramganga
• Kali (Sharda).

Climate: The climate of the state is generally temperate but varies greatly from tropical to severe cold, depending upon altitude. Different parts of the state experience temperature variations due to difference in elevation. Summers are pleasant in the hilly regions but in the Doon area, it can get very hot. It can get even hotter in the plains of the state. Temperature drops to below freezing point not only at high altitudes but also at places like Dehradun in the winters. Average rainfall experienced in the state is around 1079mm. Average temperature ranges between a minimum of 1.9°C and a maximum of 40.5°C.

Flora and Fauna:
Flora: Different types of forests found in the state are: deodar forests, blue pine forests, chir forests, teak forests, bamboo forests, oak forests, fir and spruce forests, and sal forests.

The region is also rich in medicinal plants. These can be classified on the basis of the altitude at which they can be found growing.

1. Medicinal plants growing upto 1000m: bel, chitrak, kachnar, pipali, babul, ashok, amaltas, sarpagandha, bhringraj, harar, behera, malu, siris, amla and mossli.

2. Medicinal plants growing from 1000m to 3000m: banspa, sugandhabala, tejpat, dalchini, jhoola, kuth, timru and painya.

3. Medicinal plants growing above 3000m: atis, mitha, gugal, jamboo, mamira, gandrayan, bajradanti and salammishri.

Fauna: The animal population of Uttaranchal includes tiger, leopard, other members of the cat family, Indian elephant, dhole (wild dog), antelopes like nilgai and ghoral, Himalayan tahr, deer like hog deer, sambar, chital or spotted deer and barking deer and primates like rhesus monkey and langur. Other animals found in the state include jackals, foxes, civets, wild boar, sloth bear and black bear. Reptiles like the cobra and python are found in the state. Ramganga river is home to two species of crocodile, namely gharial and mugger, as well as fishes like the famous mahaseer and the malee.

Uttaranchal is also home to hundreds of species of birds including water fowl, many types of woodpecker and predatory birds like the Pallas's fishing eagle, harriers and kites. Peafowl, kalij pheasant, chir pheasant, red jungle fowl, minivets, shrikes, cuckoos, drongos and barbets are also found in the state. Corbett National Park is home to various species of birds like brown fish owl, Himalayan kingfisher, brown dipper and plumbeous/white-capped redstarts. The bird population of the National Park also includes the little/staty backed forktails and mountain/rufous-bellied hawk-eagles, blue whistling thrush and red jungle fowl, oriental white-eye, jungle owlet, Alexandrine parakeet, Himalayan swiftlet, lesser fish-eagle and great thick-knee, stork-billed kingfisher.

History

Uttaranchal has been mentioned in ancient texts as Kedarkhand and Kurmanchal. The region's history is older than that of the *Ramayana* and the *Mahabharata*. It is also a site of popular myths, like that of Lord Shiva appearing as Kirat, of Urvashi, Shakuntala as well as the Kauravas and Pandavas. In those days, the area that is today Garhwal was known as Kedarkhand, or the region of Kedarnath. On the other hand, Kumaon was Kurmanchal, the land of the Kurmavatar—Lord Vishnu in his incarnation as tortoise.

Rock paintings, rock shelters, palaeoliths and megaliths bear evidence of human habitation in this region from the prehistoric period. Various texts also mention a number of tribes that inhabited the region. These include the Sakas, Kol-Munds, the Nagas, Khasas, Hunas, Kirats, Gujars and Aryans. After the era of the Kols and the Kirats, the Khasas attained a position of dominance in the Garhwal and Kumaon Himalayas, till the arrival of the Rajputs and Brahmins from the plains.

With the arrival of the Aryans came the establishment of later Vedic culture and most of these people got absorbed into the caste system. The sages living in the region made it an important point of origin of Indo-Aryan culture.

What is Uttaranchal today was earlier a part of the United Provinces of Agra and Awadh. This province came into existence in 1902 and in 1935, it was renamed United Provinces. In 1950, it was renamed once again, this time as Uttar Pradesh. The socio-economic disparities of this region led to a demand for a separate state for many years. The students' protest at Pauri in August 1994 against 27 per cent OBC reservation in education subsequently led to widespread agitations. Later on, it turned into a full-fledged mass movement for a separate state.

Uttaranchal came into existence on 9 November 2000 as the 27th state of the Indian Union. Nityanand Swami was the first Chief Minister of the state.

Politics

The first demand for a separate Uttarakhand state was voiced by P.C.

Joshi, a member of the Communist Party of India (CPI), in 1952. However, a movement did not develop in earnest until 1979 when the Uttarakhand Kranti Dal (Uttarakhand Revolutionary Front) was formed to fight for separation. In 1991 the Uttar Pradesh Legislative Assembly passed a resolution supporting the idea, but nothing came of it. In 1994 student agitation against the state's implementation of the Mandal Commission report increasing the number of reserved government positions and university places for lower caste people (the largest caste of Kumaon and Garhwal is the high-ranking Rajput Kshatriya group) expanded into a struggle for statehood. Violence spread on both sides, with attacks on police, police firing on demonstrators, and rapes of female Uttarakhand activists. In 1995 the agitation was renewed, mostly peacefully, under the leadership of the Uttarakhand Samyukta Sangharsh Samiti (Uttarakhand United Struggle Association), a coalition headed by the Uttarakhand Kranti Dal.

The Bharatiya Janata Party (BJP), seeing the appeal of statehood to its high-caste constituencies, also supported the movement, but wanted to act on its own. To distinguish its activities, the BJP wanted the new state to be called Uttaranchal, meaning 'northern border or region,' essentially a synonym for Uttarakhand. In 1995 various marches and demonstrations of the Uttarakhand movement were tense with the possibility of conflict not just with the authorities, but also between the two main political groups. Actual violence, however, was rare. A march to New Delhi in support of statehood was being planned later in the year. An interesting development was that women were playing an active leadership role in the agitation. Later on, it turned into a

full-fledged mass movement for a separate state. Uttaranchal became the 27th state of the Republic of India on 9 November 2000. On the same day, the BJP came to power under the leadership of Nityanand Swamy in the newly born state of Uttaranchal.

Uttaranchal Legislative Assembly is one of the youngest Legislative Assemblies in India. The state of Uttaranchal was carved out of Uttar Pradesh by the enactment of the Uttar Pradesh Reorganisation Act, 2000 by the Parliament. Uttaranchal has a unicameral legislature. With a nominated member from Anglo-Indian community, it has a total strength of 71 members. The Bharatiya Janata Party replaced Nityanand Swamy with Bhagat Singh Koshiyari as Uttaranchal Chief Minister on 30 October 2001. In the 2002 Assembly elections to the Uttaranchal Legislative Assembly INC secured 36 seats and BJP 18. Narain Dutt Tiwari was sworn in as the Chief Minister on 2 March 2002.

Culture

The arts, crafts, dance forms and music of Uttaranchal revolve around gods and goddesses and seasonal cycles. In recent times, however, historical events of the freedom struggle and national life have come to be based as the topic for art forms.

Fairs and festivals:

1. Almora: Shrawan Mela (Jageshwar), Doonagiri Mela (Ranikhet), Gananath Mela, Dwarhat Mela, Kasar Devi Mela, Somnath Fair.

2. Bageshwar: Uttarayani Mela, Shivratri Fair, Kartik Purnima, Dussehra Fair.

3. Champawat: Purnagiri Fair, Devidhura Fair, Mata Murti Ka Mela.

4. Dehradun: Jhanda Fair, Tapakeshwar Fair, Lakshman Siddha

Fair, Bissu Fair, Mahasu Devta's Fair, Shadheed Veer Kesari Chand's Fair, Lakhawar Fair, Hanol Mela, Neelkanth Mahadev Mela.

5. **Hardwar:** Ardh Kumbh and Kumbh Mela, Kavand Mela.

6. **Nainital:** Vasantotsav, Nandadevi Fair, Hariyali Devi Fair, Ranibagh Fair, Chhota Kailash Fair, Garjiadevi Fair, Sharadotsav, Holi Mahotsav.

7. **Pithoragarh:** Jauljibi and Thal Fairs, Punyagiri Mela, Hatkalika Fair.

8. **Tehri Garhwal:** Chandrabadni Fair, Surkhanda Devi Fair, Kunjapuri Fair.

9. **Udham Singh Nagar:** Tharuwat Buxad Mahotsav, Ataria Fair, Chaiti Fair, Terai Utsav.

10. **Uttarkashi:** Magh Mela.

Economy, Industry and Agriculture

Economy: The net state domestic product at current prices in 2001–02 was Rs 11,361 crores. The per capita net state domestic product at current prices in 2001–02 was Rs 13,260.

Minerals and industry: Sheep development, weaving and fruit processing are the predominant industries of this industrially backward state. Most of the industrial enterprises of the state belong to the small-scale and household sector like khadi and handicrafts.

According to estimates, there are deposits of limestone, dolomite, magnesite, rock phosphate, gypsum and soapstone in different areas of the state.

Agriculture: Agriculture is the main source of livelihood of the rural population. The state grows foodgrains (like rice, wheat, barley, jowar, bajra, maize, manduwa, sanwan and kodo). The state also grows pulses (like urad, moongmoth, masoor, gram, mattar, arhar), oilseeds (like rape, mustard, sesame, groundnut, sunflower and soyabean). Besides these, sugar cane, potato, tobacco and cotton are also grown.

Power: The state's power requirements are mainly met by hydroelectric power plants. The state is home to the Tehri Dam Project.

Education

Educational institutions:

• Hemwati Nandan Bahuguna Garhwal University, Srinagar
• G.B. Pant Kumaon University, Nainital
• Gurukul Kangri University, Hardwar
• G.B. Pant University of Agriculture and Technology, Pantnagar
• Roorkee Engineering University, Roorkee
• Forest Research Institute, Dehradun
• Indian Institute of Petroleum, Dehradun
• Keshav Dev Malviya Institute of Petroleum Exploration, Dehradun
• Oil and Natural Gas Corporation Ltd., Dehradun
• Wadia Institute of Himalayan Geology, Dehradun
• Wildlife Institute of India, Dehradun
• Indira Gandhi National Forest Academy, Dehradun
• Survey of India, Dehradun
• Indian Institute of Remote Sensing, Dehradun
• Instrument Research and Development Establishment, Dehradun
• L.B.S. National Academy of Administration, Mussoorie
• Defence Electronics Applications Laboratory, Dehradun
• Indian Military Academy, Dehradun
• Central Soil and Water Conservation Research and Training Institute, Dehradun
• National Institute of Visually Handicapped, Dehradun
• Rashtriya Indian Military College,

Dehradun
• Nehru Institute of Mountaineering, Uttarkashi
• Central Building Research Institute, Roorkee.

Tourism

Major tourist attractions:

I. Nature tourism:

   a. Wildlife: Askot Sanctuary, Corbett National Park, Govind Wildlife Sanctury, Nanda Devi National Park, Rajaji National Park, Valley of Flowers, Assan Barrage.

   b. Glaciers: Bandarpunch Glacier, Chorbari Bamak Glacier, Dokriani Glacier, Doonagiri Glacier, Gangotri Glacier, Pindari Glacier, Maiktoli Glacier, Sunderdhunga Glacier, Milam Glacier, Ralam Glacier, Namik Glaciers, Khatling Glaciers, Nandadevi Glacier, Satopnath, Bhagirathi-Khark Glacier, Tiprabamak Glacier.

II. Pilgrimage tourism:

   a. Yatras: Char Dham Yatra, Nanda Devi Yatra, Kailash Mansarovar Yatra.

   b. Pilgrimage centres

   i. Almora: Doonagiri Temple, Jageshwar Temple, Chitai Temple, Hairakhan.

   ii. Bageshwar: Bagnath Temple, Chandika Temple, Shri Haru Temple, Gauri Udiyar.

   iii. Chamoli: Badrinath, Hemkund Saheb, Gopeshwar, Prayags.

   iv. Champawat: Baleshwar Temple, Gwal Devta, Devidhura, Kranteshwar Mahadev, Meetha Reetha Saheb, Purnagiri.

   v. Dehradun: Bhadraj Temple, Surkhanda Devi, Jwalaji Temple, Nag Devta Temple, Parkasheshwar Temple, Bharat Mandir, Kailash Niketan Mandir, Satya Narayan Temple, Shatrughan Temple, Neelkanth Mahadev.

   vi. Haridwar: Har ki Pauri, Sapt Rishi Ashram and Sapt Sarovar, Mansa Devi Temple, Chandi Devi Temple, Maya Devi Temple, Daksha Mahadev Temple.

   vii. Nainital: Garjiya Devi Temple, Naina Devi Temple, Seeta Bani Temple.

   viii. Pauri: Siddhibali Temple, Durga Devi Temple, Medanpuri Devi Temple, Shri Koteshwar Mahadev, Tarkeshwar Mahadev, Keshorai Math, Kamleshwar Temple, Shankar Math, Devalgarh, Dhar Devi.

   ix. Pithoragarh: Dhwaj Temple, Narayan Ashram, Patal Bhaubaneshwar, Thal Kedar, Kapileshwar Mahadev.

   x. Rudraprayag: Kedarnath Temple, Shankaracharya Samadhi, Gaurikund, Son Prayag, Panch Kedar, Madmaheshwar, Tungnath, Koteshwar, Guptkashi.

   xi. Tehri Garhwal: Surkhanda Devi Temple.

   xii. Udham Singh Nagar: Atariya Temple, Nanak Matta, Purnagiri, Chaiti.

   xiii. Uttarkashi: Gangotri, Yamunotri.

III. Adventure tourism:

   a. Skiing: Auli, Mundali, Dayara Bagyal, Munsya.

   b. Water sports:

   i. Still water sports: Asan Barrage Water Sports Resort, Nainital Lake Paradise, Nanaksagar Matta.

   ii. Rafting:

   a. Garhwal: River Yamuna: Barkot to Bernigad, Damta to Yamuna Bridge, Mori to Tuni (Khoonigad). River Alaknanda: Kaliasaur to Srinagar, Srinagar to Bagwan, Kaliasaur to Rishikesh. River Bhagirathi: Matli to Dunda, Harsil to Uttarkashi, Dharasu to Chham, Jangla to Jhala, Bhaldyana to Tehri. River Bhilangana: Ghansali to Gadolia. River Mandakini: Chandrapuri to Rudraprayag.

   b. Kumaon: River Maha Kali, Kaudiyala Rafters Camp.

Airports:
• Dehradun

• Pant Nagar.

National Parks:
• Corbett National Park in Nainital and Garhwal districts (520.82 sq. km)
• Gangotri National Park in Uttarkashi district (1,552 sq. km)
• Govind National Park in Uttarkashi district (472.08 sq. km)
• Nanda Devi National Park in Chamoli district (630.00 sq. km)
• Rajaji National Park in Dehradun Garhwal and Haridwar districts (820.00 sq. km)
• Valley of Flowers National Park in Chamoli district (87.50 sq. km).

Administration

Legislature: Uttaranchal has a unicameral legislature of 70 seats of which 12 are reserved for SCs and 3 for STs. The term of the current house ends on 17 March 2007. The present party position is as under:

Name of Party	Seats
Indian National Congress	36
Bharatiya Janata Party	19
Bahujan Samaj Party	7
Uttarakhand Kranti Dal	4
Nationalist Congress Party	1
Independent	3
Total	**70**

Judiciary: The High Court of Uttaranchal is at Nainital. The chief justice is Cyriac Joseph.

Districts:

District	Area (sq. km)	Population	Headquarters	Urban Agglomerations
Almora	3,082.8	630,446	Almora	Almora
Bageshwar	2,302.5	249,453	Bageshwar	
Chamoli	7,613.8	369,198	Gopeshwar	
Champawat	1,781.0	224,461	Champawat	
Dehradun	3,088.0	1,279,083	Dehradun	Dehradun, Mussouri, Rishikesh
Garhwal	5,399.6	696,851	Pauri	
Hardwar	2,360.0	1,444,213	Hardwar	Hardwar, Roorkee
Nainital	3,860.4	762,912	Nainital	Nainital, Haldwani-cum-Kathgodam
Pithoragarh	7,100.0	462,149	Pithoragarh	
Rudraprayag	1,890.6	227,461	Rudraprayag	
Tehri Garhwal	4,080.0	604,608	New Tehri	
Udhamsingh Nagar (Rudrapur)	2,908.4	1,234,548	Udhamsingh Nagar	
Uttarkashi	8,016.0	294,179	Uttarkashi	

Uttar Pradesh

Key Statistics

Capital: Lucknow.

Area: 2,36,286 sq. km.

Population: Total: 166,197,921
Male: 87,565,369
Female: 78,632,552

Population density: 689 per sq. km.

Sex ratio: 898 females per 1000 males.

Principal languages: Hindi, Urdu, Punjabi.

Literacy rates: Total: 56.3%
Male: 68.8%
Female: 42.2%

Government

Governor: T.V. Rajeshwar. He was sworn in on 8 July 2004.

Chief Minister: Mulayam Singh Yadav (SP). He was sworn in on 29 August 2003.

Geography

Physical characteristics: On the basis of its physiography, the main regions of Uttar Pradesh are the central plains of the Ganga and its tributaries, the southern uplands, the Himalayan region, and the submontane region between the Himalayas and the plains.

The Gangetic Plain occupies about three-fourths of the total area of Uttar Pradesh. It largely consists of a fertile plain which is featureless, and varies in elevation, rising up to 300 metres in the northwest, and 60 metres in the extreme east. It is composed of alluvial deposits which are brought down by the Ganga and its tributaries from the Himalayas.

The southern uplands constitute a part of the Vindhya Range, which is rugged, largely dissected, and rises towards the south-east. The elevation in this region reaches up to 300 metres. The submontane region consists of the Bhabar, a narrow bed of alluvium and gravel, which along its southern fringes joins into the Terai area. The Terai area, which previously consisted of tall grass and thick forests, is a marshy and damp tract. A definite portion of the Terai region has been subject to deforestation.

The topography of the Himalayan region is vastly varied. There are deep canyons, turbulent streams, large lakes and snow-capped peaks.

Neighbouring States and Union territories:
International border:
• Nepal

States:
• Uttaranchal
• Madhya Pradesh
• Haryana
• Rajasthan
• Himachal Pradesh
• Bihar

National Capital Territory:
• Delhi

Major rivers:
• Ganga
• Yamuna
• Gomti
• Ramganga
• Ghaghara
• Chambal
• Betwa
• Ken
• Son

Climate: Uttar Pradesh has a varying climate. The Himalayan region experiences a moderately temperate climate, while the southern uplands and the central plains experience tropical monsoon. The highest temperature recorded in the state was 49.9°C at Gonda in 1958. The average temperatures in the plains vary from 12.5°C to 17.5°C in January to 27.5°C to 32.5°C in May and June.

Uttar Pradesh registers a rainfall between 1000–2000mm in the east and 600–1000mm in the west. Around 90 per cent of the rainfall occurs between June and September, during the time of the southwest monsoon. Floods are a recurring problem due to the concentrated rainfall during these four months, and cause heavy destruction to life, property and crops, especially in the eastern part of Uttar Pradesh. On the other hand, the periodic failure of monsoons leads to droughts and failure of crops.

Flora and Fauna:
Flora: The plains of Uttar Pradesh are rich in mineral vegetation, which is diminishing due to the various requirements of the people. While natural forests can be found in the mountainous regions of Uttaranchal on a very large scale, Uttar Pradesh has very few patches of natural forest that lie scattered in the plains.

Tropical moist deciduous forests grow in regions that register 1000 to 1500 mm of annual rainfall and an average temperature between 26°–27°C. In Uttar Pradesh, these forests can be found in Terai. Deciduous trees of uneven sizes grow in regions of higher altitude. This is a special feature of these forests.

In the lower regions, there are climbers, bamboo, evergreen shrubs and cand. The important trees that grow here are dhak, gular, jamun, jhingal, sal, palas, amla, and mahua semal. In all parts of the plains, especially in the central, eastern and western regions, tropical dry deciduous forests can be found, and they consist of trees that are mostly deciduous. Important trees include amaltas, anjeer, palas, bel, and sal. In other moist regions, and especially along river banks, sheesham, jamun, babool, imli (tamarind), peepal, mango, and neem can be found.

In the southwestern parts of the state can be found tropical thorny forests, which are confined to areas that experience low humidity (below 47 per cent), low annual rainfall (between 500–700mm), and a mean annual temperature between 25° to 27°C. Euphorbias, thorny legumes, babool, and especially thorny trees can be found extensively in these areas. Short grasses grow during rains. In these regions, the trees are normally small, and form open dry forests. Some of the trees that can be found in this region are kokke, khair, dhaman, neem, phulai, and danjha. These trees also produce various types of gum and resin.

Fauna: Uttar Pradesh has a variety of fauna. Important species of fish include rohu, einghi, trout, cuchia, labi, parthan, mirror carp, kata, eel, hilsa, magur, mirgal, mahaser, vittal and tengan. Birds include pigeon, vulture, owl, nightingale, sparrow, parrot, nilkanth, cheel and peacock. Other common species found in the state are black deer, nilgai, kastura, sambar, chinkara, snow leopard, hill dog, elephant, mountain goat, cheetal, hyena, tiger, and black-brown bear.

The submontane region of the state is rich in animal life. Animals like wild boars, crocodiles, sloth bears, partridges, wild ducks, quails, peafowls, woodpeckers doves, pigeons, blue jays, leopards and tigers can be found in these regions.

History

During the British rule in India, there were certain pockets in Uttar Pradesh that were governed by the English equity and common law. In 1773, the Mughal Emperor transferred the districts of Banaras and Ghazipur to the East India Company.

The East India Company acquired the area of modern-day Uttar Pradesh over a period of time. The territories occupied from the nawabs, the Scindias of Gwalior and the Gurkhas were initially placed within the Bengal Presidency. In 1833, they were separated and the North-Western Provinces, originally called Agra Presidency, were created. In 1877, the kingdom of Awadh was united with the North-Western Provinces and the province was renamed North-Western Provinces of Agra and Oudh. In 1902, the province was renamed yet again, when it became 'United Provinces of Agra and Oudh'. In 1937, the name was shortened to 'United Provinces'.

In 1947, the United Provinces became an administrative unit of Independent India. In 1949, the autonomous states of Rampur and Tehri-Garhwal were incorporated into the United Provinces. When the new Constitution was adopted in 1950, United Provinces got its present name, Uttar Pradesh. Gobind Ballabh Pant was the first Chief Minister of Uttar Pradesh

In 2000, the state of Uttaranchal was carved out from Uttar Pradesh.

Politics

United Provinces of Agra and Oudh was made a Governor's province in 1921 and after some time its capital was shifted to Lucknow. Its name was shortened to United Provinces in 1937. It got its present name of Uttar Pradesh in 1950. When the Constitution of free India came into force on 26 January 1950, Uttar Pradesh became a full-fledged state of the Republic of India. Under the Constitution of India, Uttar Pradesh has a Governor and a bicameral Legislature. The Lower House is called Vidhan Sabha and the Upper House, Vidhan Parishad.

After the constitution of the state assembly and takeover of the first Congress government under Chief Minister Govind Vallabh Pant on 1 April 1946, Uttar Pradesh has held the centre-stage in the country's politics mainly because it provides the biggest chunk of 85 MPs in the 542-member Indian Parliament. Its 425-member state assembly holds a perpetual live-wire political situation. Heavyweight Chief Ministers like Sampurnanand (1954–60), C.B. Gupta (1960–63 1st time, 1967–1967 2nd time, 1969–1970 third time), Sucheta Kriplani (1963–67), Charan Singh (1967–1968 1st time, 18 February 1970–2 Oct 1970 2nd time), Tribhuvan Narain Singh (1970–1971), Kamlapati Tripathi (1971–73), H.N. Bahuguna (1973–75) and N.D. Tiwari (1976–77) kept the Congress flag flying high for nearly 30 years. The state had by 1977 produced all the three Prime Ministers of the country till then.

By mid-March 1977, the political setting of Uttar Pradesh saw Congress as a humiliated party. The Janata Party made a clean sweep of the 85 Lok Sabha seats, with 68 per cent of the voters backing it. Subsequent state elections proved no different for the Congress. The Janata Party won 352 seats of the 425 seats of UP assembly. But soon infighting and bickering crippled the Janata Party. The going proved tough for the first backward Chief Minister Ram Naresh Yadav. Already bogged down with Shia-Sunni riots of October 1977, Yadav seemed completely at a loss with the outbreak of communal violence in Varanasi on Dushera day. Banarsi Das was the Chief Minister from 1979 to 1980. This was a period of political instability. At this time Sanjay Gandhi capitalized on Janata Party's failures and helped his mother Indira Gandhi to take over the reins of the country for the second time in January 1980. The Congress won 51 of the 85 U.P. Lok Sabha seats. The Janata experiment had failed and so had the belief that there could be a viable alternative to the Congress party.

Vishwanath Pratap Singh set his foot in big time politics on 9 June 1980 as the new Chief Minister of Uttar Pradesh. Sanjay Gandhi himself hand-picked his huge 61-member ministry. The air crash on 23 June abruptly ended Sanjay Gandhi's soaring rise. This presented Singh with unexpected challenges from within the Congress in the state. Many severe tests were waiting. The violent Moradabad riots, which started off on 13 August 1980, proved the worst ever. The riot continued for more than 45 days and necessitated intermittent curfew situations in and around the district. A visibly upset V.P. Singh tendered his resignation but it was not accepted.1981 was even worse for V.P. Singh. Sripati Misra was chosen as Singh's alternative in 1982. A virtual revolt by Congress MLAs sealed Misra's fate. The Congress chose its old hand N.D. Tiwari, a union minister, to replace Misra in August 1984. The Vishwa Hindu Parishad had launched Ek-atmata Yatras in late 1983. These yatras criss-crossed Uttar Pradesh to receive an overwhelming response. There were repeated religious build-ups in Ayodhya. Under obvious prompting from his central leaders especially state home minister Arun Nehru, as a senior minister in Misra and Tiwari's cabinet Bir Bahadur Singh had also made attempts to please the majority community.

The Vishwa Hindu Parishad's major onslaught was unveiled with the announcement of a Ram Janm Bhumi Mukti (freeing of the temple) agitation on 7 October 1984. A huge crowd of karsevaks (RSS volunteers) collected at the banks of the Sarayu River in Ayodhya and vowed to sacrifice their lives for the cause. A truck carrying idols of Ram and Sita, called the Ram Rath yatra, started from Ayodhya to Lucknow the next day on its way to Delhi. The yatra had to be abandoned in Ghaziabad, on the Delhi borders, as Indira Gandhi was assassinated, riddled with bullets by her own bodyguards.

Rajiv Gandhi's entry worked as a soothing balm for hurt sentiments. The eighth Lok Sabha elections proved that Rajiv's magic wand had made inroads into people's hearts. The Congress won a whopping 415 of the total 542 Lok Sabha seats; the biggest ever haul by a single party. Uttar Pradesh responded in Rajiv's favour almost unilaterally. The party lost just 3 of the 85 Lok Sabha seats in the state with an incredible 50.71% votes. The BJP, in turn, stood nowhere with merely

6.37% votes. The Dalit Mazdoor Kisan Party (DMKP), formed by dissolving Lok Dal, was the only party which survived the hurricane with only 3 seats but a more respectable vote percentage of 24.47%. But the Congress could not fare well in the Vidhan Sabha elections in 1985. One reason for the Congress's dip in performance compared to 1980 elections could have been Rajiv's determination of lending a clean image to the party. Nearly half the 306 MLAs of 1980 were denied tickets and they worked against the party's interest in most cases during the campaign. The Congress won 268 seats though it marginally increased its vote-kitty from 37.5% in 1980 to 39.3% in 1985. It was time for Narayan Datt Tiwari to move out. He made way for Bir Bahadur Singh as Chief Minister.

The National Front of seven parties had been formed on 6 August 1988 and the Janata Dal was formed on 11 October the same year following the merger of V.P. Singh's Jan Morcha, Congress-S, Janata Party and the Lok Dal. In September 1989 the National Front and the BJP agreed to have seat adjustments by not fielding candidates against each other in most of the seats. Playing the pivotal role, the National Front also arrived at a similar agreement with the Left parties, though on a much smaller scale. Though the Congress remained the single largest party in the Lok Sabha with 197 seats (39.5% votes), the National Front with 146 seats was able to form the government with the support of BJP's 86 and Left Front's 52 seats. The outcome was more pronounced in Uttar Pradesh with the Janata Dal bagging 204 seats of the 422 for which elections were held. The Congress went down from 268 seats of 1985 to merely 94 seats with a nearly 10% loss of votes. The BJP increased its tally from 15 to 58 seats with an increase of 2% votes. The BSP also carved out its niche in the state's politics by winning 13 seats. The Congress downfall in UP had begun. And so had the era of political instability in Uttar Pradesh.

Mulayam Singh Yadav became the Chief Minister and remained in the post till 1991. On 5 November 1990 the Janata Dal split and Chandra Shekhar with a group of 58 JD MPs was on his way to replace V.P. Singh as the Prime Minister. Mulayam Singh Yadav formed the Samajvadi Janata Party (SJP) with 120 of the 204 JD MLAs. The Congress, supporting both the centre and the state governments, first brought about the downfall of the Chandra Shekhar government on 5 March 1991 and then Mulayam's government on 4 April. Mulayam Singh Yadav was succeeded by Kalyan Singh on 24 June 1991. The Kalyan Singh government was dismissed on 6 December 1992 after the demolition of the Babri Masjid and a Governor's rule imposed. Two Governors—Satyanarain Reddy and Motilal Vora—ruled the state in the interim nine months. Motilal Vora's style of functioning, which involved opening of the huge Raj Bhawan gates to the general public and personalized interaction with all sections of people, went a long way in putting the state back on its course. On 5 December 1993 Mulayam Singh Yadav was back on the seat of Chief Minister. He remained in office till 3 June 1995. Mayawati became the Chief Minister on 3 June 1995 and remained in office till 18 October 1995.

The 13th Vidhan Sabha was constituted on 17 October 1997. It was a hung assembly; BJP got 173, Samajvadi Party 108, BSP 66 and the Congress 33 in a house of 425. The central gov-

ernment annulled the Governor's Rule, constituted the assembly afresh and then placed it under suspension to make a case for the re-imposition of Governor's Rule. A notification was issued reimposing Governor's Rule. Romesh Bhandari was the Governor. After some time the BJP and the BSP carved out a peculiar unheard of arrangement—the Chief Minister's position was to be shared by the two parties in rotation in the block period of six months each. The BSP was to get the CM's position first and in lieu of that the party had to back the election of a BJP Vidhan Sabha speaker. Mayawati took over the CM's position once again on 20 March 1997. Kalyan Singh took over on 21 September 1997 and reversed some of the decisions made by the Mayawati government. Mayawati withdrew support from the Kalyan Singh government on 19 October. On 21 February 1998, twelve members of the rebel Congress group Loktantrik Congress Party (LCP), which was supporting the BJP government, called on the Governor along with some other rebel MLAs of other splinter groups along with Mayawati and Congress Legislature Party leader Pramod Tewari. Representatives of the Samajvadi Party were also in the delegation. Congress MLAs submitted a memorandum claiming that the LCP had withdrawn support from the BJP. The Governor of U.P. Romesh Bhandari immediately invited Jagdambika Pal of Samajwadi Party to form the government. Jagdambika Pal was sworn in as the new CM at 10.30 p.m. the same day. On 22 February the court reinstated the Kalyan Singh government by setting the Governor's order null and void. But the state witnesses a weird situation in the interim period. Two Chief Ministers reached the same office. Pal was the first to grab the CM's chair at 10 a.m. on 22 February. A few hours later Kalyan Singh marched in with the court orders. Pal then had no options but to withdraw. Pal moved the Supreme Court against the High Court order but the apex court refused to interfere but suggested a 'composite' floor test. The Vidhan Sabha met on 26 February as both the Chief Minister occupied the podium along with the Speaker. Kalyan Singh scored an outright victory by getting support of 225 members against Pal's 196. Kalyan Singh was back in the saddle. On 12 June 1999 Ram Prakash Gupta succeeded Kalyan Singh and he remained in office till 28 October 2000. In 2000, the Parliament of India carved out the northern part of Uttar Pradesh to form the state of Uttaranchal.

Rajnath Singh was the Chief Minister from 28 October 2000 to March 2002. Again Mayawati came to power for the third time on 3 May 2002. She was succeeded by Mulayam Singh Yadav on 29 August 2003.

Culture

Apart from possessing a variety of geographical regions and cultures, Uttar Pradesh is also one of the most ancient centres of Indian culture. The antiquities discovered at Mirzapur, Meerut and Banda or Bundelkhand connect its history to the early stone age and the Harappan culture. In the Vindhyan Range, chalk drawings or dark red drawings by primitive men can be found.

The state also features popular holy shrines and pilgrim centres, and also plays an important role in education, culture, politics, tourism, industry, and agriculture. It is also well known for the contribution of its people to the national freedom movement.

Fairs and festivals: There are about 2250 fairs that are held every year in Uttar Pradesh. Mathura has the largest number of fairs (86). Other major venues of fairs are Kanpur, Hamirpur, Jhansi, Agra and Fatehpur.

The Kumbh Mela at Prayag (Allahabad) attracts pilgrims and tourists from around the world. At Prayag, the Kumbh fair is held once in twelve years, and the Ardh Kumbh is held every six years.

Festivals of other religions are also celebrated in Uttar Pradesh, and it is renowned for its composite culture. As many as 40 festivals are celebrated by various communities. Hindu festivals include Shivaratri, Makar Sankranti, Krishna Janmashtami, Karthik Purnima, Vijaya Dashmi, Holi, Deepawali, Ganesha Chaturthi, Ganga Dashahara, Ram Navami, Vaishakhi Purnima, Raksha Bandhan, Sheetla Ashtami, Naag Panchami, and Vasant Panchami. Major Muslim festivals celebrated in the state are Shab-e-Barat, Barawafat, Bakr-Id, Id and Muharram. Christian festivals include Christmas, Good Friday, Easter and New Year's Day.

Some of the important fairs and festivals held in Uttar Pradesh include the Bateshwar Fair, festivals organised by the UP Tourism Department, the Ganga Mahotsava at Varanasi, the Buddha Mahotsava at Sarnath and Kushinagar, and the Water Sports Festival at Allahabad.

Economy, Industry and Agriculture

Economy: The net state domestic product at current prices for 2002–03 (provisional) was Rs 176,076 crores. The per capita net state domestic product at current prices for 2002–03 (provisional) was Rs 10,289.

Minerals and industry: Textiles and

sugar refining, both long-standing industries in Uttar Pradesh, employ nearly one-third of the state's total factory labour. Most of the mills, however, are old and inefficient. Other resource-based industries in Uttar Pradesh include vegetable oil, jute and cement.

A number of large factories manufacturing heavy equipment, machinery, steel, aircraft, telephone and electronics equipment, and fertilizers have been set up in the state. An oil refinery at Mathura and the development of coalfields in the southeastern district of Mirzapur are also major Union government projects.

The state government has promoted medium and small scale industries. Industries that contribute most to the state's exports include handicrafts, carpets, brassware, footwear, and leather and sporting goods. Carpets from Bhadohi and Mirzapur are prized worldwide. Silks and brocades of Varanasi, ornamental brassware from Moradabad, chikan (a type of embroidery) work from Lucknow, ebony work from Nagina, glassware from Firozabad, and carved woodwork from Saharanpur are also important.

Tourism in the state has great potential, but much of it is untapped.

The minerals found in Uttar Pradesh include limestone, dolomite, glass-sand, marble, bauxite and uranium

Agriculture: The economy of Uttar Pradesh is largely dependent on agriculture. The main crops are rice, sugar cane, millet, wheat and barley. High-yielding varieties of seed for rice and wheat were introduced in the 1960s, along with a greater availability of fertilizers, and an increased use of irrigation in the state.

Two chief problems still affect the farmers, namely small, non-economic landholdings and lack of resources needed to invest in the state's technology, in order to increase production. The yield of milk is low, but livestock and dairy still manage to provide a supplementary means of income. Most of the agricultural landholdings are insufficient for the subsistence of the farmers in the state.

Forests in the state yield timber, which is used in construction, and also as firewood and raw materials for producing a number of industrial products like paper, matches and plywood. The government's reforestation programmes in Uttar Pradesh have contributed to some increase in the forest area, and the subsequent availability of forest products useful for industries.

Power: Uttar Pradesh is mainly dependent on thermal power, which provides bulk of the energy to the state. However, hydroelectric and nuclear power (from the Narora Atomic Power Station) also contribute to the total power scenario.

Education

Educational institutes:
• Aligarh Muslim University (Aligarh)
• University of Allahabad
• Babasaheb Bhimrao Ambedkar University (Lucknow)
• Banaras Hindu University (Varanasi)
• Bundelkhand University (Jhansi)
• Central Institute of Higher Tibetan Studies (Varanasi)
• Ch. Charan Singh University (Meerut)
• Chandra Shekhar Azad University of Agriculture and Technology (Kanpur)
• Chhatrapati Sahu Ji Maharaj Kanpur University (Kanpur)
• Dayalbagh Educational Institute (Agra)
• Deendayal Upadhyaya Gorakhpur University (Gorakhpur)
• Dr Bhim Rao Ambedkar University (Agra)

- Dr Ram Manohar Lohia Avadh University (Faizabad)
- Indian Institute of Technology (Kanpur)
- Indian Veterinary Research Institute (Izatnagar)
- University of Lucknow
- Mahatma Gandhi Kashi Vidyapeeth (Varanasi)
- M.J.P. Rohilkhand University (Bareilly)
- Narendra Deva University of Agriculture and Technology (Faizabad)
- Purvanchal University (Jaunpur)
- University of Roorkee
- Sampurnanand Sanskrit Vishwavidyalaya (Varanasi)
- Sanjay Gandhi Postgraduate Institute of Medical Sciences (Lucknow)

Tourism

Major tourist attractions: Chitrakoot, Ayodhya, Jhansi, Kushinagar, Kapilavastu, Varanasi, Sarnath, Fathepur Sikri, Braj-Bhoomi, Vrindavan, Agra.

Airports:
- Lucknow
- Kanpur
- Varanasi
- Agra.

National Parks: Dudhwa National Park in Lakhimpur Kheri district (490.00 sq. km).

Administration

Legislature: Uttar Pradesh has a bi-cameral legislature. The Lower House is called Vidhan Sabha and the Upper House Vidhan Parishad. The state legislative assembly has 403 seats, of which 89 are reserved for the SCs. No seats are reserved for STs. The present party positions are:

Name of Party	Seats
Samajwadi Party	143
Bahujan Samaj Party	98
Bharatiya Janata Party	88
Indian National Congress	25
Rashtriya Lok Dal	14
Rashtriya Kranti Party	4
Apna Dal	3
Communist Party of India (Marxist)	2
Akhil Bhartiya Lok Tantrik Congress	2
Janata Dal (United)	2
Akhil Bharat Hindu Mahasabha	1
Janata Party	1
Lok Jan Shakti Party	1
National Loktantrik Party	1
Rashtriya Parivartan Dal	1
Samajwadi Janata Party (Rashtriya)	1
Independent	16
Total	**403**

Judiciary: The Allahabad High Court is the seat of judiciary. A.N. Roy is the chief justice.

Districts:

District	Area (sq. km)	Population	Headquarters	Urban Agglomerations
Agra	4,027.0	3,611,301	Agra	Agra
Aligarh	3,747.0	2,990,388	Aligarh	
Allahabad	5,425.1	4,941,510	Allahabad	Allahabad
Ambedkar Nagar	2,372.0	2,025,373	Akbarpur	
Auraiya	2,051.9	1,179,496	Auraiya	
Azamgarh	4,210.0	3,950,808	Azamgarh	Mubarakpur
Baghpat	1,389.4	1,164,388	Baghpat	
Bahraich	5,751.0	2,384,239	Bahraich	
Ballia	2,981.0	2,752,412	Ballia	
Balrampur	2,927.0	1,684,567	Balrampur	
Banda	4,418.1	1,500,253	Banda	Banda
Barabanki	3,825.0	2,673,394	Barabanki	Barabanki
Bareilly	4,120.0	3,598,701	Bareilly	Bareilly
Basti	3,033.8	2,068,922	Basti	
Bijnor	4,561.0	3,130,586	Bijnor	Bijnor, Kiratpur, Seohara
Budaun	5,168.0	3,069,245	Budaun	
Bulandshahar	3,717.7	2,923,290	Bulandshahar	
Chandauli	2,554.1	1,639,777	Chandauli	Mughalsarai
Chattrapati Shahuji Maharaj Nagar			Gauriganj	
Chitrakoot	3,205.9	800,592	Chitrakoot	
Deoria	2,535.0	2,730,376	Deoria	
Etah	4,446.0	2,788,270	Etah	
Etawah	2,288.2	1,340,031	Etawah	
Faizabad	2,764.0	2,087,914	Faizabad	Faizabad
Farrukhabad	2,279.5	1,577,237	Fatehgarh	Farrukhabad-cum-Fatehgarh
Fatehpur	4,152.0	2,305,847	Fatehpur	
Firozabad	2,361.0	2,045,737	Firozabad	Firozabad, Sirsaganj, Tundla
Gautam Buddha Nagar	1,268.6	1,191,263	Noida	
Ghaziabad	1,955.8	3,289,540	Ghaziabad	Modinagar
Ghazipur	3,377.0	3,049,337	Ghazipur	Ghazipur
Gonda	4,425.0	2,765,754	Gonda	
Gorakhpur	3,321.0	3,784,720	Gorakhpur	
Hamirpur	4,316.5	1,042,374	Hamirpur	
Hardoi	5,986.0	3,397,414	Hardoi	
Hathras	1,751.0	1,333,372	Hathras	Hathras, Sasni
Jalaun	4,565.0	1,455,859	Orai	
Jaunpur	4,038.0	3,911,305	Jaunpur	
Jhansi	5,024.0	1,746,715	Jhansi	Jhansi
Jyotiba Phule Nagar	2,320.5	1,499,193	Amroha	

Kannauj	1,994.5	1,385,227	Kannauj	
Kanpur Dehat	3,146.0	1,584,037	Akbarpur	
Kanpur Nagar	3,030.0	4,137,489	Kanpur	Kanpur
Kaushambi	1,835.9	1,294,937	Kaushambi	
Kheri	7,680.0	3,200,137	Kheri	
Kushinagar	2,910.0	2,891,933	Padarauna	
Lalitpur	5,039.0	977,447	Lalitpur	
Lucknow	2,528.0	3,681,416	Lucknow	Lucknow
Maharajganj	2,951.0	2,167,041	Maharajganj	
Mahoba	2,849.6	708,831	Mahoba	
Mainpuri	2,746.0	1,592,875	Mainpuri	Mainpuri
Mathura	3,332.0	2,069,578	Mathura	Mathura
Mau	1,713.0	1,849,294	Mau	Muhammadabad Gohna
Meerut	2,521.6	3,001,636	Meerut	Meerut
Mirzapur	4,522.0	2,114,852	Mirzapur	
Moradabad	3,646.5	3,749,630	Moradabad	Bilari
Muzaffarnagar	4,008.0	3,541,952	Muzaffarnagar	Muzaffarnagar, Purquazi
Pilibhit	3,499.0	1,643,788	Pilibhit	
Pratapgarh	3,717.0	2,727,156	Pratapgarh	
Rae Bareli	4,586.0	2,872,204	Rae Bareli	
Rampur	2,367.0	1,922,450	Rampur	
Saharanpur	3,689.0	2,848,152	Saharanpur	
Sant Kabir Nagar	1,442.3	1,424,500	Khalilabad	
Sant Ravidas Nagar	959.8	1,352,056	Bhadohi	
Shahjahanpur	4,575.0	2,549,458	Shahjahanpur	Shahjahanpur
Shravasti	1,126.0	1,175,428	Shravasti	
Siddharth Nagar	2,752.0	2,038,598	Navgarh	
Sitapur	5,743.0	3,616,510	Sitapur	
Sonbhadra	6,788.0	1,463,468	Robertsganj	Renukoot
Sultanpur	4,436.0	3,190,926	Sultanpur	
Unnao	4,558.0	2,700,426	Unnao	
Varanasi	1,578.0	3,147,927	Varanasi	Varanasi

West Bengal

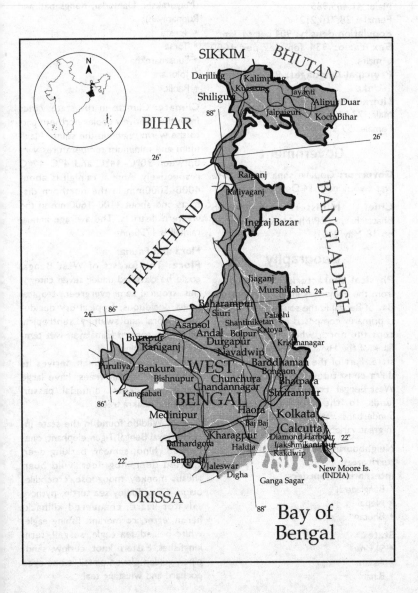

Key Statistics

Capital: Kolkata.

Area: 88,752 sq. km.

Population: Total: 80,176,197
Male: 41,465,985
Female: 38,710,212

Population density: 904 per sq. km.

Sex ratio: 934 females per 1000 males.

Principal languages: Bengali, Hindi, Urdu.

Literacy rates: Total: 68.6%
Male: 77.0%
Female: 59.6%

Government

Governor: Gopalkrishna Gandhi. He was sworn in on 14 December 2004.

Chief Minister: Buddhadeb Bhattacharya (CPIM). He was sworn in on 18 May 2001.

Geography

Physical characteristics: Stretching from the Himalayas in the north to the Bay of Bengal in the south, West Bengal is primarily composed of plain land, except the north where the southern flank of the Himalayas extends into the state. Part of the Ganga–Brahmaputra delta constitutes the eastern part of West Bengal. From the northern highlands to the tropical forests of Sunderbans, variations in altitude result in great variety in nature and climate.

Neighbouring States and Union territories:
International borders:
• Bangladesh
• Nepal
• Bhutan

States:
• Sikkim
• Assam
• Bihar
• Jharkhand
• Orissa

Major rivers:
• Hooghly and its tributaries (Mayurakshi, Damodar, Kangsabati and Rupnarayan)
• Teesta
• Torsa
• Subarnarekha
• Joldhara
• Ranjit

Climate: Climate in the state varies from the relatively cooler northern part to the warm region in the south. Maximum and minimum temperatures vary between 30°C–44°C and 4°C–12°C respectively. Annual rainfall is about 4000–5000mm in the northern districts and about 1100–1600mm in the western districts. The average annual rainfall is 1750mm.

Flora and Fauna:
Flora: The forests of West Bengal could be classified under seven categories: tropical semi-evergreen, tropical moist deciduous, tropical dry deciduous, littoral and swampy, subtropical hill forest, eastern Himalayan wet temperate, and alpine.

The Sunderbans, which derives its name from sundari trees, have large numbers of genwa, dhundal, passur, garjan and kankra trees.

Fauna: Wildlife found in the state include Royal Bengal Tiger, elephant, one-horned rhino, sambar, barking deer, spotted deer, hog deer, wild boar, rhesus monkey, mongoose, crocodile, bison, Olive Ridley sea turtle, python, salvator lizard, chequered killback, heron, egret, cormorant, fishing eagle, white-bellied sea eagle, seagull, tern, kingfisher, Eastern knot, curlew, sandpiper, golden plover, pintail, white-eyed pochard and whistling teal.

History

The state gets its name from the ancient kingdom of Vanga, or Banga. Around 3 BC, it formed part of the extensive Mauryan empire. The region was then taken over into the Gupta empire and later came under the rule of the Pala dynasty. From the 13th to the 18th centuries Bengal was under Muslim rule, and came under British control following Robert Clive's conquest over the region in 1757.

In 1773, Warren Hastings, the governor of Bengal, became the first Governor General of Bengal with powers over the Madras and Bombay Presidencies as well. In 1905, Bengal was partitioned into two provinces in spite of violent protests. Continued opposition to the partition led to the reunification of the state in 1911.

At the time of independence, the eastern part of Bengal became East Pakistan (later Bangladesh) and the western part became the Indian state of West Bengal. The princely state of Cooch Behar was integrated with West Bengal in 1950. The state also gained some territory from Bihar after the reorganization of Indian states in 1956.

Politics

After India's independence partition led to two nations—India and Pakistan with two halves—East Pakistan and West Pakistan. Bengal was partitioned again and the western half became the state of West Bengal in the Indian Union. The eastern half of Bengal became East Pakistan and in 1971, became an independent nation—Bangladesh. The state legislature of West Bengal is unicameral and is known as the Vidhan Sabha.

The first Chief Minister of the state of West Bengal, Dr Prafulla Chandra Ghosh was sworn in as the Chief Minister on 14 January 1948 and he resigned on 15 January 1948. Dr Bidhan Chandra Ray (1882–1962) became the new Chief Minister on 23 January 1948. Dr B.C. Ray is credited with the planning and implementation of many of West Bengal's major projects. In 1962, with the death of Dr B.C. Ray, Prafulla Chandra Sen, the food minister, became the Chief Minister and his government lasted till 1967.

During the late sixties and early seventies, widespread poverty and dissatisfaction led to a major political turbulence in the state. The breakdown of infrastructure and resentment against the Delhi-based Congress government led to the strengthening of the Left parties in West Bengal. The Communist Party of India (CPI) was formed in 1920. The party split in 1964 and the Communist Party of India (Marxist) (CPIM) was formed. The United Front, a combination of Left and other parties, came to power in 1967. Ajoy Mukherjee of the Bangla Congress became the new Chief Minister in the UF government. The government was short lived and Dr Prafulla Chandra Ghosh (the first Chief Minister and the food minister in Ajoy Mukherjee's cabinet) formed the Progressive Democratic Front and became the new Chief Minister. In 1969 the United Front returned to power with Ajoy Mukherjee as the Chief Minister for a second time. The second UF government survived till 1971 followed by a Congress coalition with Ajoy Mukherjee remaining the Chief Minister. Congress Party returned to power in 1972 under the leadership of Sidhartha Shankar Ray.

A Leftist movement called the Naxalite movement (named after its birthplace Naxalbari in West Bengal) gathered huge support amongst the frustrated urban youth. The leader of this movement was Charu Chandra Majumder. The uprising was clamped down with a heavy hand leading to widespread middle class resentment. The period of uncertainty, instability and lawlessness led to an economic decline as major companies and business houses shifted their investments and offices from Calcutta to other states. Meanwhile Indira Gandhi imposed a national emergency and censorship on 25 June 1975. However she was forced to withdraw the Emergency and call for national elections in 1977. Mrs Gandhi lost the elections and her party was routed in the general elections. In West Bengal the state elections were won by the Left Front, a coalition of ten parties. The CPI(M) led by Jyoti Basu was the dominant party in the coalition. Jyoti Basu was elected Chief Minister and remained in that position till 2000. The turbulent situation of the seventies slowly improved and from the late eighties the political situation in the state has stabilized. Today West Bengal is one of the few remaining strongholds of the Left parties of India.

In the year 2000, the Left Front completed 24 years of rule under the leadership of Chief Minister Jyoti Basu. Buddhadeb Bhattacharya succeeded Basu as the Chief Minister of West Bengal. The main opposition in the state—the Indian National Congress (INC)—suffered a setback when a former Congress party member and popular leader, Mamata Bannerjee founded her own Trinamool (grassroots) Congress (TMC) Party in 1997. In the 1998 and the 1999 national elections she allied with the Bharatiya Janata Party. It is interesting to note that the BJP (founded in 1980) has its origins in the Bharatiya Jana Sangha which was founded by prominent Bengali leader Dr

Shymaprasad Mukherjee (1901-1953). The 1999 national elections saw the Left maintaining its comfortable lead from the state, followed by the TMC, the INC and the BJP. The TMC won all three seats from Calcutta. In 1999 Calcutta's name was changed to Kolkata by the state legislature and in December 2000, the new name was accepted by the Central government. Just before the 2001 state assembly elections there was a realignment of political parties with the TMC dumping the BJP and joining hands with the INC. The Kolkata media had predicted a tough fight by the TMC - INC alliance and a possibility of the government changing hands. However the Left Front won 199 of the 294 seats and was voted back to power for a record sixth time. Buddhadeb Bhattacharya is the current Chief Minister of the state. After the electoral losses, the TMC broke its alliance with the INC and realigned with the BJP.

Culture

The rich traditions in art and culture in West Bengal are reflected in numerous ways in theatre, folk music, literature, films and paintings. The state has seen many great writers and artists, including the Nobel prize-winning poet Rabindranath Tagore.

Jatra, the hugely popular theatre form, has a range of themes: from mythological to historical to contemporary. Rabindrasangeet, consisting of songs written and composed by Tagore, has a strong influence on Bengali culture. Bengali filmmakers— most notably Satyajit Ray, Tapan Sinha and Mrinal Sen—have also earned worldwide acclaim.

Popular handicrafts include leather craft, brass and bell metal, articles from bamboo and cane, clay dolls, jute products and silver filigree. Handloom saris, notably the Baluchari and Dhakai, are well known.

Fairs and festivals: Important festivals of West Bengal include Durga Puja, Id, Diwali, Rasajatra, Navanna, Christmas, Saraswati Puja, Vasanta Utsav, Holi and Charak. Important fairs include Gangasagar Mela, Kenduli Mela, Jalpesh Mela, Rash Mela and Poush Mela.

Economy, Industry and Agriculture

Economy: The net state domestic product at current prices for 2002–03 (provisional) was Rs 153,781 crores. The per capita net state domestic product at current prices for 2002–03 (provisional) was Rs 18,756.

Minerals and industry: Major industries in the state include chemicals, cotton textiles, coal, iron and steel products, heavy and light Engineering products, leather and footwear, papers, tea, jute products, breweries, drugs and pharmaceuticals, electrical and electronics, plastics, software and infotech, locomotives, vegetable oils, gems and jewellery, poultry products and frozen marine products.

The state is rich in coal deposits located in the districts of Bardhaman and Birbhum. Other mineral deposits include iron ore, manganese, silica, limestone, China clay and dolomite.

Agriculture: Principal crops include rice, food grains, oilseeds, jute, potato, tea, mango, pineapple, banana, papaya, orange, guava and litchi. With an annual production of 58,000 tonnes, floriculture is another important activity.

Power: With an installed capacity of 6877 MW, West Bengal is a power surplus state. It supplies power to its neighbouring states. Most of the state's power comes from thermal power plants, and a small amount from hydroelectric plants.

Education

Educational institutes:
• University of Calcutta, Kolkata
• Jadavpur University, Kolkata
• Visva Bharati, Santiniketan
• Rabindra Bharati University, Kolkata
• Indian Institute of Technology, Kharagpur
• Indian Institute of Management, Kolkata
• Indian Statistical Institute, Kolkata
• Bengal Engineering College, Howrah
• University of Burdwan, Burdwan
• Netaji Subhash Open University, Kolkata
• University of North Bengal, Darjeeling
• Vidyasagar University, Medinipur
• Marine Engineering and Research Institute, Kolkata
• West Bengal University of Animal and Fisheries Sciences, Kolkata.

Tourism

Major tourist attractions:
1. Kolkata and Howrah: Victoria Memorial, Indian Museum, Kalighat Temple, Dakshineswar Kali Temple, Belur Math, Ramakrishna Mission Institute of Culture, St. John's Church, Birla Planetarium, Shahid Minar, Howrah Bridge (Rabindra Setu), Vidyasagar Setu, Science City, Botanical Gardens.
2. Santiniketan.
3. Darjeeling: Tiger Hill, Batasia Loop, Lloyds Botanical Garden.
4. Murshidabad: Nimak Haram Deohri, Khusbagh, Hazarduari, Plassey.
5. Dooars Valley: Jaldapara, Buxa Tiger Project, Gorumara and Chapramari Wildlife Sanctuaries.
6. Kalimpong: Dr Graham's Homes, Durpin Dara, Kalibari, Thongsha Gumpha, Tharpa Choling Monastery.

7. Vishnupur: Rasmancha, Pancha Ratna Temple, Jorebangla Temple.

8. Siliguri.

9. Beaches: Digha, Shankarpur, Junput, Bakkhali, Sagardwip.

Airports:
International: Kolkata.

Domestic: Bagdogra.
National Parks:
• Neora Valley National Park (Darjeeling)—88.00 sq. km
• Singalila National Park (Darjeeling)—78.60 sq. km
• Sunderbans Tiger Reserve (South 24 Paraganas)—1330.10 sq. km
• Buxa Tiger Reserve (Jalpaiguri)—117.10 sq. km
• Gorumara National Park (Jalpaiguri)—79.45 sq. km.

Administration

Legislature: The unicameral West Bengal legislature comprises 294 elected seats, of which 59 are reserved for SCs and 17 for STs. One member can be nominated by the governor to represent the Anglo-Indian community. The term of the current house expires on 13 June 2006. The present party-wise break-up is as follows:

Name of Party	Seats
Communist Party of India (Marxist)	143
All India Trinamool Congress	60
Indian National Congress	26
All India Forward Bloc	25
Revolutionary Socialist Party	17
Communist Party of India	7
West Bengal Socialist Party	4
Gorakha National Liberation Front	3
Independent	9
Total	**294**

Judiciary: The Calcutta High Court is the seat of judiciary. The present chief justice is V.S. Sirpurkar.

Districts:

District	Area (sq. km)	Population	Headquarters	Urban Agglomerations
Bankura	6,882.0	3,191,822	Bankura	
Bardhaman	7,024.0	6,919,698	Bardhaman	Asansol, Kalna, Katwa
Birbhum	4,545.0	3,012,546	Suri	
Cooch Behar	3,387.0	2,478,280	Cooch Behar	Dinhata, Cooch Behar
Darjeeling	3,149.0	1,605,900	Darjeeling	Darjeeling
East Midnapore	NA	NA	NA	NA
Hooghly	3,149.0	5,040,047	Chinsurah	Kolkata
Howrah	1,467.0	4,274,010	Howrah	Kolkata
Jalpaiguri	6,227.0	3,403,204	Jalpaiguri	Alipurduar
Kolkata	185.0	4,580,544	Kolkata	Kolkata
Maldah	3,733.0	3,290,160	English Bazar	English Bazar
Murshidabad	5,324.0	5,863,717	Behrampore	Behrampore
Nadia	3,927.0	4,603,756	Krishnanagar	Birnagar, Chakdaha, Kolkata, Krishnanagar, Nabadwip, Ranaghat
North Twenty Four Parganas	4,094.0	8,930,295	Barasat	Gobardanga, Habra, Kolkata
North Dinajpur	3,140.0	2,478,280	Raiganj	Raiganj
Puruliya	6,259.0	2,535,233	Puruliya	
South Twenty Four Parganas	9,960.0	6,909,015	Alipur	Kolkata
South Dinajpur	2,219.0	1,502,647	Balurghat	Balurghat, Jaynagar-Mazilpur
West Midnapore	NA	NA	NA	NA

NATIONAL CAPITAL
TERRITORY

Delhi

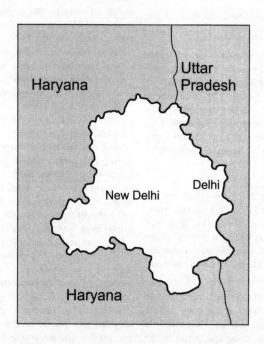

Key Statistics

Capital: Delhi.
Area: 1483 sq. km.
Population: Total: 13,850,507
Male: 7,607,234
Female: 6,243,273
Population density: 9294 per sq. km.
Sex ratio: 821 females per 1000
  males
Principal languages: Hindi, Punjabi,
  Urdu.
Literacy rates: Total: 81.7%
Male: 87.3%
Female: 74.7%

Government

Lt Governor: Banwari Lal Joshi. He
was sworn in as Lt Governor on 9 June
2004.

Chief Minister: Sheila Dikshit (INC).
She was sworn in on 15 December
2003.

Geography

Physical characteristics: Delhi, the
National Capital Territory of India, is
divided into two zones: the extension
of the Aravali Hills and the plains. Alti-

tudes vary between 200 to 300 metres.

Neighbouring States and Union territories:
States:
• Haryana
• Uttar Pradesh

Major rivers: Yamuna.

Climate: Delhi witnesses hot summers characterized by extreme dryness, with maximum temperatures going up to 46°C. Cold waves from the north make winters in Delhi very chilly, with minimum temperatures of around 4°C. Winters also witness thick fog on some mornings. Rainfall varies between 400–600mm.

Flora and Fauna:
Flora: Forest and tree cover constitutes about 151 sq. km of the area. The Ridge, with trees like dhak and amaltas, is classified as a tropical thorn forest. Delhi is also known for numerous flowering plants, mainly chrysanthemums, verbenas, violas, and phlox.

Fauna: The Indira Priyadarshini Wildlife Sanctuary at Asola is the main habitat for most animal species. These include nilgai, common mongoose, small Indian civet, porcupine, rufus tailed hare and monitor lizards. There's also a variety of birds including cormorants, egrets, grebes, falcons, partridges, quail, peafowl, waterhens, lapwings, sandpipers, woodpeckers, doves, parakeets, cuckoos, owls, nightjars, barbets, swallows, shrikes, orioles, drongos, mynahs, flycatchers, warblers, babblers, wagtails, pipits and buntings.

History

The earliest historical reference to Delhi date back to the first century BC, when Raja Dhilu built a city near the site of present-day Qutab Minar

and named it after himself. Around AD 12, the city became the capital of Prithviraj Chauhan and passed into Muslim rule by the end of that century. It became the capital of Qutab-ud-din Aibak. The city was then ruled by the Khaljis followed by the Tughluqs. Babur established Mughal rule in India in 1526 with Delhi as the seat of his empire.

Mughal emperors Akbar and Jahangir moved their headquarters to Fatehpur Sikri and Agra respectively, but the city was restored to its former glory in 1638, when Shah Jahan laid the foundations of Shahjahanabad, which is now known as Old Delhi.

After the fall of the Mughal Empire during the mid-18th century, Delhi faced many raids by the Marathas and an invasion by Nadir Shah before the British rise to prominence in 1803. In 1912 the British moved the capital of British India from Calcutta to Delhi.

After independence, Delhi remained a chief commissioner's province till 1956, when it was converted into a Union territory. The chief commissioner was replaced by a Lt Governor.

In 1991, the National Capital Territory Act was passed by the Parliament and the elected government was given wider powers.

Delhi was divided into nine revenue districts in 1997.

Politics

After Independence, Delhi was given the status of a Part-C state. The Delhi State Legislative Assembly came into being on 7 March 1952 under the Government of India Part-C States Act, 1951. In 1951 Indian National Congress won 39 seats out of a total of 42 in the first Delhi Legislative Assembly. Bharatiya Jan Sangh, the earlier avatar of BJP had secured five seats. The 1952 Assembly consisted of 48 members. There was a provision for a council of Ministers to aid and advise the Chief Commissioner in the exercise of his functions in relation to matters in respect of which the state Assembly was given powers to make laws. The first Council of Ministers was headed by Ch. Braham Prakash. However, legislative powers granted to Part-C states were limited and the legislative powers of Delhi Assembly had been further curtailed as is evident from the proviso to Section 21 of the Part C States Act, 1951. In pursuance of the recommendations of the State Reorganisation Commission (1955), Delhi ceased to be a Part-C state with effect from 1 November 1956. The Delhi Legislative Assembly and the Council of Ministers were abolished and Delhi became a Union Territory under the direct administration of the President. In accordance with another recommendation of the Commission, the Delhi Municipal Corporation Act, 1957 was enacted constituting a Municipal Corporation for the whole of Delhi with members elected on the basis of adult franchise. There was considerable pressure of public opinion for providing a democratic set up and a responsive administration for Delhi. In partial fulfilment of this demand and on the basis of recommendations of Administrative Reforms Commission, the Delhi Administration Act, 1960 was enacted. The Act provided for a deliberative body called Metropolitan Council having recommendatory powers. At the top, there was the Lt. Governor or Administrator who was appointed by the President of India under Article 239 of the Constitution. The Metropolitan Council was a unicameral democratic body consisting of 61 members—56 elected and 5 nominated by the President. The Metropolitan Council set-up suffered from many inherent deficiencies. It had no legislative powers and it had only an advisory role in the governance of Delhi. There was, therefore, a continuous demand for a ful-fledged state Assembly with Council of Ministers to aid and advice the Lt. Governor.

Accordingly, on 24 December 1987, the Government of India appointed the Sarkaria Committee (later on called Balakrishan Committee) to go into the various issues connected with the administration of the Union Territory of Delhi and to recommend measures for streamlining the administrative set up. The Committee submitted its report on 14 December 1989. After detailed enquiries and examinations, it recommended that Delhi should continue to be a Union Territory but should be provided with a Legislative Assembly and a Council of Ministers responsible to such an Assembly with appropriate powers to deal with matters of concern to the common man. The Committee also recommended that with a view to ensuring stability and permanence, the arrangements should be incorporated in the Constitution to give the National Capital a special status among the Union Territories. Delhi was granted a special statehood and an elected legislative assembly in 1991 under the 69th Constitutional amendment. Delhi is headed by a Lieutenant Governor nominated by the President of India and is administered by a Chief Minister appointed from the elected party. The Legislative Assembly of Delhi has powers to make laws in respect of all the 68 matters in the State list excepting public sector, police and land. The annual budget is laid before the Legislative Assembly by the Lt. Governor with the previous sanction of the President as this is mandatory under article 239 (1) of the Constitution according to which the President is responsible for the administration of every Union Territory. Additional demand for expenditure upon the consolidated fund of the Capital is made on the recommendation of the Lt. Governor.

In 1993, BJP wrested the state from the Congress in a big way securing 49 of the 70 seats while Congress got just 14. Four seats went to Janata Dal while Independents bagged three seats. The veteran BJP leader Madanlal Khurana became the Chief Minister. Sahib Singh Verma replaced him after a few years following intense infighting. Finally, just months before the 1998 poll the high profile Union Minister Sushma Swaraj was brought in as the Chief Minister. The ruling BJP led by Sushma Swaraj was routed in the polls bagging just 15 seats while the Congress walked away with 52 seats. One seat was won by Janata Dal while two seats went to Independents. The credit for the Congress victory went to its Delhi chief Sheila Dikshit, who eventually became the Chief Minister. In the state Assembly Elections held in 2003 the Congress became victorious once more and again Sheila Dikshit became the Chief Minister of the National Capital Territory of Delhi.

Culture

Migrations from various parts of India has led to pockets of diverse culture coming together in Delhi. Many of the country's prominent cultural institutions are located in Delhi. Popular handicrafts include zari zardozi, stone carving, paper craft and papier mache, and metal engraving.

Fairs and festivals: Major festivals and fairs include Holi, Dussehra, Lohri, Deepawali, Qutub festival, Phoolwalon Ki Sair, Roshnara and Shalimar Bagh festivals, and Mango festival.

Economy, Industry and Agriculture

Economy: The net state domestic product at current prices in 2002–03 (provisional) was Rs 68,747 crores. The per capita state domestic product at current prices in 2002–03 (provisional) was Rs 47,477.

Minerals and industry: Delhi is the largest centre of small industries in India. These manufacture a wide variety of goods like plastic and PVC goods, sports goods, radio and TV parts, razor blades, textiles, chemicals, fertilizers, soft drinks, and hand and machine tools. The new industrial policy focuses on areas like electronics, telecommunications, software and IT-enabled services.

Agriculture: The main crops are wheat, jawar, bajra and paddy. Vegetable cultivation, floriculture and mushroom cultivation are also important activities. The main livestock products are milk, eggs and meat.

Power: Delhi's own resources amount to an installed capacity of about 1000 MW, all of which come from thermal power plants. The balance of the power demand, which exceeds 3000 MW, is met by purchases from NTPC and other sources.

Education

Educational institutes:
• All India Institute of Medical Sciences
• University of Delhi
• Indian Agricultural Research Institute
• Indian Institute of Technology, Delhi
• Indira Gandhi National Open University
• Jamia Millia Islamia
• Jawaharlal Nehru University

- School of Planning and Architecture
- Shri Lal Bahadur Shastri Rashtriya Sanskrit Vidyapeetha
- TERI School of Advanced Study
- Indian Institute of Foreign Trade

Tourism

Major tourist attractions: Red Fort, Puarana Qila, Qutab Minar (World Heritage Site), India Gate, Bahai's House Of Worship, Rashtrapati Bhavan, Rajghat, Humayun's Tomb (World Heritage Site), Parliament House, Jama Masjid, Jantar Mantar, Firoz Shah Kotla, Safdurjung's Tomb, Dilli Haat, Mughal Gardens, Lodi Gardens, National Museum.

Airports:
International: Indira Gandhi International Airport.
Domestic:
- Palam Airport
- Safdarjung Airport.

National Parks: None.

Administration

Legislature: Two acts passed by the Parliament have been instrumental in providing for a legislative assembly for Delhi and supplementing the provisions relating to it: the Constitution (69th Amendment) Act, 1991; and the Government of National Capital Territory of Delhi Act, 1991.

The Delhi Legislative Assembly has 70 members, all chosen by direct election from as many constituencies, of which 13 are reserved for SCs. The term of the present house ends on 17 December 2008. Party position in the present assembly is as follows:

Name of Party	Seats
Indian National Congress	47
Bharatiya Janata Party	20
Nationalist Congress Party	1
Janata Dal (Secular)	1
Independent	1
Total	**70**

Judiciary: The Delhi High Court was established in 1966. The present chief justice is B.C. Patel.

Districts:

District	Area (sq. km)	Population
Central	25	644,005
East	64	1,448,770
New Delhi	35	171,806
North	60	779,788
North East	60	1,763,712
North West	440	2,847,395
South	250	2,258,367
South West	420	1,749,492
West	129	2,119,641

UNION TERRITORIES

Andaman and Nicobar Islands

Key Statistics

Capital: Port Blair.
Area: 8,249 sq. km.
Population: Total: 356,152
Male: 192,972
Female: 163,180
Population density: 43 per sq. km.
Sex ratio: 846 females per 1000 males.

Principal languages: Bengali, Tamil, Hindi.
Literacy rates: Total: 81.3%
Male: 86.3%
Female: 75.2%

Government

Lieutenant Governor: Prof. Ramchandra Ganesh Kapse. He was sworn in on 5 January 2004.

Geography

Physical characteristics: The Andaman and Nicobar Islands lie along an arc in a long broken chain, approximately north–south over a distance of about 800km.

The Andamans are a group of more than 300 islands and islets, of which only 26 are inhabited. The three main islands, namely North, Middle and South Andaman, are collectively known as Great Andaman, since they are closely positioned. The Andaman Islands have a rough landscape, with hills enclosing its longitudinal, narrow valleys. The islands are covered by dense tropical forests. The deeply indented coral-fringed coasts form tidal creeks and harbours, which are surrounded by mangrove swamps. Saddle Peak (737m) is the highest in the Andaman Islands. About 135 km from Port Blair is Barran Island, India's only active volcano.

The Nicobar Islands consist of a group of islands, of which 12 are inhabited and seven are uninhabited. The uninhabited islands in the central and southern group are Battimay, Tileangchong and Merore, Trak, Treis, Menchal and Kabna respectively. Inhabited islands include Kamorta and Nancowry, which form the central group; Car Nicobar, which belongs to the northern group; and Great Nicobar, the largest and the southernmost of all. Undulating landscapes and intervening valleys characterize the physiography of these islands. However, Car Nicobar and Trinket are flat islands.

The Great Nicobar is hilly, and contains many fast-flowing streams. A few of the other islands have flat surfaces covered with coral. Great Nicobar rises to a height of 642m. It is isolated from the Nicobars and the Nancowries group by the Sombero channel.

The Ten Degree Channel (145 km wide) separates the Andamans from the Nicobars. The principal harbours in Andaman and Nicobar are Port Blair, Neil, Diglipur, Mayabandar and Rangat in the Andamans and Car Nicobar and Kamorta in the Nicobars. The Union Territory has a total of 572 islands and islets. To the extreme south of the Nicobars is Indira Point, the southernmost point of India.

Neighbouring States and Union territories: The Andaman and Nicobar Islands have no neighbouring states or union territories. They lie on the south-eastern margins of the Bay of Bengal. Port Blair is connected to Kolkata and Chennai by air as well as by sea routes.

Major rivers:
• Alexendra
• Dagmar
• Galathea rivers (Great Nicobar)
• Kalpong (North Andaman) are the perennial freshwater rivers in these islands.

Climate: The Andaman and Nicobar Islands enjoy warm, moist and tropical climate. The abundant rainfall and the presence of the sea prevent the islands from experiencing extremes of heat, though the amount of rainfall may vary from island to island. Humidity is high, and varies from 66 per cent to 85 per cent. The temperature ranges from 18°C to 34°C. The islands receive an average annual rainfall of about 3000mm from southwest and northeast monsoons, extending over a period of about eight months.

A reporting station was set up at Port Blair in 1868, in order to provide accurate meteorological data for shipping in the Bay of Bengal.

Flora and Fauna:
Flora: The Andaman and Nicobar Isalnds are covered with evergreen

tropical rainforests containing some 2200 varieties of plants. Out of these, 200 are endemic and 1300 cannot be found in mainland India. North Andamans have wet evergreen forests that contain plenty of woody climbers. South Andaman forests have a luxuriant growth of orchids, ferns and other epiphytic vegetation, while the Middle Andamans mostly contain deciduous forests.

Evergreen forests are absent in north Nicobar, including Battimaly and Car Nicobar, but form the dominant vegetation in central and southern Nicobar. Grasslands, not found in the Andamans, are present in the Nicobar group, whereas deciduous forests common in Andamans, can hardly be found in the Nicobars.

This uncharacteristic forest coverage consists of different types, including the giant evergreen forest, the southern hilltop tropical evergreen forest, the wet bamboo brakes, the Andaman tropical evergreen forest, the Andaman semi-evergreen forests and the cane brakes.

Andaman forest is abundant in timber of more than 200 species. Of these, 30 varieties are considered to be commercial. Major commercial varieties are padauk (*Pterocarpus dalbergioides*), and gurjan. There are a few kinds of ornamental wood noted for their pronounced grain formation. These include silver grey, kokko, padauk, chooi and marble wood.

Fauna: The Andaman and Nicobar Islands have a rich variety of animal species. These include about 50 varieties of forest mammals, most of which have been brought in from outside. Rats constitute the largest group of animals (26 species), followed by 14 species of bat. The larger mammals include two endemic varieties of wild

pig, the spotted deer, sambar, barking deer and elephants.

Other than mammals, there are more than 225 species of moths and butterflies in the Andaman and Nicobar islands. Shells, corals and fishes are also found in abundance.

History

The Andaman and Nicobar islands have been the home of aboriginals since prehistoric times. According to a British Survey conducted here in 1777, Negritos and Mongoloids occupied the Islands for many centuries, till people from outside arrived.

The history of these islands can be divided into four broad periods: British intrusion and settlement, the Japanese regime, and the post-independence period. In 1788, the Governor General of India, Lord Cornwallis, according to the recommendation of two of his navy officers, founded the British settlement in 1789 on Chatham Island near Port Cornwallis (which is now Port Blair, named after Lt. Reginald Blair who conducted a survey of the area in 1789).

After the Revolt of 1857, the British government wanted to establish a penal settlement here, which they did in 1858. Two hundred prisoners, mostly rebels from the Indian Army, were kept in a jail at Viper island, which had a jail, gallows, and areas for residence. This jail was later abandoned in favour of the Cellular Jail built at Port Blair in 1906.

During the Second World War, the Japanese occupied Andamans on 21 March 1942 and kept the region under their control till 1945. Many innocent people were killed by the Japanese, including the massacre at Humfreygunj. The Japanese occupation however made the Andamans self-sufficient, in terms of food production. On 30 December 1943, Subhash Chandra Bose hoisted the National Flag at Port Blair, making it the first instance during British rule in India. The Japanese finally surrendered to the South East Asia Command at Port Blair on 8 October 1945.

The Andaman and Nicobar Islands together with the rest of India became independent on 15 August 1947.

Culture

Two distinct native cultures dominate the Andaman and Nicobar Islands. One is that of the Negrito population, and the other is of the Mongoloid Nicobarese and Shompen. Both before and after independence, these cultures retained their separate identities.

The Onges of Negrito origin form the main aboriginal group in the Andamans. Their main occupations include honey collecting, fishing and food gathering and hunting. They are the only tribe who accept contact with people from outside the islands. Till 1998, the Jarwas remained hostile but now they voluntarily seek medical assistance.

In the Nicobars, the Shompens are the only aboriginals. They are averse to contact with people from outside the island. The largest group, the Nicobarese are probably a mixture of Malay, Mon, Shan and Burmese origins. They still engage in the barter system.

Fairs and Festivals: The noteworthy fairs and festivals in these islands include the Island Tourism Festival, Subhash Mela (organized to commemorate the birth anniversary of Subhash Chandra Bose) and Vivekananda Mela. Festivals like Panguni Uthiram and Pongal for the Tamils, Durga Puja for the Bengalis, and Onam for the Malayalis are also celebrated.

Economy, Agriculture and Industry

Economy: The net state domestic product at current prices for 2000–01 (new series) was Rs 872 crores (provisional). The per capita net state domestic product at current prices for 2000–01 (new series) was Rs 24,560 (provisional).

Minerals and industry: The main industry is fisheries which, the Union territory occupying a coastline of 1912 km, has potential for further development. More than 1100 species of fish are identified in these islands of which about 30 species are commercially exploited at present. The estimated annual exploited stock is around 1.6 lakh tonnes, while the level of exploitation is only 26,000 tonnes. Fish culture, fish processing and other industries like fish meal, fish pickling, and fish oil are encouraged.

Another important industry is tourism, with the islands coming up as major tourist attractions. This also generates large employment. The other industries include production of cane, bamboo, coir, coconut and rubber. Industries like boat building, automobile body building, electronics and packaging are also coming up. The mineral wealth is negligible.

Agriculture: Paddy is the main food crop of the Andaman Islands. About 50,000 hectares of land is cultivated. Areca nut and coconut are the main cash crops of the Nicobar group of islands. Fruits such as sapota, pineapple, mango, papaya, orange and root crops are also grown in these islands. Coffee, rubber and tapioca are also important. About 7,171 sq. km of the total area is under forest cover.

Power: Presently, diesel power generation meets the requirements of commercial and household establishments in the territory.

Education

Educational institutes: The Andaman and Nicobar Islands has a few colleges affiliated to the Pondicherry University, and two polytechnics—the Dr B.R. Ambedkar Government Polytechnic at Port Blair, and the Second Government Polytechnic at Port Blair.

Tourism

Major tourist attractions:
1. Andaman: Long Island, Neil Island, Mayabander, Rangat, Diglipur, Little Andaman Island, Cellular Jail, Sippighat Farm, National Memorial Museum, Ross Island, Andaman Water Sports Complex.
2. Nicobar: Car Nicobar, Katchal, Great Nicobar. Scuba-diving and snorkelling are added attractions here.

Airports:
• Port Blair
• Car Nicobar.

National Parks:
 Andaman district:
• Mahatma Gandhi Marine National Park (281.50 sq. km)
• Rani Jhansi Marine National Park (256.14 sq. km)
• Middle Button Island National Park (0.64 sq. km)
• Mount Harriet National Park (0.46 sq. km)
• North Button Island National Park (0.44 sq. km)
• Saddle Peak National Park (32.54 sq. km)
• South Button Island National Park (0.03 sq. km).
 Nicobar district:
• Campbell Bay National Park (426.23 sq. km)
• Galathea National Park (110.00 sq. km).

Administration

Legislature: The territory is administered by a lieutenant governor, appointed by the President of India.

Judiciary: The Union territory of Andaman and Nicobar Islands is under the jurisdiction of the Calcutta High Court. The chief justice of the Calcutta High Court is V.S. Sirpurkar.

Districts:

District	Area (sq. km)	Population	Headquarters	Urban Agglomerations
Andaman	6,408	314,239	Port Blair	–
Nicobar	1,841	42,026	Car Nicobar	–

Chandigarh

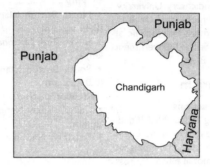

Key Statistics

Capital: Chandigarh.

Area: 114 sq. km.

Population: Total: 900,635
Male: 506,938
Female: 393,697

Population density: 7,902 per sq. km.

Sex ratio: 777 females per 1000 males.

Principal languages: Hindi, Punjabi, Tamil.

Literacy rates: Total: 81.9%
Male: 86.1%
Female: 76.5%

Government

Administrator: Gen. (Retd) S.F. Rodrigues. He was sworn in on 16 November 2004.

Geography

Physical characteristics: Situated at the foot of the Shivalik Range, Chandigarh lies on the Indo-Gangetic plain. The Union territory is positioned between two seasonal hill torrents: the Patiali Rao and the Sukhna Choe.

The city of Chandigarh (area 56 sq. km) covers about half of the land area of the territory. It has the distinction of being the first planned city of independent India. The city, built in 47 rectangular sectors, has a modern infrastructure. No sector was given the unlucky number '13'. Every sector consists of shopping centres and marketplaces, and the sectors are interconnected by buses and auto-rickshaws. Most of the important government buildings are in Sector 1, in the northern part of the city, whereas the industrial areas are mainly located in the south-east.

Neighbouring States and Union territories:
States:
• Haryana
• Punjab.

Major rivers: There are no major rivers.

Climate: Chandigarh has hot summers and cold winters. During summer, the maximum temperature goes up to 44°C, the temperature range being 37°C–44°C. In winter, the temperature is generally within 4°C–14°C. Chandigarh sees monsoon from July to September, with an average annual rainfall of 1110mm.

Flora and Fauna: The Union territory of Chandigarh has 3,245 hectares under forest area. These forest areas are mostly situated around Patiala ki Rao, Sukhna Choe and Sukhna Lake. On the outskirts of Chandigarh towards the hills, next to the village of Kansal, is a reserve forest. Another reserve forest, known as Nepli, is located at a short distance from Kansal forest, and has a variety of wild life including hyena, antelopes, jackals, nilgais, and hares.

History

After India attained independence in 1947, the province of Punjab was divided and its capital Lahore fell within the Pakistani borders. As a result, the Indian state of Punjab was left without a capital and the need to construct a new capital city was felt. In March 1948, a 114.59 sq. km tract of land at the foot of the Shivalik Hills was approved for the purpose. The chosen site was a tract of agricultural land marking the sites of 24 villages—one of which was called 'Chandigarh' since it had a temple dedicated to the goddess Chandi. The chosen site got its name from that village.

American town planner Albert Mayer was initially approached by the Government of Punjab to create the new capital. Though he showed a lot of initial interest and also conceived a master plan for the city, he could not continue with the project due to the death of Matthew Nowicki, an architect who was involved with Mayer in the execution of the plan. In 1950, renowned French architect Le Corbusier was selected to replace Mayer, which he successfully did, giving India its first 'planned' city. Other than Corbusier, the work was carried out by three other foreign architects—Maxwell Fry, his wife Jane Drew and Corbusier's cousin Pierre Jeanneret.

On 21 September 1953, the capital of Punjab was officially shifted to Chandigarh from Shimla, and President Dr Rajendra Prasad inaugurated the city on 7 October 1953. When Punjab was again divided in 1966, leading to the creation of Haryana, Chandigarh became the capital of both Punjab and Haryana. However, the city became a Union territory, administered by the Government of India, and Mani Majra town and some villages of Kharar tehsil of Ambala district were added to the city.

Culture

The city of Chandigarh has a cosmopolitan character. It is home to many painters and writers, and houses frequently held exhibitions and performances by musicians, dancers, singers and actors. The city also has many associations and halls devoted to the culture of other states. Numerous institutions in the city offer instruction in classical, folk and instrumental music. Chandigarh also has several noted potters, sculptors, photographers and graphic designers. Street theatre is quite popular in Chandigarh, and there are many active groups in the realm of theatre.

Fairs and festivals: Other than the traditional religious festivals, Chandigarh celebrates several unique festivals. The Festival of Gardens (initially called the Rose Festival) is one of the main cultural events in Chandigarh and attracts thousands of visitors. On April Fools' Day, poets from all over the country gather to take part in the 'Maha Moorkh Sammelan'. The other popular festivals are Baisakhi, the Mango Festival, Indo-Pak Mushaira, Teej, the Plaza Carnival, the Chrysanthemum Show and the Chandigarh Carnival.

Economy, Industry and Agriculture

Economy: The net state domestic product at current prices for 2001–02 was Rs 935 crores. The per capita net state domestic product at current prices for 2002–03 was Rs 52,795.

Minerals and industry: Chandigarh has about 15 medium and large-scale industrial units. These units mainly manufacture steel and wooden furniture, antibiotics, electric meters, electronic components and equipment, machine tools, soaps and detergents, biomedical equipment, tractor parts, cement pipes and tiles, washing machines, sports goods, plastic goods etc. These units employ close to 30,000 people. There are also about 20 major exporting units. The mineral wealth is negligible.

Agriculture: The agricultural produce in Chandigarh includes crops like wheat, maize and rice. Fruits like lemon, litchi, mango, orange, guava, pear, plum, grape and peach are also cultivated.

Power: In order to meet its power requirement, Chandigarh gets power from Central generation projects and neighbouring states.

Education

Educational institutes:
• Punjab University

• Post Graduate Institute of Medical Education and Research
• The Government Medical College
• Punjab Engineering College
• Chandigarh College of Architecture
• The Government College of Art
• Chandigarh College of Engineering and Polytechnic (The Central Polytechnic College)
• The Government Polytechnic for Women
• Industrial Training Institute
• The Government Central Crafts Institute for Women and the Food Craft Institute

Tourism

Major tourist attractions: Government Museum and Art Gallery, Museum of the Evolution of Life, International Dolls Museum, Punjab Kala Kendra, The Rock Garden, Sukhna Lake, Zakir Rose Garden, Leisure Valley.

Airports: Chandigarh.

National Parks: There are no national parks. The Sukhna Lake Wildlife Sanctuary was established in 1986 and has an area of 25.42 sq. km.

Administration

Legislature: Chandigarh has no legislature; instead, it is administered by an administrator appointed by the President of India (under the provisions of Article 239 of the Constitution). The Parliament is directly responsible for legislating for Chandigarh, and administrative control of the Union territory rests with the Union ministry of home affairs. Regarding policy matters concerning Chandigarh, the ministry receives advice from a committee constituted by the Union home minister.

Judiciary: The High Court of Punjab and Haryana is at Chandigarh. The chief justice is D.K. Jain.

Districts:

District	Area (sq. km)	Population	Headquarters	Urban Agglomerations
Chandigarh	114	900,635	Chandigarh	Chandigarh

Dadra and Nagar Haveli

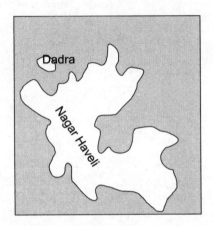

Key Statistics

Capital: Silvassa.
Area: 491 sq. km.
Population: Total: 220,490
Male: 121,666
Female: 98,824.
Population density: 449 per sq. km.
Sex ratio: 812 females per 1000 males.
Principal languages: Gujarati, Hindi, Konkani.
Literacy rates: Total: 57.6%
Male: 71.2%
Female: 40.2%.

Government

Administrator: Arun Mathur.

Geography

Physical characteristics: Reaching elevations of about 305m in the northeast and east near the Western Ghats, the territory of Dadra and Nagar Haveli is hilly and undulating. The lowland areas are generally restricted to the central plains.

Neighbouring States and Union territories:
States:
• Maharashtra
• Gujarat.

Union territories: Daman and Diu.

Major rivers: The Damanganga is the only navigable river in Dadra and Nagar Haveli. It flows through the territory towards Daman in the north-west.

Climate: From November to March, the climate is very pleasant in Dadra and Nagar Haveli. The region otherwise experiences hot summers with the average maximum temperature in May approaching 34°C. Most of the rainfall takes place between June and September, averaging about 3000mm annually.

Flora and Fauna:

Flora: Around 40 per cent of the total geographical area spread over 58 villages is covered with forests. Teak, khair, sisam, sadra and mahara constitute the main vegetation of the territory, of which teak and khair are the most predominant. Teak is the main source of timber, whereas a forest-based industry producing 'Katha' from khair wood helps the local economy.

History

The recorded history of Dadra and Nagar Haveli starts from the medieval period. A Rajput invader became the ruler of a small state called Ramnagar (which included Nagar Haveli in its territory) in AD 1262, by defeating the Koli chieftains of the area. The region continued to remain under Rajput rule till the mid-18th century, when it was conquered by the Marathas. In 1783, Nagar Haveli was ceded to the Portuguese, as compensation for a Portuguese vessel that the Maratha navy had destroyed. In 1785, Dadra was also acquired by the Portuguese. After the independence of India, Goan nationalists tried to break away from Portuguese control, and their first success was the possession of Dadra on 21 July 1954. Two weeks later, they also captured Nagar Haveli, and a pro-Indian administration was formed in Dadra and Nagar Haveli. On 1 June 1961, the administration requested accession to the Indian Union, and the government of India that had already acknowledged their induction to the union from the day of liberation, made it official on 11 August 1961.

Culture

The Dhol dance (incorporating aerobatics and rhythm), the Gheria dance of the Dubla tribe, the Mask dance or Bhavada, the Bohada mask dance performed by the Koknas and the human pyramid formations by the Tur dancers are some of the prominent dance forms.

Fairs and festivals: The Union territory of Dadra and Nagar Haveli normally celebrates all festivals of Hindus, Muslims and Christians, while the tribal communities celebrate their own festivals. The Dhodia and Varli tribes celebrate Diwaso, while the Dhodia tribe also celebrates Raksha Bandhan. The 'Gram Devi' and 'Khali Puja' are celebrated by all tribes before and after harvest respectively.

Economy, Industry and Agriculture

Economy: The net state domestic product at current prices is not available.

Minerals and industry: There was no industry in Dadra and Nagar Haveli before 1965–66, except for a few traditional craftsmen who made pots, leather items and some other items made of bamboo. It was only between 1967–68 that industrial development started on a low-key basis. An industrial estate was established under the cooperative sector by Dan Udyog Sahakari Sangh Ltd, after which three Government Industrial Estates were developed at Masat, Silvassa and Khadoli. As on March 2003, there were 1617 industries in the region including cottage, village and small scale industries, and 406 medium scale industries in engineering, textiles, electronics, pharmaceuticals and plastics.

Agriculture: Dadra and Nagar Haveli is mainly rural, with 79 per cent of its population consisting of tribals. There are about 22,850 hectares of area under cultivation. Paddy, small millets, pulses and ragi are the main crops, and the agricultural production is mainly dependent on rain, and mostly on a single crop system. Other than the main crops, additional crops like wheat, jowar, tuvr, sugar cane and oilseeds are also cultivated. Among vegetables, cauliflower, brinjal, tomato, and cabbage are grown. The tribals have been given exclusive rights for collection of minor forest produce for free, since they depend mainly on forests.

Power: The Central sector power generating stations located in the western region handle the power requirement of the territory.

Education

Educational institutes:
• Lions English School
• Prabhat Scholar's Academy

Tourism

Major tourist attractions: Khanvel; The Tribal Cultural Museum, Silvassa; Vanganga Lake.

Airports: None.

National Parks: There are no National Parks in Dadra and Nagar Haveli, and there is only one wildlife sanctuary—the Dadra and Nagar Haveli Wildlife Sanctuary. It has an area of 92.16 sq. km and is located in the Dadra and Nagar Haveli district.

Administration

Legislature: An administrator, appointed by the Government of India, heads the Union territory.

Judiciary: Dadra and Nagar Haveli comes under the jurisdiction of the Bombay High Court. The chief justice of the Bombay High Court is Dalveer Bhandari.

Districts: There is only one district, which is Dadra and Nagar Haveli.

District	Area (sq. km)	Population	Headquarters	Urban Agglomerations
Dadra and Nagar Haveli	491	220,490	Silvassa	–

Daman and Diu

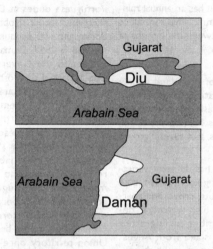

Key Statistics

Capital: Daman.
Area: 112 sq. km.
Population: Total: 158,204
Male: 92,512
Female: 65,692
Population density: 1411 per sq. km.
Sex ratio: 710 females per 1000
males.
Principal languages: Gujarati, Hindi,
Marathi.
Literacy rates: Total: 78.2%
Male: 86.8%
Female: 65.6%

Government

Administrator: Arun Mathur.

Geography

Physical characteristics: Daman is
situated on an alluvial coastal plain, even
though headlands and low plateaus are
created in the area due to outcrops of
basalt. The area surrounding the town
of Daman is traversed by River
Damanganga which flows through the
territory. A marshy creek separates the
island of Diu from the Kathiawar Peninsula in Gujarat, though the territory of
Diu also encompasses a small part of
the mainland. The island is about 11
km long and 2 km wide.

**Neighbouring States and Union
territories:**
States:
• Gujarat
• Maharashtra.

Union territories: Dadra and Nagar
Haveli.

Major rivers:
• Damanganga
• Kalai
• Kolak.

Climate: In Daman, the average daily maximum temperatures range from 29°C in January to 34°C in May, which is quite similar to that of Diu. However, Daman receives more rainfall than Diu; it averages 2000mm annually in Daman whereas Diu has an annual rainfall of about 585mm. The rainfall is mainly received between the months of June and September.

Flora and Fauna:

Flora: The flora of the island mainly consists of vegetation ranging from fuliflora, tortolis, acasias, palm trees (locally referred to as hokka), casuarina, equistifolia, procofis, and several groves of coconut palms.

Fauna: The island has different varieties of birds, including koels, doves, blue rock pigeons, parrots, crows and sparrows, making it a bird watchers' delight. A large number of migratory birds fly into the island from August and stay on until February, which constitutes a major attraction. The inland and the coastal waters are rich in fishes, especially hilsa, Bombay duck, shark, dara, prawns, and the popular pomfret.

History

The town of Daman possibly gets its name from the Damanganga River, whereas 'Diu' is derived from the Sanskrit word 'dvipa', which means 'island'. Daman, in the 13th century, formed part of the state of Ramnagar, which then became a tributary of the sultans of Gujarat. Diu was taken over by the sultan of Gujarat in the 15th century, which until then had been ruled over by many dynasties of Kathiawar (Saurashtra). Both Daman and Diu were acquired by the Portuguese in order to control the trade of the Indian Ocean. The Portuguese in 1535 signed a treaty with Bahadur Shah of Gujarat in order to build a fort at Diu. Towards the middle of the 1550s, all Gujarati ships entering and leaving the Gulf of Khambhat (Cambay) ports were required to pay Portuguese duties at Diu. Daman was renowned for its shipbuilding yards and docks, and was conquered by the Portuguese in 1559. Daman and Diu were subject to the Governor General of Goa as part of the Portuguese province Estado da India (State of India). The Portugese ruled them for more than four centuries, and they remained as outposts of Portuguese overseas territory until December 1961, when 'Operation Vijay' was launched by India restoring Daman and Diu to India to make them an integral part of the country. It initially became part of the erstwhile Union territory of Goa, Daman and Diu, but became a separate Union territory once statehood was given to Goa on 30 May 1987.

Culture

Dance and music are a part of the daily life of the people of Daman. Different Portuguese dances are still widely prevalent and performed, and they reflect the distinct fusion of tribal, urban, European and Indian cultures.

Fairs and festivals: Some of the important festivals in Daman and Diu are Holi, Diwali, Bhai Duj, Raksha Bandhan, Id-ul-Fitr, Navratri, Moharram, Id-ul-Zuha, Carnival, Feast of St Francis Xavier, Good Friday and Easter.

Economy, Industry and Agriculture

Economy: The net state domestic product at current prices is not available.

Minerals and industry: Daman and Diu has 2707 small and medium-scale industries. Omnibus Industrial Development Corporation at Daman has developed two industrial areas. The other industrial areas are Kadaiya, Bhimpore, Kanchigam and Dabhel.

Agriculture: The important crops of Daman include rice, ragi (finger millet), beans and pulses (legumes); however, Diu only has 20 per cent of cultivated land area, and crops such as wheat and bajra (pearl millet) are more suited to the dry climate.

Power: The Central sector power stations in the western region have granted power allocation to the Union territory of Daman and Diu, with which all villages have been electrified.

Education

Educational institute: Daman Government Arts College.

Tourism

Major tourist attractions: Fort of Moti Daman, Jampore Beach, Kadaiya Lake Garden.

Airports: Daman, Diu.

National Parks: Though there are no National Parks here, it has a wildlife sanctuary—Fudam Wildlife Sanctuary (area 2.18 sq. km in Diu).

Administration

Legislature: Daman and Diu does not have a legislative assembly. They are each organized as administrative districts and the Government of India appoints an administrator to govern these districts.

Judiciary: The Union Territory of Daman and Diu is under the jurisdiction of the Bombay High Court. The chief justice is Dalveer Bhandari.

Districts:

District	Area (sq. km)	Population	Headquarters	Urban Agglomerations
Daman	72	113,949	Daman	–
Diu	40	44,110	Diu	–

Lakshadweep

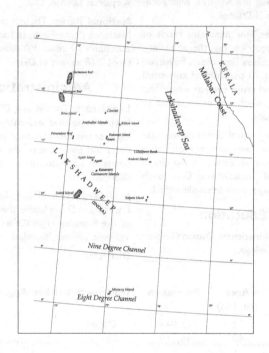

Key Statistics

Capital: Kavaratti.
Area: 32 sq. km.
Population: Total: 60,650
Male: 31,131
Female: 29,519
Population density: 1,894 per sq. km.
Sex ratio: 948 females per 1000 males.
Principal languages: Malayalam, Tamil, Hindi.
Literacy rates: Total: 86.7%
Male: 92.5%
Female: 80.5%

Government

Administrator: Parimal Rai. He assumed charge on 22 November 2004.

Geography

Physical characteristics: Lakshadweep is an archipelago of 12 atolls, three reefs and five submerged banks. It lies scattered over 45,000 sq. km of the Indian Ocean. There are 27 coral islands—India's only coral islands. In all, there are 10 inhabited islands, 17 uninhabited islands with attached islets, four newly formed islets and five submerged reefs. The easternmost island lies about 300 km off the western coast of Kerala. Lakshadweep has a lagoon area of about 4,200 sq. km and territorial waters of 20,000 sq. km. Only 10 of the islands are inhabited. The 10 inhabited islands are Andrott, Amini, Agatti, Bitra, Chetlat, Kadmath, Kalpeni, Kavaratti, Kiltan and Minicoy. Bitra is the smallest of all, with a nominal population. The main islands are Kavaratti, Minicoy and Amini.

The Amindivis are the northernmost islands of the group and Minicoy Island the southernmost. The eastern sides of the islands are higher and hence more suitable for human habitation. The low-lying lagoons on the western sides protect the islanders from the south-west monsoon. None of the islands exceed 1.5 km in width. They have sandy soils, derived from corals.

Neighbouring States and Union territories: None. The Union Territory lies in the Indian Ocean with no land borders. However, Kerala is the closest state. Kochi in Kerala is the usual point of origin for scheduled ships and aircraft travelling to the state.

Major rivers: There are no major rivers.

Climate: Lakshadweep has a tropical climate. Summer temperatures range between 22°C and 35°C while winter temperature varies between 20°C and 32°C. The monsoon season is between October and November. Normal rainfall is around 1600mm in the Minicoy group of islands and 1500mm in the Amindivi group of islands.

Flora and Fauna:
Flora: Coconut is the only crop of economic importance in the Union territory. Different varieties of coconut found in Lakshadweep include Laccadive micro, Laccadive ordinary and green dwarf. Banana, vazha, breadfruit, chakka, colocassia, chambu, drumstick moringakkai and wild almond grow extensively in Lakshadweep. It is also home to shrub jungle plants like kanni, chavok, punna and cheerani. Two different varieties of sea grass are seen adjacent to the beaches. These prevent sea erosion and movement of the beach sediments.

Fauna: The seas around Lakshadweep are rich in marine life. Sharks, tuna, flying fish, devil ray, bonito, octopus, sail fish, turtles, sea cucumber and snapper are found here. Colourful coral fish such as butterfly fish, parrotfish and surgeonfish are also found in plenty. Oceanic birds are also found in Lakshadweep. These include tharathasi and karifetu. Other species of birds found in Lakshadweep include seagull, tern, teal, heron and water heron. Money cowry is widely found in the shallow lagoons and reefs. The hermit crab is commonly found.

History

It is commonly believed that Cheraman Perumal, the last king of Kerala, set up the first settlement on what is today Lakshadweep, after he was shipwrecked. However, there are historical records to show that a Muslim saint named Ubaidullah was shipwrecked around the 7th century and it was he who converted the inhabitants to Islam.

Control over the islands remained with the Hindu ruler of Chirakkal for some years, after which it passed on to the Muslim rulers of Arakkal, in Cannanore, around the middle of the 16th century. The oppressive nature of the Arakkal rule resulted in the islanders seeking refuge with

in 1783. Tipu Sultan was on friendly terms with the Beebi of Arakkal and the Amini islands passed into his control. After Tipu Sultan's defeat at the battle of Seringapattam in 1799, the British East India Company annexed the islands and administered them from Mangalore.

In 1847, a severe cyclone hit the island of Andrott. When the Raja of Chirakkal found it difficult to pay for the damages, the East India Company granted a loan. The Raja was however unable to repay the loan or the mounting interest and in 1854 all the remaining islands were handed over to the British, who administered the islands till India became independent in 1947. Till 1956, the islands were a part of the erstwhile Madras state. On 1 November 1956, the islands became a Union territory of the Indian Union. The headquarters of the administration was shifted from Kozhikode/Calicut in Kerala to Kavaratti Island in March 1964. Between 1956 and 1973, the territory was called Laccadive, Minicoy, and Amindivi Islands. In 1973, it was renamed Lakshadweep.

Culture

Most of the people on Lakshadweep are Muslims with a small number of Hindus. The commonly spoken languages include Mahl, similar to old Sinhalese. The Hindu society is characterized by the matrilineal system of kinship and a rigid caste system. The folklore and customs are largely derived from the sea. Kiltan Island has a rich tradition of folk dances, namely kolkali and parichakali. Other dance forms of the Union territory include Lava dance, Ulakamut, Bhandiya, Kottuvili, Oppana, Duff and Attam. Opana is a well-known form of music performed at marriages. The Union territory is noted for carpentry and woodcarving. A variety of handicrafts are also made out of material like tortoise-shell, coconut shell, co-

conut fibre and corals. However, picking of corals from their natural habitat is a punishable offence.

Fairs and festivals: Id-ul-Fitr, Bakrid, Muharram, Id-e-Milad-un-Nabi and Dussehra are important festivals of Lakshadweep.

Economy, Industry and Agriculture

Economy: Figures not available.

Minerals and industry: The two most important industries of the state revolve around the coconut plant and fishes. Extraction of coconut fibre and its conversion into fibre products is a main industry of Lakshadweep. There are many fibre factories, coir production-cum-demonstration centres and fibre curling units in different islands. Fishing is the other important industrial activity. The huge potential that Lakshadweep possesses in fishing has resulted in the setting up of boat-building yards, fish-processing factories and the adoption of mechanized fishing boats. Tourism is also a major industry. Two handicaraft training centres were established at Kavaratti and Kalpeni in 1973 and 1979 respectively. A hosiery factory was established in 1967 at Kalpeni.

Agriculture: Agriculture is the most important component of the economy of Lakshadweep. The key products are coconut and coir. Coconut is the Union territory's only major crop.

Power: Lakshadweep gets most of its power supply from diesel generating sets. There are a few solar power plants while wind power plants are also planned for the Union territory.

Education

There are no universities or major institute of higher education in the Union territory.

Tourism

Major tourist attractions: Lighthouse, Minicoy; Ujra Mosque, Kavaratti; Hazrat Ubaidullah, Andrott; Buddhist archaeological remains, Andrott; Water Sport Institute, Kadmat.

Airports: Agatti.

National Parks: None.

Administration

Legislature: The President of India appoints an administrator to govern the territory.

Judiciary: Lakshadweep is under the jurisdiction of the High Court of Kerala. The acting chief justice is K.S. Radhakrishnan.

Districts:

District	Area (sq. km)	Population	Headquarters	Urban Agglomerations
Lakshadweep	32	60,650	Kavaratti	–

Pondicherry

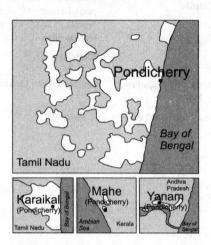

Key Statistics

Capital: Pondicherry.
Area: 492 sq. km.
Population: Total: 974,345
Male: 486,961
Female: 487,384
Population density: 2029 per sq. km.
Sex ratio: 1001 females per 1000 males.
Principal languages: Tamil, Malayalam, Telugu.
Literacy rates: Total: 81.2%
Male: 88.6%
Female: 73.9%

Government

Lieutenant Governor: Lt. Gen. (Retd.) M.M. Lakhera was sworn in on 3 June 2004.

Chief Minister: Thiru N. Rangasamy. He was sworn in on 27 October 2001.

Geography

Physical characteristics: The Union territory of Pondicherry has four constituent parts: Pondicherry, Karaikal, Mahe and Yanam. Podicherry and Karaikal are bordering Tamil Nadu, Mahe is situated on the Malabar Coast surrounded by the state of Kerala and Yanam is surrounded by the East Godavari district of Andhra Pradesh.

A canal divides the town of Pondicherry into two parts. The main streets run parallel to one another. The port of Pondicherry does not have a harbour and ships are anchored at some distance offshore. The Pondicherry area has about 300 villages.

Karaikal lies on Coromandel Coast, about 300km south of Chennai, at a distance of about 135km from Pondicherry town. It is located near the mouth of River Arasalar, in the Kaveri delta. The Nagappattinam and Thiruvarur districts of Tamil Nadu surround Karaikal.

Mahe consists of two parts. The town of Mahe lies on the left bank of River Mahe near its mouth while the area called Naluthrara is on the right bank and consists of the villages of Chambara, Chalakara, Palour, and Pandaquel. Mahe town is situated 647km away from Pondicherry town, between Badagara and Thalassery.

The town of Yanam lies at the spot where River Koringa (Atreya) branches off from Gauthami into two parts, about 870km from Pondicherry town.

Neighbouring States and Union territories:

1. Karaikal
   States: Tamil Nadu.
2. Mahe
   States: Kerala.
3. Pondicherry
   States: Tamil Nadu.
4. Yanam
   States: Andhra Pradesh.

Major rivers:
- Arasalar (Karaikal)
- Mahe (Mahe)
- Koringa
- Gauthami (Yanam).

Climate: Pondicherry has a hot and humid climate for most of the year. Temperature varies between 26°C and 38°C. It is mostly dry. The short monsoon season is between July and September. The months of May and June can be very humid. The summer is between March and July, when temperatures can touch 40°C and higher, mainly in May and June. On the west coast (Mahe), the monsoon season lasts between July and October. The winter usually starts in November, but sometime in mid-October, which is also when the north-east monsoon brings some rainfall. Temperatures remain in the region of 30°C.

Flora and Fauna:
Flora: The flora of Pondicherry can be listed under seven categories. These are: hydrophytes (aquatic plants), halophytes (plants that grow in salty soil), plants on sand dunes, plants on sandstones, avenue trees, hedge plants and ornamental plants.

Hydrophytes or aquatic plants found in Pondicherry include the lotus, akasathamarai and vettiver. Halophytes found in the Union territory include muttaikkorai, sattaranai, thakkali, thumbai, kanavalai, mayil kondai pul, karisalankanni, tutti and gilugilupai. Plants on sand dunes occurring in Pondicherry include woody plants like casuarina and eucalyptus. They grow along the sea coast. This category of plants also includes some herbs. The vegetative landscape of Pondicherry comprises mostly tall palms.

The Union territory also possesses a limited variety of mangrove species, mainly in the estuaries and the riverine sides of Ariyankuppam river and Malattar. A mangrove patch is also present in Thengaithittu and Murthikuppam.

Another striking feature of the flora of Pondicherry is the sacred groves. Pondicherry does not have natural forest cover. However, there are patches of sacred groves. These may be termed as natural islands of vegetation that are maintained and preserved for centuries for a religious purpose. Such groves are usually looked after by the local communities. The distribution of species varies from grove to grove.

Pondicherry is also home to some tropical dry evergreen species and some medicinal plants.

Fauna: The marine biodiversity of the Union territory include mackerel, shrimps, sardines, perches, ribbonfish and flying fish.

History

Remains of an ancient port town have been excavated at Arikamedu, 6 km from Pondicherry town. There are evidences here to suggest that it had trade connections with Rome and Greece around the period between 100 BC and AD 100. Pondicherry flourished during the Chola period, as indicated by the discovery of the Chola coins from the 11th and 12th centuries. Karaikal was also a part of the Chola empire but was successively occupied by the Vijayanagar, Marathas, Muslims and finally the French.

The history of modern Pondicherry starts with the arrival of the French in 1673, who ruled for most of the next 281 years. In 1674, the French East India Company established a settlement at Pondicherry. Mahe was founded in 1725, Yanam in 1731, and Karaikal in 1739.

Mahe was the site of prolonged conflict between the British and French troops in the 18th and 19th centuries. In 1726, the French captured the town. Later however, it was added several times to the British Madras Presidency. It was finally restored to the French in 1817.

Yanam was also a part of the Chola empire but came under Muslim occupation in the 16th century. In the 17th and 18th centuries it was the scene of conflict between Muslim, British, and French troops. When much of the coastal plain region that includes Yanam was incorporated into the Madras Presidency in 1765, Yanam remained a French enclave.

At the time of independence in 1947, the French restored Pondicherry, Mahe, Karaikal and Yanam to the Union of India. De facto transfer of these four French possessions to the Union of India took place on 1 November 1954 while de jure transfer took place on 28 May 1956. The instruments of ratification were signed on 16 August 1962.

Politics

With India becoming independent in August 1947, the citizens of French India hoisted the Indian national flag all over the French settlements. The Jaipur session of Indian National Congress passed a resolution for the peaceful merger of Pondicherry with India. The Indo-French agreement of June 1948 was signed and the French gave freedom to the French Indian population to choose their political status by a referendum. While Chandennagar (another French colony) merged with India on the basis of referendum, Pondicherry could not enjoy that facility because of a different system and practice of elections. On 23 March 1954, Nettapakkam and Madurai areas were liberated and a French India Liberation Government was set up on 16 May 1954. As per the understanding reached between the Government of India and France, the question of the merger of Pondicherry with the Indian Union was referred to the elected representatives of the people for decision in a secret ballot on 18 October 1954. 170 out of 178 elected representatives favoured the merger. This was the de facto transfer of power, which took place on 1 November 1954 and the de jure transfer took place on 16 August 1962. As the people aspired for a popular government, the Parliament enacted the Government of Union Territories Act, 1963 which came into force on 1 July 1963, and the pattern of government prevailing in the rest of the country was introduced in this territory also, subject to certain limitations. Under Article 239 of the Constitution, the President appoints an Administrator to head the administration of the territory. The President appoints the Chief Minister. The other Ministers are also appointed by the President on the advice of the Chief Minister.

The Congress has consistently won the elections ever since the former French enclave became a part of the Indian Union. In the 12 elections held between 1962 and 1999, the Congress won nine times, the All India Anna Dravida Munnetra Kazhagam (AIADMK) twice and the DMK once. On 1 July 1963 Edouard Goubert became the first Chief Minister of Pondicherry and he remained in power till 11 September 1964. He was succeeded by V. Venkatasuba Reddiar. He had two tenures as Chief Minister. The first tenure was from 11 September 1964 to 9 April 1967 and the second tenure was from 6 March 1968 to 18 September 1968. M.O. Hasan Farook Maricar was the Chief Minister from 9 April 1967 to 6 March 1968 and second time from 17 March 1969 to 3 January 1974. Hasan Farook Maricar was succeeded by Subramanyan Ramaswamy. He was elected twice and remained in office from 6 March 1974 to 12 November 1978. D. Ramachandran became Chief Minister of Pondicherry twice; first time from 16 January 1980 to 24 June 1983 and again from 5 March 1990 to 12 January 1991. Between D. Ramchandran's two tenures M.O. Hasan Farook Maricar again came to power on 16 March 1985. On 4 July 1991 V. Vaithilingam became the Chief Minister and remained in power till 14 May 1996. He was succeeded by R.V. Janakiraman who served as the Chief Minister of Pondicherry from 26 May 1996 to 18 March 2000. On 22 March 2000 P. Shanmugam was sworn in as the Chief Minister. On 27 October 2001 N. Rangaswamy became the Chief Minister.

Culture

There is a strong French influence in Pondicherry even today. Pondicherry was home to the famous poets, Subramania Bharathi and Bharathidasan. Pondicherry is also famous for the Aurobindo Ashram and Auroville. Pondicherry is well known for its handmade paper, the use of dried flowers on stationery items, aromatic candles and candles with pressed-in dried flowers. Incense sticks made at the Ashram and in Auroville are also famous.

Fairs and festivals: Festivals of Pondicherry are unique in the sense that the French influence still remains in its festivals and celebrations. The mask festival, Masquerade, is held in March–April. During this festival, the inhabitants wear costumes and masks and dance down the streets to accompanying music. On the eve of Bastille Day (14 July), retired soldiers parade in the streets singing the French and Indian national anthems. The Maasi Magam Festival is celebrated during the full moon period around mid-March. In Yanam, Vishnu Festival is celebrated in March. In March–April (first week after Easter), the Villianur Lourdes Festival is held. The Chitrai Kalai Vizha summer festival is held in April. The Villianur Temple Car Festival is usually celebrated around the middle of May but its exact date depends on the appearance of the full moon. During the Mangani Festival Karaikal experiences a month-long period of festivity that accompanies a feast dedicated to Karaikal Ammaiyar. The Virampattinam Car Festival takes place in August while the Fete de Pondicherry coincides with the Indian Independence Day. Other festivals celebrated in the Union territory are St Theresa Festival in Mahe and Isai Vizha, both celebrated in October.

Economy, Industry and Agriculture

Economy: The net state domestic product at current prices (new series) in 2002–03 (advance estimates) was Rs 3828 crores. The per capita state domestic product at current prices (new series) in 2002–03 (advance estimates) was Rs 38,162.

Minerals and industry: The significant industrial products of the Union territory include food products, cotton products, wood products, paper products, leather, rubber, plastic products, chemical and chemical products, non-metallic mineral products, metal products and machinery products. There are seven industrial estates in Pondicherry.

Agriculture: Around 35 per cent of the population is dependent on agriculture. Paddy is the most important crop in the territory, followed by pulses. Coconut, spices, condiments and areca nut are grown in Mahe while Yanam grows spices, chilli, pulses and groundnut.

Power: Pondicherry draws its power requirements from the southern grid. A gas-based power plant is being established at Karaikal.

Education

Educational institutes:
• Pondicherry University is at Pondicherry
• Ecole Français d' Extrème Orient Institute for Indology
• French Institute
• Jawaharlal Institute of Post-graduate Medical Education and Research (JIPMER)
• Pondicherry Institute of Linguistics and Culture
• Vinayaka Mission Medical College (Karaikal)

Tourism

Major tourist attractions:
1. Pondicherry: Auroville and Shri Aurobindo Ashram, Pondicherry Museum, Botanical Garden, Sri Gokilambal Thirukameswarar Temple, Mansion of Ananda Rangapillai, Eglise De Sacre Coeur De Jesus.
2. Karaikal: Lord Darbaraneswara Temple, Karaikal Ammaiyar Temple, Jadaayupureeswar Temple, Dargah of Mastan Syed Dawood, Our Lady Angel's Church.
3. Mahe: Tagore Park, St Theresa's Church, Puthalam, Othenan's Fort, St George Fort, Sree Krishna Temple, Choodikotta.
4. Yanam: Annavaram, Draksharamam, Padagaya Temple.

Airports: None.

National Parks: None.

Administration

Legislature: Pondicherry has a 30-seat legislative assembly of which five seats are reserved for SCs. The tenure of the current house expires on 8 June 2006. The present party position is as under:

Name of Party	Seats
Indian National Congress	11
Dravida Munnetra Khazagam	7
Pudhucherry Makkal Congress	4
All India Anna Dravida Munnetra Khazagam	3
Tamil Maanila Congress (Moopanar)	2
Bharatiya Janata Party	1
Independent	2
Total	**30**

Judiciary: Pondicherry falls under the jurisdiction of the Madras High Court. The chief justice is Thiru Markandey Katju.

Districts:

District	Area (sq. km)	Population	Headquarters	Urban Agglomerations
Karaikal	161.0	31,362	Karaikal	–
Mahe	9.0	36,823	Mahe	–
Pondicherry	290.0	735,004	Pondicherry	Pondicherry
Yanam	20.0	170,640	Yanam	–

APPENDIX I

States at a Glance

States at a Glance

State	Capital	Governor	Chief Minister
Andhra Pradesh	Hyderabad	Sushilkumar Shinde	Y.S. Rajasekhar Reddy
Arunachal Pradesh	Itanagar	S.K. Singh	Gegong Apang
Assam	Dispur	Lt Gen (Retd) Ajai Singh	Tarun Gogoi
Bihar	Patna	Buta Singh	
Chhattisgarh	Raipur	Lt Gen (Retd) K.M. Seth	Raman Singh
Goa	Panaji	S.C. Jamir	Pratapsingh Rane
Gujarat	Gandhinagar	Nawal Krishna Sharma	Narendra Modi
Haryana	Chandigarh	A.R. Kidwai	Bhupinder Singh Hooda
Himachal Pradesh	Shimla	Vishnu Sadashiv Kokje	Virbhadra Singh
Jammu and Kashmir	Srinagar/Jammu	Lt Gen (Retd) S.K. Sinha	Mufti Mohammed Sayeed
Jharkhand	Ranchi	Syed Sibtey Razi	Arjun Munda
Karnataka	Bangalore	T.N. Chaturvedi	N. Dharam Singh
Kerala	Thiruvananthapuram	R.L. Bhatia	Oommen Chandy
Madhya Pradesh	Bhopal	Balram Jakhar	Babulal Gour
Maharashtra	Mumbai	S.M. Krishna	Vilasrao Deshmukh
Manipur	Imphal	Shivinder Singh Sidhu	Okram Ibobi Singh
Meghalaya	Shillong	Mundakkal Matthew Jacob	D. Dethwelson Lapang
Mizoram	Aizawl	Amolak Rattan Kohli	Pu Zoramthanga
Nagaland	Kohima	Shyamal Datta	Neiphi-u Rio
Orissa	Bhubaneswar	Rameshwar Thakur	Naveen Patnaik
Punjab	Chandigarh	Gen (Retd) S.F. Rodrigues	Capt Amarinder Singh
Rajasthan	Jaipur	Pratibha Patil	Vasundhara Raje Scindia
Sikkim	Gangtok	V. Rama Rao	Pawan Kumar Chamling
Tamil Nadu	Chennai	Surjeet Singh Barnala	J. Jayalalithaa
Tripura	Agartala	Dinesh Nandan Sahaya	Manik Sarkar

State	Capital	Governor	Chief Minister
Uttaranchal	Dehradun	Sudarshan Agarwal	N.D. Tiwari
Uttar Pradesh	Lucknow	T.V. Rajeswar	Mulayam Singh Yadav
West Bengal	Kolkata	Gopalkrishna Gandhi	Buddhadeb Bhattacharya
National Capital Territory		**Lt Governor**	**Chief Minister**
Delhi	Delhi	Banwari Lal Joshi	Sheila Dikshit
Union Territory		**Lt Governor/Administrator**	
Andaman and Nicobar	Port Blair	Ramchandra Ganesh Kapse	
Chandigarh	Chandigarh	Gen (Retd) S.F. Rodrigues	
Dadra and Nagar Haveli	Silvassa	Arun Mathur	
Daman and Diu	Daman	Arun Mathur	
Lakshadweep	Kavaratti	Parimal Rai	
Pondicherry	Pondicherry	Lt Gen (Retd) M.M. Lakhera	Thiru N. Rangasamy

APPENDIX II

Comparison Tables

Area

Name	Area (sq. km.)
State	
Rajasthan	342239
Madhya Pradesh	308000
Maharashtra	307713
Andhra Pradesh	276754
Uttar Pradesh	236286
Jammu and Kashmir	222236
Gujarat	196024
Karnataka	191791
Orissa	155707
Chhattisgarh	135191
Tamil Nadu	130058
Bihar	94163
West Bengal	88752
Arunachal Pradesh	83743
Jharkhand	79714
Assam	78438
Himachal Pradesh	55673
Uttaranchal	53483
Punjab	50362
Haryana	44212
Kerala	38863
Meghalaya	22429
Manipur	22327
Mizoram	21087
Nagaland	16579
Tripura	10491
Sikkim	7096
Goa	3702
National Capital Territory	
Delhi	1483
Union Territory	
Andaman and Nicobar	8249
Pondicherry	492
Dadra and Nagar Haveli	491
Chandigarh	114
Daman and Diu	112
Lakshadweep	32

Population

Name	Population

State

Uttar Pradesh	166197921
Maharashtra	96878627
Bihar	82998509
West Bengal	80176197
Andhra Pradesh	76210007
Tamil Nadu	62405679
Madhya Pradesh	60348023
Rajasthan	56507188
Karnataka	52850562
Gujarat	50671017
Orissa	36804660
Kerala	31841374
Jharkhand	26945829
Assam	26655528
Punjab	24358999
Haryana	21144564
Chhattisgarh	20833803
Jammu and Kashmir	10069917
Uttaranchal	8489349
Himachal Pradesh	6077900
Tripura	3199203
Meghalaya	2318822
Manipur	2166788
Nagaland	1990036
Goa	1347668
Arunachal Pradesh	1097968
Mizoram	888573
Sikkim	540851

National Capital Territory

Delhi	13850507

Union Territory

Pondicherry	974345
Chandigarh	900635
Andaman and Nicobar	356152
Dadra and Nagar Haveli	220490
Daman and Diu	158204
Lakshadweep	60650

Population Density

Name	Population Density (persons per sq. km.)

State

West Bengal	904
Bihar	880
Kerala	819
Uttar Pradesh	689
Punjab	482
Tamil Nadu	478
Haryana	477
Goa	363
Assam	340
Jharkhand	338
Maharashtra	314
Tripura	304
Andhra Pradesh	275
Karnataka	275
Gujarat	258
Orissa	236
Madhya Pradesh	196
Rajasthan	165
Uttaranchal	159
Chhattisgarh	154
Nagaland	120
Himachal Pradesh	109
Manipur	107
Meghalaya	103
Jammu and Kashmir	99
Sikkim	76
Mizoram	42
Arunachal Pradesh	13

National Capital Territory

Delhi	9294

Union Territory

Chandigarh	7902
Pondicherry	2029
Lakshadweep	1894
Daman and Diu	1411
Dadra and Nagar Haveli	449
Andaman and Nicobar	43

Literacy Rate

Name	Literacy Rate (%)
State	
Kerala	90.9
Mizoram	88.5
Goa	82.3
Maharashtra	76.9
Himachal Pradesh	76.5
Tamil Nadu	73.5
Tripura	73.2
Uttaranchal	71.6
Manipur	70.5
Punjab	69.7
Gujarat	69.1
Sikkim	68.8
West Bengal	68.6
Haryana	67.9
Karnataka	66.6
Nagaland	66.6
Chhattisgarh	64.7
Madhya Pradesh	63.7
Assam	63.3
Orissa	63.1
Meghalaya	62.6
Andhra Pradesh	60.5
Rajasthan	60.4
Uttar Pradesh	56.3
Jammu and Kashmir	54.4
Arunachal Pradesh	54.3
Jharkhand	53.6
Bihar	47
National Capital Territory	
Delhi	81.7
Union Territory	
Lakshadweep	86.7
Chandigarh	81.9
Andaman and Nicobar	81.3
Pondicherry	81.2
Daman and Diu	78.2
Dadra and Nagar Haveli	57.6

Net State Domestic Product

Name	Net State Domestic Product (Rs crores)
State	
Maharashtra	263225
Uttar Pradesh	176076
West Bengal	153781
Andhra Pradesh	143975
Tamil Nadu	135252
Gujarat	114405
Karnataka	100406
Rajasthan	75048
Madhya Pradesh	71387
Kerala	71064
Punjab	64621
Haryana	57937
Bihar	51345
Orissa	38737
Assam	31721
Jharkhand	27358
Chhattisgarh	25094
Himachal Pradesh	14202
Jammu and Kashmir	13697
Uttaranchal	11361
Goa	6736
Tripura	5660
Nagaland	3864
Meghalaya	3842
Manipur	3047
Mizoram	1777
Arunachal Pradesh	1747
Sikkim	1139
National Capital Territory	
Delhi	68747
Union Territory	
Pondicherry	3828
Chandigarh	935
Andaman and Nicobar	872
Dadra and Nagar Haveli	
Daman and Diu	
Lakshadweep	

Per Capita Net State Domestic Product

Name	Per capita net state domestic product (Rs)
State	
Goa	49673
Haryana	26632
Maharashtra	26386
Punjab	25855
Himachal Pradesh	22576
Gujarat	22047
Kerala	21853
Tamil Nadu	21433
Sikkim	20456
Mizoram	19696
Nagaland	18911
West Bengal	18756
Andhra Pradesh	18661
Karnataka	18521
Tripura	17459
Meghalaya	15983
Arunachal Pradesh	15616
Jammu and Kashmir	13320
Uttaranchal	13260
Rajasthan	12753
Manipur	12230
Chhattisgarh	11893
Assam	11755
Madhya Pradesh	11438
Orissa	10340
Uttar Pradesh	10289
Jharkhand	9955
Bihar	6015
National Capital Territory	
Delhi	47477
Union Territory	
Chandigarh	52795
Pondicherry	38162
Andaman and Nicobar	24560
Dadra and Nagar Haveli	
Daman and Diu	
Lakshadweep	

Statehood

Name	Statehood (Year)
State	
Andhra Pradesh	1956
Arunachal Pradesh	1987
Assam	1950
Bihar	1950
Chhattisgarh	2000
Goa	1987
Gujarat	1960
Haryana	1966
Himachal Pradesh	1971
Jammu and Kashmir	1957
Jharkhand	2000
Karnataka	1950
Kerala	1956
Madhya Pradesh	1950
Maharashtra	1950
Manipur	1972
Meghalaya	1972
Mizoram	1987
Nagaland	1963
Orissa	1950
Punjab	1950
Rajasthan	1956
Sikkim	1975
Tamil Nadu	1950
Tripura	1972
Uttaranchal	2000
Uttar Pradesh	1950
West Bengal	1950
National Capital Territory	**NCT Status**
Delhi	1992
Union Territory	**UT Status**
Andaman and Nicobar	1956
Chandigarh	1996
Dadra and Nagar Haveli	1961
Daman and Diu	1987
Lakshadweep	1956
Pondicherry	1963

Number of Assembly Seats

Name	Number of Seats
State	
Andhra Pradesh	295
Arunachal Pradesh	60
Assam	126
Bihar	243
Chhattisgarh	90
Goa	40
Gujarat	182
Haryana	90
Himachal Pradesh	68
Jammu and Kashmir	87
Jharkhand	81
Karnataka	225
Kerala	140
Madhya Pradesh	230
Maharashtra	288
Manipur	60
Meghalaya	60
Mizoram	40
Nagaland	60
Orissa	147
Punjab	117
Rajasthan	200
Sikkim	32
Tamil Nadu	234
Tripura	60
Uttaranchal	70
Uttar Pradesh	403
West Bengal	294
National Capital Territory	
Delhi	70
Union Territory	
Andaman and Nicobar	
Chandigarh	
Dadra and Nagar Haveli	
Daman and Diu	
Lakshadweep	
Pondicherry	30

Number of Lok Sabha Seats

Name	Number of Seats
State	
Andhra Pradesh	42
Arunachal Pradesh	2
Assam	14
Bihar	40
Chhattisgarh	11
Goa	2
Gujarat	26
Haryana	9
Himachal Pradesh	4
Jammu and Kashmir	6
Jharkhand	14
Karnataka	28
Kerala	19
Madhya Pradesh	29
Maharashtra	47
Manipur	2
Meghalaya	2
Mizoram	1
Nagaland	1
Orissa	21
Punjab	13
Rajasthan	25
Sikkim	1
Tamil Nadu	39
Tripura	2
Uttar Pradesh	80
Uttranchal	5
West Bengal	42
National Capital Territory	
Delhi	7
Union Territories	
Andaman and Nicobar	1
Chandigarh	1
Dadra and Nagar Haveli	1
Daman and Diu	1
Lakshadweep	1
Pondicherry	1
Others	
Nominated Members	2
Total	**542**

Number of Rajya Sabha Seats

Name	Number of Seats
State	
Andhra Pradesh	18
Arunachal Pradesh	1
Assam	7
Bihar	16
Chhattisgarh	5
Goa	1
Gujarat	11
Haryana	5
Himachal Pradesh	3
Jammu and Kashmir	4
Jharkhand	6
Karnataka	12
Kerala	9
Madhya Pradesh	11
Maharashtra	19
Manipur	1
Meghalaya	1
Mizoram	1
Nagaland	1
Orissa	10
Punjab	7
Rajasthan	10
Sikkim	1
Tamil Nadu	18
Tripura	1
Uttaranchal	3
Uttar Pradesh	31
West Bengal	16
National Capital Territory	
Delhi	3
Union Territories	
Pondicherry	1
Others	
Nominated members	12
Total	**245**

High Courts

Name	High Court

State

Andhra Pradesh	Hyderabad
Arunachal Pradesh	Gauhati
Assam	Gauhati
Bihar	Patna
Chhattisgarh	Bilaspur
Goa	Bombay
Gujarat	Ahmedabad
Haryana	Chandigarh
Himachal Pradesh	Shimla
Jammu and Kashmir	Srinagar/Jammu
Jharkhand	Ranchi
Karnataka	Bangalore
Kerala	Ernakulam
Madhya Pradesh	Jabalpur
Maharashtra	Bombay
Manipur	Gauhati
Meghalaya	Gauhati
Mizoram	Gauhati
Nagaland	Gauhati
Orissa	Cuttack
Punjab	Chandigarh
Rajasthan	Jodhpur
Sikkim	Gangtok
Tamil Nadu	Madras
Tripura	Gauhati
Uttaranchal	Nainital
Uttar Pradesh	Allahabad
West Bengal	Calcutta

National Capital Territory

Delhi	Delhi

Union Territory

Andaman and Nicobar	Calcutta
Chandigarh	Chandigarh
Dadra and Nagar Haveli	Bombay
Daman and Diu	Bombay
Lakshadweep	Ernakulam
Pondicherry	Madras

APPENDIX III

Governors and Chief Ministers
since Independence

Andhra Pradesh

1 Oct 1953	Andhra Part A State created from part of Madras
1 Nov 1956	Andhra Pradesh

Governors

1 Oct 1953–1 Aug 1957	Sir Chandulal Madhavlal Trivedi
1 Aug 1957–8 Sep 1962	Bhim Sen Sachar
8 Sep 1962–4 May 1964	Satyavant Mallannah Srinagesh
4 May 1964–11 Apr 1968	Pattom Thanu Pillai
11 Apr 1968–25 Jan 1975	Khandubhai Kasanji Desai
26 Jan 1975–10 Jan 1976	S. Obul Reddy
10 Jan 1976–16 Jun 1976	Mohan Lal Sukhadia
16 Jun 1976–17 Feb 1977	R.D. Bhandare
17 Feb 1977–5 May 1977	B.J. Diwan
5 May 1977–15 Aug 1978	Sharada Mukherjee
15 Aug 1978–15 Aug 1983	Kochakkan Chacko Abraham
15 Aug 1983–29 Aug 1984	Thakur Ram Lal
29 Aug 1984–26 Nov 1985	Shankar Dayal Sharma
26 Nov 1985–7 Feb 1990	Kumudben Joshi
7 Feb 1990–22 Aug 1997	Krishan Kant
22 Aug 1997–24 Nov 1997	Gopala Ramanujam
24 Nov 1997–3 Jan 2003	Chakravarti Rangarajan
3 Jan 2003–4 Nov 2004	Surjit Singh Barnala
4 Nov 2004–	Sushil Kumar Shinde

Chief Ministers

1 Oct 1953–15 Nov 1954	Tanguturi Prakasam
28 Mar 1955–1 Nov 1956	Bezawada Gopala Reddy
1 Nov 1956–11 Jan 1960	N. Sanjiva Reddy
11 Jan 1960–12 Mar 1962	Damodaram Sanjivayya
12 Mar 1962–29 Feb 1964	N. Sanjiva Reddy
29 Feb 1964–30 Sep 1971	Kasu Brahmananda Reddy
30 Sep 1971–10 Jan 1973	P.V. Narasimha Rao
10 Dec 1973–6 Mar 1978	Jalagam Vengala Rao
6 Mar 1978–11 Oct 1980	Marri Channa Reddy
11 Oct 1980–24 Feb 1982	Tanguturi Anjaiah
24 Feb 1982–20 Sep 1982	Bhavanam Venkatram
20 Sep 1982–9 Jan 1983	Kotla Vijaya Bhaskara Reddy
9 Jan 1983–16 Aug 1984	N.T. Rama Rao
16 Aug 1984–16 Sep 1984	N. Bhaskara Rao
16 Sep 1984–3 Dec 1989	N.T. Rama Rao
3 Dec 1989–17 Dec 1990	Marri Channa Reddy
17 Dec 1990–9 Oct 1992	N. Janardhan Reddy
9 Oct 1992–12 Dec 1994	Kotla Vijaya Bhaskara Reddy
12 Dec 1994–1 Sep 1995	N.T. Rama Rao
1 Sep 1995–14 May 2004	Nara Chandrababu Naidu
14 May 2004–	Y.S. Rajasekhara Reddy

Hyderabad

Chief Ministers

26 Jan 1950–6 Mar 1952	M.K. Vellodi
6 Mar 1952–31 Oct 1956	Burgula Ramakrishna Rao

Arunachal Pradesh

21 Jun 1972	Union territory created from part of Assam
20 Feb 1987	State

Lieutenant Governors

15 Aug 1975–18 Jan 1979	K.A.A. Raja
18 Jan 1979–23 Jul 1981	R.N. Haldipur
23 Jul 1981–10 Aug 1983	H.S. Dubey
10 Aug 1983–21 Nov 1985	Thanjavelu Rajeshwar
21 Nov 1985–20 Feb 1987	Shiva Swaroop

Governors

20 Feb 1987–19 Mar 1987	Bhishma Narain Singh (acting)
19 Mar 1987–17 Mar 1990	R.D. Pradhan
17 Mar 1990–9 May 1990	Gopal Singh (acting)
9 May 1990–17 Mar 1991	D.D. Thakur (acting)
17 Mar 1991–26 Mar 1991	Loknath Mishra (acting)
26 Mar 1991–5 Jul 1993	Surendra Nath Dwivedi
5 Jul 1993–21 Oct 1993	Madhukar Dighe (acting)
21 Oct 1993–17 May 1999	Mata Prasad
17 May 1999–2 Aug 1999	S.K. Sinha
2 Aug 1999–13 Jun 2003	Arvind Dave
13 Jun 2003–16 Dec 2004	Vinod Chandra Pande
16 Dec 2004–	S.K. Singh

Chief Ministers

13 Aug 1975–18 Sep 1979	Prem Khandu Thungon
18 Sep 1979–3 Nov 1979	Tomo Riba
18 Jan 1980–19 Jan 1999	Gegong Apang
19 Jan 1999–3 Aug 2003	Mukut Mithi
3 Aug 2003–	Gegong Apang

Assam

15 Aug 1947   Province
26 Jan 1950   State (until 1956: Part A)

Governors

15 Aug 1947–28 Dec 1948	Sir Akbar Hydari
30 Dec 1948–16 Feb 1949	Sir Ronald Francis Lodge (acting)
16 Feb 1949–27 May 1950	Sri Prakasa
27 May 1950–15 May 1956	Jairamdas Daulatram
15 May 1956–22 Aug 1959	Sir Saiyid Fazl Ali
23 Aug 1959–14 Oct 1959	Chandreswar Prasad
14 Oct 1959–12 Nov 1960	Satyavant Mallannah Srinagesh
12 Nov 1960–13 Jan 1961	Vishnu Sahay
13 Jan 1961–7 Sep 1962	Satyavant Mallannah Srinagesh
7 Sep 1962–17 Apr 1968	Vishnu Sahay
17 Apr 1968–19 Sep 1973	Braj Kumar Nehru
19 Sep 1973–10 Aug 1981	Lallan Prasad Singh
10 Aug 1981–28 Mar 1984	Prakash Chandra Mehrotra
28 Mar 1984–15 Apr 1984	T.S. Mishra
15 Apr 1985–10 May 1989	Bhishma Narain Singh
10 May 1989–21 Jul 1989	Harideo Joshi
21 Jul 1989–2 May 1990	Anisetti Roghuvir
2 May 1990–17 Mar 1991	D.D. Thakur
17 Mar 1991–1 Sep 1997	Loknath Mishra
1 Sep 1997–21 Apr 2003	S.K. Sinha
21 Apr 2003–5 Jun 2003	Arvind Dave
5 Jun 2003–	Ajai Singh

Chief Ministers

15 Aug 1947–6 Aug 1950	Gopinath Bardoloi
9 Aug 1950–28 Dec 1957	Bishnuram Medhi
28 Dec 1957–6 Nov 1970	Bimali Prasad Chaliha
11 Nov 1970–31 Jan 1972	Mahendra Mohan Choudhury
31 Jan 1972–12 Mar 1978	Sarat Chandra Sinha
12 Mar 1978–4 Sep 1979	Golap Borbora
9 Sep 1979–11 Dec 1979	Jogendra Nath Hazarika
12 Dec 1980–29 Jun 1981	Anwara Taimur
13 Jan 1982–19 Mar 1982	Keshav Chandra Gogoi
27 Feb 1983–24 Dec 1985	Hiteshwar Saikia
24 Dec 1985–27 Nov 1990	Prafulla Kumar Mahanta
30 Jun 1991–22 Apr 1996	Hiteshwar Saikia
22 Apr 1996–15 May 1996	Bhumidhar Barman
15 May 1996–18 May 2001	Prafulla Kumar Mahanta
18 May 2001–	Tarun Gogoi

Bihar

| 15 Aug 1947 | Province |
| 26 Jan 1950 | State (until 1956: Part A) |

Governors
1947	Jairamdas Daulatram
12 Jan 1948–16 Jun 1952	Madhavrao Srihari Aney
16 Jun 1952–1957	Ranganath Ramachandra Diwakar
1957–12 May 1962	Zakir Husain
12 May 1962–Dec 1967	M. Ananthasayanam Ayyangar
Dec 1967–1 Feb 1971	Nityanand Kanungo
1 Feb 1971–Feb 1973	Dev Kanta Borooah
1974–Jun 1976	R.D. Bhandare
Jun 1976–11 Sep 1979	Jagannath Kaushal
11 Sep 1979–1985	A.R. Kidwai
1985–Feb 1988	Pendekanti Venkatasubbaiah
Feb 1988–1989	Govind Narayan Singh
1989–Feb 1990	Jagannath Pahadia
Feb 1990–Feb 1991	Mohammad Yunus Saleem
Feb 1991–1991	B. Satyanarayan Reddy
1991–Aug 1993	Mohammed Shafi Qureshi
Aug 1993–Apr 1998	A.R. Kidwai
27 Apr 1998–15 Mar 1999	Sunder Singh Bhandari
15 Mar 1999–6 Oct 1999	Brij Mohan Lal (acting)
6 Oct 1999–23 Nov 1999	Suraj Bhan
23 Nov 1999–12 Jun 2003	Vinod Chandra Pande
12 Jun 2003–1 Nov 2004	M. Rama Jois
1 Nov 2004–5 Nov 2004	Ved Marwah
5 Nov 2004–	Buta Singh

Chief Ministers
15 Aug 1947–31 Jan 1961	Srikrishna Sinha
1 Feb 1961–18 Feb 1961	Deep Narayan Singh
18 Feb 1961–1 Oct 1963	Binodanand Jha
1 Oct 1963–5 Mar 1967	Krishna Ballabh Sahay
5 Mar 1967–28 Jan 1968	Mahamaya Prasad Sinha
28 Jan 1968–1 Feb 1968	Satish Prasad Sinha
1 Feb 1968–23 Feb 1968	Bindeyyeshwari Prasad Mandal
23 Feb 1968–29 Jun 1968	Bhola Paswan Shastri
29 Feb 1969–22 Jun 1969	Harihar Prasad Singh
22 Jun 1969–4 Jul 1969	Bhola Paswan Shastri
17 Feb 1970–22 Dec 1970	Daroga Prasad Rai
22 Dec 1970–2 Jun 1971	Karpoori Thakur
2 Jun 1971– 9 Jan 1972	Bhola Paswan Shastri
19 Mar 1972–2 Jul 1973	Kedar Pandey
2 Jul 1973–11 Apr 1975	Abdul Ghafoor
11 Apr 1975–30 Apr 1977	Jagannath Mishra
24 Jun 1977–21 Apr 1979	Karpoori Thakur

21 Apr 1979–17 Feb 1980	Ram Sundar Das
8 Jun 1980–14 Aug 1983	Jagannath Mishra
14 Aug 1983–25 Mar 1985	Chandra Shekhar Singh
25 Mar 1985–14 Feb 1988	Bindeshwari Dubey
14 Feb 1988–11 Mar 1989	Bhagwat Jha Azad
11 Mar 1989–6 Dec 1989	Satyendra Narain Sinha
6 Dec 1989–10 Mar 1990	Jagannath Mishra
10 Mar 1990–28 Mar 1995	Laloo Prasad Yadav
4 Apr 1995–25 Jul 1997	Laloo Prasad Yadav
25 Jul 1997–12 Feb 1999	Rabri Devi
9 Mar 1999–3 Mar 2000	Rabri Devi
3 Mar 2000–10 Mar 2000	Nitish Kumar
10 Mar 2000–7 Mar 2005	Rabri Devi

Chhattisgarh

15 Aug 1947	Province
1 Jan 1948	Part of Central Provinces and Berar (later Madhya Pradesh)
1 Nov 2000	State

Chief Commissioner

| 1947–1 Jan 1948 | S.N. Mehta |

Governors

| 1 Nov 2000–2 Jun 2003 | Dinesh Nandan Sahay |
| 2 Jun 2003– | Krishna Mohan Seth |

Chief Ministers

| 1 Nov 2000–7 Dec 2003 | Ajit Jogi |
| 7 Dec 2003– | Raman Singh |

Goa

| 16 Mar 1962 | Goa, Daman and Diu union territory (formerly Portuguese India) |
| 30 May 1987 | Split into Goa state and Daman and Diu Union territory |

Lieutenant Governors
7 Jun 1962–2 Sep 1963	Tumkur Sivasankar
2 Sep 1963–8 Dec 1964	M.R. Sachdev
12 Dec 1964–24 Feb 1965	Hari Sharma
24 Feb 1965–18 Apr 1967	Kashinath Raghunath Damle
18 Apr 1967–16 Nov 1972	Nakul Sen
16 Nov 1972–16 Nov 1977	S.K. Banerjee
16 Nov 1977–31 Mar 1981	Pratap Singh Gill
31 Mar 1981–30 Aug 1982	Jagmohan
30 Aug 1982–24 Feb 1983	Idris Hasan Latif
24 Feb 1983–4 Jul 1984	Kershasp Tehmurasp Satarawala
4 Jul 1984–24 Sep 1984	Idris Hasan Latif (acting)
24 Sep 1984–29 May 1987	Gopal Singh

Governors
30 May 1987–18 Jul 1989	Gopal Singh
18 Jul 1989–18 Mar 1991	Khurshed Alam Khan
18 Mar 1991–4 Apr 1994	Bhanu Prakash Singh
4 Apr 1994–4 Aug 1994	B. Rachaiah
4 Aug 1994–16 Jun 1995	Gopala Ramanujam
16 Jun 1995–19 Jul 1996	Romesh Bhandari
19 Jul 1996–16 Jan 1998	P.C. Alexander
16 Jan 1998–19 Apr 1998	Tumkur Ramaiya Satish Chandran
19 Apr 1998–26 Nov 1999	J.F.R. Jacob
26 Nov 1999–26 Oct 2002	Mohammed Fazal
26 Oct 2002–2 Jul 2004	Kidar Nath Sahani
2 Jul 2004–17 Jul 2004	Mohammed Fazal
17 Jul 2004–	S.C. Jamir

Chief Ministers
8 Jun 1962–2 Dec 1966	Dayanand B. Bandodkar
5 Apr 1967–12 Aug 1973	Dayanand B. Bandodkar
12 Aug 1973–27 Apr 1979	Shashikala G. Kakodkar
16 Jan 1980–27 Mar 1990	Pratapsing Rane
27 Mar 1990–14 Apr 1990	Churchill Braz Alemao
14 Apr 1990–14 Dec 1990	Luis Proto Barbosa
25 Jan 1991–18 May 1993	Ravi Naik
18 May 1993–2 Apr 1994	Wilfred D'Souza
2 Apr 1994–8 Apr 1994	Ravi Naik
8 Apr 1994–16 Dec 1994	Wilfred D'Souza
16 Dec 1994–30 Jul 1998	Pratapsing Rane
30 Jul 1998–26 Nov 1998	Wilfred D'Souza
26 Nov 1998–9 Feb 1999	Luizinho Faleiro

9 Jun 1999–24 Nov 1999   Luizinho Faleiro
24 Nov 1999–24 Oct 2000   Francisco Sardinha
24 Oct 2000–2 Feb 2005   Manohar Parrikar
2 Feb 2005–4 Mar 2005   Pratapsing Rane
7 Jun 2005–   Pratapsing Rane

Gujarat

1 May 1960   State crated from part of Bombay (see Maharashtra)

Governors

1 May 1960–1 Aug 1965	Mehdi Nawaz Jung
1 Aug 1965–7 Dec 1967	Nityanand Kanungo
7 Dec 1967–26 Dec 1967	P.N. Bhagwati (acting)
26 Dec 1967–17 Mar 1973	Shriman Narayan
17 Mar 1973–4 Apr 1973	P.N. Bhagwati (acting)
4 Apr 1973–14 Aug 1978	Kambanthodath Kunhan Vishwanatham
14 Aug 1978–6 Aug 1983	Sharada Mukherjee
6 Aug 1983–26 Apr 1984	Kizhekethil Mathew Chandy
26 Apr 1984–26 Feb 1986	Braj Kumar Nehru
26 Feb 1986–2 May 1990	Ram Krishna Trivedi
2 May 1990–21 Dec 1990	Mahipal Shastri
21 Dec 1990–1 Jul 1995	Sarup Singh
1 Jul 1995–1 Mar 1996	Naresh Chandra
1 Mar 1996–25 Apr 1998	Krishna Pal Singh
25 Apr 1998–16 Jan 1999	Anshuman Singh
16 Jan 1999–18 Mar 1999	K.G. Balakrishnan (acting)
18 Mar 1999–7 May 2003	Sunder Singh Bhandari
7 May 2003–2 Jul 2004	Kailashpati Mishra
2 Jul 2004–24 Jul 2004	Balram Jakhar
24 Jul 2004–	Nawal Kishore Sharma

Chief Ministers

1 May 1960–18 Sep 1963	Jivraj Mehta
18 Sep 1963–19 Sep 1965	Balwantrai Mehta
1 Oct 1965–13 May 1971	Hitendra Kanaiyalal Desai
17 Mar 1972–20 Jul 1973	Ghanshyam Oza
20 Jul 1973–9 Feb 1974	Chimanbhai Patel
18 Jun 1975–12 Mar 1976	Babubhai Jashbhai Patel
24 Dec 1976–11 Apr 1977	Madhavsinh Solanki
11 Apr 1977–17 Feb 1980	Babubhai Jashbhai Patel
7 Jun 1980–6 Aug 1985	Madhavsinh Solanki
6 Aug 1985–10 Dec 1989	Amarsinh Chaudhary
10 Dec 1989–4 Mar 1990	Madhavsinh Solanki
4 Mar 1990–17 Feb 1994	Chimanbhai Patel
17 Feb 1994–14 Mar 1995	Chhabildas Mehta
14 Mar 1995–21 Oct 1995	Keshubhai Patel
21 Oct 1995–19 Sep 1996	Suresh Chandra Mehta
23 Oct 1996–28 Oct 1997	Shankersinh Vaghela
28 Oct 1997–4 Mar 1998	Dilip Parikh
4 Mar 1998–7 Oct 2001	Keshubhai Patel
7 Oct 2001–	Narendra Modi

Saurashtra

Chief Ministers

1948–1954	Uchharangray Navalshankar Dhebar
19 Dec 1954–1956	Rasiklal Umedchand Parikh

Haryana

1 Nov 1966   State created from part of Punjab

Governors

1 Nov 1966–15 Sep 1967	Dharma Vira
15 Sep 1967–27 Mar 1976	Birendra Narayan Chhakravarti
27 Mar 1976–14 Aug 1976	Ranjit Singh Narula
14 Aug 1976–24 Sep 1977	Jaisukh Lal Hathi
24 Sep 1977–10 Dec 1979	Harcharan Singh Brar
10 Dec 1979–28 Feb 1980	S.S. Sandhawalia
28 Feb 1980–14 Jun 1984	Ganpatrao Devji Tapase
14 Jun 1984–22 Feb 1988	S.M.H. Burney
22 Feb 1988–7 Feb 1990	Hara Anand Barari
7 Feb 1990–14 Jun 1995	Dhanik Lal Mandal
14 Jun 1995–19 Jun 2000	Mahabir Prasad
19 Jun 2000–2 Jul 2004	Babu Parmanand
2 Jul 2004–7 Jul 2004	Om Prakash Verma
7 Jul 2004–	A.R. Kidwai

Chief Ministers

1 Nov 1966–24 Mar 1967	Bhagwat Dayal Sharma
24 Mar 1967–21 Nov 1967	Rao Birendra Singh
21 May 1968–7 Dec 1975	Bansi Lal
7 Dec 1975–21 May 1977	Banarsi Das Gupta
21 May 1977–28 Jun 1979	Devi Lal
28 Jun 1979–5 Jul 1985	Bhajan Lal
5 Jul 1985–19 Jun 1987	Bansi Lal
17 Jul 1987–2 Dec 1989	Devi Lal
2 Dec 1989–22 May 1990	Om Prakash Chautala
22 May 1990–12 Jul 1990	Banarsi Das Gupta
12 Jul 1990–17 Jul 1990	Om Prakash Chautala
17 Jul 1990–22 Mar 1991	Hukam Singh
22 Mar 1991–6 Apr 1991	Om Prakash Chautala
23 Jul 1991–11 May 1996	Bhajan Lal
11 May 1996–24 Jul 1999	Bansi Lal
24 Jul 1999–5 Mar 2005	Om Prakash Chautala
5 Mar 2005–	Bhupinder Singh Hooda

Himachal Pradesh

15 Apr 1948   Province
26 Jan 1950   Part C state
1 Nov 1956   Union territory
25 Jan 1971   State

Chief Commissioners
Apr 1948–1951   E.P. Menon
1951–1952   Bhagwan Sahay

Lieutenant Governors
1 Mar 1952–1 Jan 1955   M.S. Himmatsinhji
1 Jan 1955–14 Aug 1963   Bajrang Bahadur Singh Bhadri
14 Aug 1963–26 Feb 1966   Bhagwan Sahay
26 Feb 1966–7 May 1967   Venkata Vishwanathan
7 May 1967–16 May 1967   Om Prakash
16 May 1967–25 Jan 1971   Kanwar Bahadur Singh

Governors
25 Jan 1971–17 Feb 1977   Subramaniam Chhakravarti
17 Feb 1977–26 Aug 1981   Aminuddin Ahmad Khan
26 Aug 1981–16 Apr 1983   Asoka Nath Banerji
16 Apr 1983–8 Mar 1986   Hokishe Sema
8 Mar 1986–17 Apr 1986   Prabodh Dinkarrao Desai (acting)
17 Apr 1986–16 Feb 1990   Rustom Khusro Shampoorjee Gandhi
16 Feb 1990–20 Dec 1990   B. Rachaiah
20 Dec 1990–30 Jan 1993   Virendra Verma
30 Jan 1993–11 Feb 1993   Surendra Nath
11 Feb 1993–30 Jun 1993   Bali Ram Bhagat
30 Jun 1993–27 Nov 1993   Gulsher Ahmed
27 Nov 1993–10 Jul 1994   Surendra Nath
10 Jul 1994–30 Jul 1994   Viswanathan Ratnam
30 Jul 1994–18 Sep 1995   Sudhakarrao Naik
18 Sep 1995–17 Nov 1995   Mahabir Prasad
17 Nov 1995–23 Apr 1996   Sheila Kaul
23 Apr 1996–26 Jul 1997   Mahabir Prasad
26 Jul 1997–2 Dec 1999   V.S. Rama Devi
2 Dec 1999–24 Nov 2000   Vishnu Kant Shastri
24 Nov 2000–8 May 2003   Suraj Bhan
8 May 2003–   Vishnu Sadashiv Kokje

Chief Ministers
8 Mar 1952–1956   Yashwant Singh Parmar
1 Jul 1963–28 Jan 1977   Yashwant Singh Parmar
28 Jan 1977–22 Jun 1977   Ram Lal Chauhan
22 Jun 1977–14 Feb 1980   Shanta Kumar
14 Feb 1980–8 Apr 1983   Thakur Ram Lal
8 Apr 1983–5 Mar 1990   Virbhadra Singh
5 Mar 1990–3 Dec 1993   Shanta Kumar
3 Dec 1993–24 Mar 1998   Virbhadra Singh
24 Mar 1998–6 Mar 2003   Prem Kumar Dhumal
6 Mar 2003– Virbhadra Singh

Jammu & Kashmir

Governors

30 Mar 1965–15 May 1967	Karan Singh
15 May 1967–3 Jul 1973	Bhagwan Sahay
3 Jul 1973–22 Feb 1981	Lakshmi Kant Jha
22 Feb 1981–26 Apr 1984	Braj Kumar Nehru
26 Apr 1984–Jul 1989	Jagmohan
Jul 1989–19 Jan 1990	K.V. Krishna Rao
19 Jan 1990–26 May 1990	Jagmohan
26 May 1990–12 Mar 1993	Girish Chandra Saxena
12 Mar 1993–2 May 1998	K.V. Krishna Rao
2 May 1998–4 Jun 2003	Girish Chandra Saxena
4 Jun 2003–	S.K. Sinha

Prime Ministers

11 Aug 1947–15 Oct 1947	Janak Singh (acting)
15 Oct 1947–5 Mar 1948	Meher Chand Mahajan
5 Mar 1948–9 Aug 1953	Sheikh Mohammad Abdullah
9 Aug 1953–12 Oct 1963	Bakshi Ghulam Mohammad
12 Oct 1963–29 Feb 1964	Khwaja Shams-ud-Din
29 Feb 1964–30 Mar 1965	Ghulam Mohammad Sadiq

Chief Ministers

30 Mar 1965–12 Dec 1971	Ghulam Mohammad Sadiq
12 Dec 1971–25 Feb 1975	Syed Mir Qasim
25 Feb 1975–26 Mar 1977	Sheikh Mohammad Abdullah
9 Jul 1977–8 Sep 1982	Sheikh Mohammad Abdullah
8 Sep 1982–2 Jul 1984	Farooq Abdullah
2 Jul 1984–6 Mar 1986	Ghulam Mohammad Shah
7 Nov 1986–19 Jan 1990	Farooq Abdullah
9 Oct 1996–18 Oct 2002	Farooq Abdullah
2 Nov 2002–	Mufti Mohammad Sayeed

Jharkhand

15 Nov 2000   State created from part of Bihar

Governors

15 Nov 2000–1 Feb 2002	Prabhat Kumar
1 Feb 2002–15 Jul 2002	Vinod Chandra Pande
15 Jul 2002–12 Jun 2003	M. Rama Jois
12 Jun 2003–10 Dec 2004	Ved Marwah
10 Dec 2004–	Syed Sibtey Razi

Chief Ministers

15 Nov 2000–18 Mar 2003	Babulal Marandi
18 Mar 2003–2 Mar 2005	Arjun Munda
2 Mar 2005–12 Mar 2005	Shibu Soren
12 Mar 2005–	Arjun Munda

Karnataka

| 15 Aug 1947 | Mysore state (1950–56: part B) |
| 1 Nov 1973 | Renamed Karnataka |

Rajpramukh

| 1947–1 Nov 1956 | Jayachamarajendra Wodeyar |

Governors

1 Nov 1956–4 May 1964	Jayachamarajendra Wodeyar
4 May 1964–2 Apr 1965	Satyavant Mallannah Srinagesh
2 Apr 1965–13 May 1967	Varahagiri Venkata Giri
13 May 1967–30 Aug 1969	Gopal Swarup Pathak
23 Oct 1969–1 Feb 1972	Dharma Vira
1 Feb 1972–10 Jan 1976	Mohan Lal Sukhadia
10 Jan 1976–2 Aug 1977	Uma Shankar Dikshit
2 Aug 1977–15 Apr 1983	Govind Narain Singh
16 Apr 1983–25 Feb 1988	Asoka Nath Banerji
26 Feb 1988–5 Feb 1990	Pendekanti Venkatasubbaiah
8 May 1990–6 Jan 1991	Bhanu Pratap Singh
6 Jan 1991–2 Dec 1999	Khurshed Alam Khan
2 Dec 1999–21 Aug 2002	V.S. Rama Devi
21 Aug 2002–	T.N. Chaturvedi

Chief Ministers

1946–25 Oct 1947	Arcot Ramaswami Mudaliar
25 Oct 1947–30 Mar 1952	Kysasambally Chengalaraya Reddy
30 Mar 1952–19 Aug 1956	Kengal Hanumanthaiah
19 Aug 1956– 1 Nov 1956	Kadidal Manjappa
1 Nov 1956–16 May 1958	Siddhavvanahalli Nijalingappa
16 May 1958– 9 Mar 1962	Basappa Danappa Jatti
14 Mar 1962–21 Jun 1962	Shivalingappa Rudrappa Kanthi
21 Jun 1962–3 Mar 1967	Siddhavvanahalli Nijalingappa
29 May 1968–27 Mar 1971	Veerendra Patil
20 Mar 1972–31 Dec 1977	Devaraj Urs
28 Feb 1978–12 Jan 1980	Devaraj Urs
12 Jan 1980–10 Jan 1983	R. Gundu Rao
10 Jan 1983–13 Aug 1988	Ramakrishna Hegde
13 Aug 1988–21 Apr 1989	Somappa R. Bommai
30 Nov 1989–10 Oct 1990	Veerendra Patil
17 Oct 1990–20 Nov 1992	S. Bangarappa
20 Nov 1992–11 Dec 1994	M. Veerappa Moily
11 Dec 1994–31 May 1996	H.D. Deve Gowda
31 May 1996–11 Oct 1999	Jayadevappa Halappa Patel
11 Oct 1999–28 May 2004	S.M. Krishna
28 May 2004–	Dharam Singh

Coorg

Chief Minister

| 17 Mar 1952–1956 | Cheppudira Muthana Poonacha |

Kerala

1 Jul 1949	Travancore-Cochin state formed (from 1950: Part B)
1 Nov 1956	Kerala state

Rajpramukh

1 Jul 1949–31 Oct 1956	Sir Bala Rama Varma II

Governors

22 Nov 1956–1 Jul 1960	Burgula Ramakrishna Rao
1 Jul 1960–2 Apr 1965	Varahagiri Venkata Giri
2 Apr 1965–6 Feb 1966	Ajit Prasad Jain
6 Feb 1966–15 May 1967	Bhagwan Sahay
15 May 1967–1 Apr 1973	Venkata Vishwanathan
1 Apr 1973–14 Oct 1977	Niranja Nath Wanchoo
14 Oct 1977–27 Oct 1982	Jyoti Venkatachalam
27 Oct 1982–23 Feb 1988	Parthasarathy Ramachandran
23 Feb 1988–12 Feb 1990	Ram Dulari Sinha
12 Feb 1990–20 Dec 1990	Sarup Singh
20 Dec 1990–12 Nov 1995	B. Rachaiah
12 Nov 1995–4 May 1996	P. Shiv Shanker
4 May 1996–25 Jan 1997	Khurshed Alam Khan
25 Jan 1997–18 Apr 2002	Sukhdev Singh Kang
18 Apr 2002–23 Feb 2004	Sikander Bakht
25 Feb 2004–23 Jun 2004	T.N. Chaturvedi
23 Jun 2004–	Raghunandan Lal Bhatia

Chief Ministers (of Travancore to 1 Jul 1949)

24 Mar 1948–20 Oct 1948	Pattom Thanu Pillai
20 Oct 1948– Jan 1951	T.K. Narayan Pillai
Jan 1951–12 Mar 1952	C. Kesavan
12 Mar 1952–16 Mar 1954	Anapparambul Joseph John
16 Mar 1954–10 Feb 1955	Pattom Thanu Pillai
10 Feb 1955–23 Mar 1956	Panampilly Govinda Menon
5 Apr 1957–31 Jul 1959	E.M. Sankaran Namboodiripad
22 Feb 1960–25 Sep 1962	Pattom Thanu Pillai
25 Sep 1962– 9 Sep 1964	R. Sankar
5 Mar 1967– 1 Nov 1969	E.M. Sankaran Namboodiripad
1 Nov 1969– 4 Aug 1970	C. Achutha Menon
4 Oct 1970–11 Apr 1977	C. Achutha Menon
11 Apr 1977–25 Apr 1977	K. Karunakaran
25 Apr 1977–29 Oct 1978	A.K. Antony
29 Oct 1978–12 Oct 1979	P.K. Vasudevan Nair
12 Oct 1979– 5 Dec 1979	C.H. Mohammed Koya
25 Jan 1980–20 Oct 1981	E.K. Nayanar
28 Dec 1981–17 Mar 1982	K. Karunakaran
24 May 1982–25 Mar 1987	K. Karunakaran
25 Mar 1987–24 Jun 1991	E.K. Nayanar
24 Jun 1991–22 Mar 1995	K. Karunakaran
22 Mar 1995–20 May 1996	A.K. Antony
20 May 1996–18 May 2001	E.K. Nayanar
18 May 2001–31 Aug 2004	A.K. Antony
31 Aug 2004–	Oommen Chandy

Madhya Pradesh

15 Aug 1947	Central Province and Berar
26 Jan 1950	Madhya Pradesh state (until 1956: Part A)

Governors

1947–1952	Mangaldas Mancharam Pakvasa
1952–14 Jun 1957	B. Pattabhi Sitaramayya
14 Jun 1957–11 Feb 1965	Hari Vinayaha Pataskar
11 Feb 1965–8 Mar 1971	Kysasambally Chengalaraya Reddy
8 Mar 1971–14 Oct 1977	Satya Narayan Sinha
14 Oct 1977–17 Aug 1978	Niranja Nath Wanchoo
17 Aug 1978–30 Apr 1980	Cheppudira Muthana Poonacha
30 Apr 1980–15 May 1984	Bhagwat Dayal Sharma
15 May 1984–31 Mar 1989	Kizhekethil Mathew Chandy
31 Mar 1989–6 Feb 1990	Serla Grewal
6 Feb 1990–24 Jun 1993	Kunwar Mahmood Ali Khan
24 Jun 1993–22 Apr 1998	Mohammed Shafi Qureshi
22 Apr 1998–7 May 2003	Bhai Mahavir
7 May 2003–1 May 2004	Ram Prakash Gupta
2 May 2004–30 Jun 2004	Krishna Mohan Seth
30 Jun 2004–	Balram Jakhar

Chief Ministers

15 Aug 1947–31 Dec 1956	Ravi Shankar Shukla
1 Jan 1957–31 Jan 1957	Bhagwantrao Mandloi
31 Jan 1957–11 Mar 1962	Kailash Nathi Katju
11 Mar 1962–30 Sep 1963	Bhagwantrao Mandloi
30 Sep 1963–30 Jul 1967	Dwarka Prasad Mishra
30 Jul 1967–13 Mar 1969	Govind Narayan Singh
13 Mar 1969–26 Mar 1969	Raja Naresh Chandra Singh
26 Mar 1969–29 Jan 1972	Shyama Charan Shukla
29 Jan 1972–23 Dec 1975	Prakash Chandra Sethi
23 Dec 1975–29 Apr 1977	Shyama Charan Shukla
26 Jun 1977–18 Jan 1978	Kailash Chandra Joshi
18 Jan 1978–20 Jan 1980	Virendra Kumar Saklecha
20 Jan 1980–17 Feb 1980	Sunderlal Patwa
9 Jun 1980–14 Mar 1985	Arjun Singh
14 Mar 1985–14 Feb 1988	Motilal Vora
14 Feb 1988–25 Jan 1989	Arjun Singh
25 Jan 1989– 9 Dec 1989	Motilal Vora
9 Dec 1989– 5 Mar 1990	Shyama Charan Shukla
5 Mar 1990–15 Dec 1992	Sunderlal Patwa
7 Dec 1993–8 Dec 2003	Digvijay Singh
8 Dec 2003–23 Aug 2004	Uma Bharti
23 Aug 2004–	Babulal Gaur

Madhya Bharat

Chief Ministers

Jan 1948– May 1949	Lilasthar Joshi
May 1949–18 Oct 1950	Gopikrishnan Vijayavargiya
18 Oct 1950–3 Mar 1952	Takhatmal Jain
3 Mar 1952–16 Apr 1955	Mishrilal Gangwal
16 Apr 1955–31 Oct 1956	Takhatmal Jain

Bhopal

Chief Ministers

Apr 1948–Jan 1949	Oudhnarain Bisatya
Jan 1949–1952	Pandit Chatur Narain Malviya
1952–1956	Shankar Dayal Sharma

Vindhya Pradesh

Chief Ministers

1948–1949	Awadesh Pratap Singh
13 Mar 1952–31 Oct 1956	Shambhunath Shukla

Maharashtra

15 Aug 1947	Bombay province
26 Jan 1950	State (unitl 1956: Part A)
1 May 1960	Divided into Maharashtra and Gujarat

Governors

15 Aug 1947–6 Jan 1948	David John Colville, Baron Clydesmuir
Jan 1948–30 May 1952	Raja Maharaj Singh
30 May 1952–5 Dec 1954	Sir Girja Shankar Bajpai
5 Dec 1954–1 Mar 1955	Mangaldas Mancharam Pakvasa
1 Mar 1955–14 Oct 1956	Harekrushna Mahatab
14 Oct 1956–10 Dec 1956	Mohomedali Currim Chagla
10 Dec 1956–16 Apr 1962	Sri Prakasa
16 Apr 1962–6 Oct 1962	P. Subbarayan
6 Oct 1962–5 Dec 1962	H.K. Chainani
5 Dec 1962–5 Sep 1963	Vijaya Lakshmi Pandit
5 Sep 1963–18 Dec 1963	H.K. Chainani
18 Dec 1963–8 Oct 1964	Vijaya Lakshmi Pandit
8 Oct 1964–14 Nov 1964	Mangaldas Mancharam Pakvasa
14 Nov 1964–9 Nov 1969	P.V. Cherian
9 Nov 1969–26 Feb 1970	S.P. Kotval
26 Feb 1970–11 Dec 1976	Ali Yavar Jung Bahadur
12 Dec 1976–30 Apr 1977	R.M. Kantawala
30 Apr 1977–3 Nov 1980	Sadiq Ali
3 Nov 1980–5 Feb 1982	Om Prakash Mehra
6 Mar 1982–18 Apr 1985	Idris Hasan Latif
18 Apr 1985–30 May 1985	K. Madhava Reddy
30 May 1985–3 Apr 1986	Kona Prabhakara Rao
3 Apr 1986–3 Sep 1987	Shankar Dayal Sharma
3 Sep 1987–6 Nov 1987	S.K. Desai
6 Nov 1987–20 Feb 1988	Chittatosh Mookerjee
20 Feb 1988–15 Feb 1989	Kasu Brahmananda Reddy
15 Feb 1989–12 Jan 1993	Chidambaram Subramaniam
12 Jan 1993–13 Jul 2002	P.C. Alexander
13 Jul 2002–10 Oct 2002	C.K. Thakkar (acting)
10 Oct 2002–6 Dec 2004	Mohammed Fazal
6 Dec 2004–	S.M. Krishna

Chief Ministers

15 Aug 1947–21 Apr 1952	Bal Gangadhar Kher
21 Apr 1952–1 Nov 1956	Morarji Desai
1 Nov 1956–19 Nov 1962	Yashwantrao Balwantrao Chavan
19 Nov 1962–25 Nov 1963	Marotrao Sambashio Kannamwar
5 Dec 1963–20 Feb 1975	Vasantrao Phulsing Naik
20 Feb 1975–1 Apr 1977	Shankarrao Chavan
1 Apr 1977–18 Jul 1978	Vasantrao Patil
18 Jul 1978–9 Jun 1980	Sharad Pawar
9 Jun 1980–20 Jan 1982	Abdul Rahman Antulay

20 Jan 1982–2 Feb 1983	Babasaheb Bhosale
2 Feb 1983–2 Jun 1985	Vasantrao Patil
2 Jun 1985–13 Mar 1986	Shivajirao Patil Nilangekar
13 Mar 1986–24 Jun 1988	Shankarrao Chavan
25 Jun 1988–25 Jun 1991	Sharad Pawar
25 Jun 1991–3 Mar 1993	Sudhakarrao Naik
3 Mar 1993–14 Mar 1995	Sharad Pawar
14 Mar 1995–1 Feb 1999	Manohar Joshi
1 Feb 1999–18 Oct 1999	Narayan Rane
18 Oct 1999–18 Jan 2003	Vilasrao Deshmukh
18 Jan 2003–1 Nov 2004	Sushil Kumar Shinde
1 Nov 2004–	Vilasrao Deshmukh

Manipur

15 Oct 1949	State (from 1950: Part C)
1 Nov 1956	Union territory
21 Jan 1972	State

Chief Commissioners (from 19 Dec 1969, lieutenant governors)
15 Oct 1949–18 Oct 1949	Rawal Amar Singh
18 Oct 1949–Dec 1950	Himmat Singh K. Maheswari
Jan 1951–22 Sep 1952	E.P. Moon Jan
22 Sep 1952–3 Jan 1955	Rameshwar Prasad Bharagava
3 Jan 1955–25 Apr 1958	P.C. Mathew
26 Apr 1958–23 Nov 1963	Jagat Mohan Raina
23 Nov 1963–Jan 1970	Baleshwar Prasad
Jan 1970–21 Jan 1972	Dalip Rai Kohli

Governors
21 Jan 1972–21 Sep 1973	Braj Kumar Nehru
21 Sep 1973–12 Aug 1981	Lallan Prasad Singh
12 Aug 1981–12 Jun 1984	S.M.H. Burney
12 Jun 1984–10 Jul 1989	K.V. Krishna Rao
10 Jul 1989–20 Mar 1993	Chintamani Panigrahi
20 Mar 1993–31 Aug 1993	K.V. Raghunatha Reddy
31 Aug 1993–23 Dec 1994	V.K. Nayar
23 Dec 1994–2 Dec 1999	Oudh Narain Shrivastava
2 Dec 1999–12 Jun 2003	Ved Marwah
12 Jun 2003–6 Aug 2004	Arvind Dave
6 Aug 2004–	Shivinder Singh Sidhu

Chief Ministers
1 Jul 1963–12 Jan 1967	M. Koireng Singh
20 Mar 1967–4 Oct 1967	M. Koireng Singh
13 Oct 1967–25 Oct 1967	Longjam Thambou Singh
19 Feb 1968–17 Oct 1969	M. Koireng Singh
23 Mar 1972–28 Mar 1973	Mohammed Alimuddin
4 Mar 1974–10 Jul 1974	Mohammed Alimuddin
10 Jul 1974–6 Dec 1974	Yangmasho Shaiza
6 Dec 1974–16 May 1977	R.K. Dorendra Singh
29 Jun 1977–14 Nov 1979	Yangmasho Shaiza
14 Jan 1980–27 Nov 1980	R.K. Dorendra Singh
27 Nov 1980–28 Feb 1981	Rishang Keishing
19 Jun 1981–4 Mar 1988	Rishang Keishing
4 Mar 1988–23 Feb 1990	R.K. Jaichandra Singh
23 Feb 1990–7 Jan 1992	Raj Kumar Ranbir Singh
8 Apr 1992–11 Apr 1993	R.K. Dorendra Singh
11 Apr 1993–31 Dec 1993	Dasarath Deb
14 Dec 1994–16 Dec 1997	Rishang Keishing
16 Dec 1997–15 Feb 2001	W. Nipamacha Singh
15 Feb 2001–2 Jun 2001	Radhabinod Koijam
7 Mar 2002–	Okram Ibobi Singh

Meghalaya

| 2 Apr 1970 | State within Assam |
| 21 Jan 1972 | Separate state |

Governors

1970–Sep 1973	Braj Kumar Nehru
Sep 1973–10 Aug 1980	Lallan Prasad Singh
10 Aug 1980–1984	Prakash Chandra Mehotra
1984	Triveni Sahai Misra
1984–1989	Bhishma Narain Singh
1989	Harideo Joshi
1 Jul 1989–1990	Abubakar Abdul Rahim
1990–1995	Madhukar Dighe
19 Jun 1995–	M.M. Jacob

Chief Ministers

2 Apr 1970–10 Mar 1978	Williamson A. Sangma
10 Mar 1978–7 May 1979	Darwin Diengdoh Pugh
7 May 1979–7 May 1981	Brington Buhai Lyngdoh
7 May 1981–2 Mar 1983	Williamson A. Sangma
2 Mar 1983–2 Apr 1983	Brington Buhai Lyngdoh
2 Apr 1983–6 Feb 1988	Williamson A. Sangma
6 Feb 1988–26 Mar 1990	Purno Agitok Sangma
26 Mar 1990–11 Oct 1991	Brington Buhai Lyngdoh
5 Feb 1992–19 Feb 1993	D.D. Lapang
19 Feb 1993–10 Mar 1998	Salseng C. Marak
10 Mar 1998–8 Mar 2000	Brington Buhai Lyngdoh
8 Mar 2000–8 Dec 2001	E.K. Mawlong
8 Dec 2001–4 Mar 2003	Flinder Anderson Khonglam
4 Mar 2003–	D.D. Lapang

Mizoram

21 Jan 1972   Union territory created from part of Assam
20 Feb 1987   State

Chief Commissioner
21 Jan 1972–24 Apr 1972   S.J. Das

Lieutenant Governors
24 Apr 1972–13 Jun 1974   Shanti Priya Mukherjee
13 Jun 1974–27 Sep 1977   S.K. Chhibbar
27 Sep 1977–1980   Mohan Prakash Mathur
1980–16 Apr 1981   K.A.A. Raja
16 Apr 1981–10 Aug 1983   S.N. Kohli
10 Aug 1983–11 Dec 1986   Mari Shankar Dhube
11 Dec 1986–20 Feb 1987   Hiteshwar Saikia

Governors
20 Feb 1987–30 Apr 1989   Hiteshwar Saikia
1 Jul 1989–8 Feb 1990   Williamson A. Sangma
8 Feb 1990–10 Feb 1993   Swaraj Kaushal
10 Feb 1993–29 Jan 1998   Paty Ripple Kyndiah
29 Jan 1998–2 May 1998   Arun Prasad Mukherjee
2 May 1998–22 Nov 2000   Anandam Padmanabhan
22 Nov 2000–18 May 2001   Ved Marwah
18 May 2001–   Amolak Rattan Kohli

Chief Ministers
3 May 1972–10 May 1977   L. Chal Chhunga
2 Jun 1978–10 Nov 1978   Thenphunga Sailo
8 May 1979–4 May 1984   Thenphunga Sailo
5 May 1984–20 Aug 1986   Lal Thhanhawla
21 Aug 1986–7 Sep 1988   Laldenga
24 Jan 1989–3 Dec 1998   Lal Thhanhawla
3 Dec 1998–   Zoramthanga

Nagaland

1 Dec 1963   State created from part of Assam

Governors

1 Dec 1963–17 Apr 1968	Vishnu Sahay
17 Apr 1968–19 Sep 1973	Braj Kumar Nehru
19 Sep 1973–10 Aug 1981	Lallan Prasad Singh
10 Aug 1981–13 Jun 1984	S.M.H. Burney
13 Jun 1984–20 Jul 1989	K.V. Krishna Rao
20 Jul 1989–4 May 1990	Gopal Singh
4 May 1990–9 May 1990	Chintamani Panigrahi
9 May 1990–13 Apr 1992	M.M. Thomas
13 Apr 1992–2 Oct 1993	Loknath Mishra
2 Oct 1993–5 Aug 1994	V.K. Nayar
5 Aug 1994–12 Nov 1996	Oudh Narain Shrivastava
12 Nov 1996–28 Jan 2002	Om Prakash Sharma
28 Jan 2002–	Shyamal Datta

Chief Ministers

1 Dec 1963–14 Aug 1966	Shilu Ao
14 Aug 1966–22 Feb 1969	T.N. Angami
22 Feb 1969–26 Feb 1974	Hokishe Sema
26 Feb 1974–10 Mar 1975	Vizol
10 Mar 1975–22 Mar 1975	John Bosco Jasokie
25 Nov 1977–18 Jan 1980	Vizol
18 Jan 1980–18 Apr 1980	George A. Pang
18 Apr 1980–5 Jun 1980	S.C. Jamir
5 Jun 1980–18 Nov 1982	John Bosco Jasokie
18 Nov 1982–29 Oct 1986	S.C. Jamir
29 Oct 1986–7 Aug 1988	Hokishe Sema
25 Jan 1989–15 May 1990	S.C. Jamir
15 May 1990–19 Jun 1990	K.L. Chishi
19 Jun 1990–2 Apr 1992	Vamuzo Phesao
22 Feb 1993–6 Mar 2003	S.C. Jamir
6 Mar 2003–	Neiphiu Rio

Orissa

| 15 Aug 1947 | Province |
| 26 Jan 1950 | State (unitl 1956: Part A) |

Governors

15 Aug 1947–20 Jun 1948	Kailash Nathi Katju
21 Jun 1948–6 Jun 1952	Janab M. Asaf Ali
7 Jun 1952–9 Feb 1954	Sir Saiyid Fazl Ali
10 Feb 1954–11 Sep 1956	Poosapati S. Kumaraswamy Raja
12 Sep 1956–31 Jul 1957	Bhim Sen Sachar
31 Jul 1957–15 Sep 1962	Yeshwant Narayan Sukthankar
16 Sep 1962–30 Jan 1968	Ajudhia Nath Khosla
31 Jan 1968–20 Sep 1971	Shaukatullah Shah Ansari
20 Sep 1971–30 Jun 1972	Sardar Jogendra Singh
1 Jul 1972–8 Nov 1972	Gatikrisina Misra (acting)
8 Nov 1972–20 Aug 1974	Basappa Danappa Jatti
21 Aug 1974–25 Oct 1974	Gatikrisina Misra (acting)
25 Oct 1974–17 Apr 1976	Akbar Ali Khan
17 Apr 1976–7 Feb 1977	Shiva Narayin Sankar (acting)
7 Feb 1977–22 Sep 1977	Harcharan Singh Brar
23 Sep 1977–30 Apr 1980	Bhagwat Dayal Sharma
30 Apr 1980–17 Aug 1983	Cheppudira Muthana Poonacha
17 Aug 1983–20 Nov 1988	Bishambhar Nath Pande
20 Nov 1988–6 Feb 1990	Nurul Hasan
7 Feb 1990–1 Feb 1993	Yagya Dutt Sharma
1 Feb 1993–31 May 1993	Nurul Hasan
1 Jun 1993–17 Jun 1995	B. Satyanarayan Reddy
18 Jun 1995–27 Apr 1998	Gopala Ramanujam
27 Apr 1998–14 Nov 1999	Chakravarti Rangarajan
15 Nov 1999–17 Nov 2004	M.M. Rajendran
17 Nov 2004–	Rameshwar Thakur

Chief Ministers

15 Aug 1947–12 May 1950	Harekrushna Mahatab
12 May 1950–15 Oct 1956	Nabakrushna Choudhury
15 Oct 1956–25 Feb 1961	Harekrushna Mahatab
28 Jun 1961–2 Oct 1963	Bijayananda Patnaik
2 Oct 1963–21 Feb 1965	Biren Mitra
21 Feb 1965–8 Mar 1967	Sadasiva Tripathy
8 Mar 1967–11 Jan 1971	Rajendra Narayana Singh Deo
3 Apr 1971–14 Jun 1972	Biswanath Das
14 Jun 1972–3 Mar 1973	Nandini Satpathy
6 Mar 1974–16 Dec 1976	Nandini Satpathy
29 Dec 1976–25 Jun 1977	Binayak Acharya
25 Jun 1977–17 Feb 1980	Nilamani Routray
9 Jun 1980–7 Dec 1989	Janaki Ballabh Patnaik
7 Dec 1989–5 Mar 1990	Hemananda Biswal
5 Mar 1990–15 Mar 1995	Bijayananda Patnaik
15 Mar 1995–15 Feb 1999	Janaki Ballabh Patnaik
15 Feb 1999–6 Dec 1999	Giridhar Gomango
6 Dec 1999–5 Mar 2000	Hemananda Biswal
5 Mar 2000–	Naveen Patnaik

Punjab

15 Aug 1947   Province
26 Jan 1950   State (until 1956: part A)

Governors

15 Aug 1947–11 Mar 1953	Sir Chandulal Madhavlal Trivedi
11 Mar 1953–15 Sep 1958	C.P.N. Singh
15 Sep 1958–1 Oct 1962	Narhar Vishnu Gadgil
1 Oct 1962–4 May 1964	Pattom Thanu Pillai
4 May 1964–1 Sep 1965	Hafiz Muhammad Ibrahim
1 Sep 1965–26 Jun 1966	Sardar Ujjal Singh
27 Jun 1966–1 Jun 1967	Dharma Vira
1 Jun 1967–16 Oct 1967	Mehar Singh
16 Oct 1967–21 May 1973	Dadasaheb Chintanani Pavate
21 May 1973–1 Sep 1977	Mahendra Mohan Choudhury
1 Sep 1977–24 Sep 1977	Ranjit Singh Narula
24 Sep 1977–26 Aug 1981	Jaisukh Lal Hathi
26 Aug 1981–21 Apr 1982	Aminuddin Ahmad Khan
21 Apr 1982–7 Feb 1983	Marri Channa Reddy
7 Feb 1983–21 Feb 1983	S.S. Sandhawalia
21 Feb 1983–10 Oct 1983	Anant Prasad Sharma
10 Oct 1983–3 Jul 1984	Bhairab Dutt Pande
3 Jul 1984–14 Mar 1985	Kershasp Tehmurasp Satarawala
14 Mar 1985–14 Nov 1985	Arjun Singh
14 Nov 1985–26 Nov 1985	Hokishe Sema
26 Nov 1985–2 Apr 1986	Shankar Dayal Sharma
2 Apr 1986–8 Dec 1989	Siddharta Shankar Ray
8 Dec 1989–14 Jun 1990	Nirmal Mukarji
14 Jun 1990–18 Dec 1990	Virendra Verma
18 Dec 1990–7 Aug 1991	Om Prakash Malhotra
7 Aug 1991–9 Jul 1994	Surendra Nath
10 Jul 1994–18 Sep 1994	Sudhakar Panditrao Kurdukar
18 Sep 1994–27 Nov 1999	B.K.N. Chhibber
27 Nov 1999–8 May 2003	J.F.R. Jacob
8 May 2003–3 Nov 2004	Om Prakash Verma
3 Nov 2004–16 Nov 2004	A.R. Kidwai
16 Nov 2004–	S.F. Rodrigues

Chief Ministers

15 Aug 1947–13 Apr 1949	Gopichand Bhargava
13 Apr 1949–18 Oct 1949	Bhim Sen Sachar
18 Oct 1949–20 Jun 1951	Gopichand Bhargava
17 Apr 1952–23 Jan 1956	Bhim Sen Sachar
23 Jan 1956–21 Jun 1964	Sardar Pratap Singh Kairon
21 Jun 1964–6 Jul 1964	Gopichand Bhargava
6 Jul 1964–5 Jul 1966	Ram Kishan
1 Nov 1966–8 Mar 1967	Gurumukh Singh Musafir
8 Mar 1967–25 Nov 1967	Sardar Gurnam Singh

25 Nov 1967–23 Aug 1968	Sardar Lachhman Singh Gill
17 Feb 1969–27 Mar 1970	Sardar Gurnam Singh
27 Mar 1970–14 Jun 1971	Prakash Singh Badal
17 Mar 1972–30 Apr 1977	Zail Singh
20 Jun 1977–17 Feb 1980	Prakash Singh Badal
6 Jun 1980–6 Oct 1983	Darbara Singh
29 Sep 1985–11 May 1987	Surjit Singh Barnala
25 Feb 1992–31 Aug 1995	Beant Singh
31 Aug 1995–21 Nov 1996	Harcharan Singh Brar
21 Nov 1996–12 Feb 1997	Rajinder Kaur Bhattal
12 Feb 1997–27 Feb 2002	Prakash Singh Badal
27 Feb 2002–	Amarinder Singh

Patiala and East Punjab States Union

Chief Ministers

22 Apr 1952–5 Mar 1953	Sardar Gian Singh Rarewala
8 Mar 1954–7 Jan 1955	Sardar Raghbir Singh
12 Jan 1955–31 Oct 1956	Brish Bhan

Rajasthan

25 Mar 1948	Rajasthan Union
18 Apr 1948	United states of Rajasthan
30 Apr 1949	United states of Greater Rajasthan (from 1950: Part B)
1 Nov 1956	Rajasthan

Rajpramukhs

25 Mar 1948–18 Apr 1948	Bhim Singh II
18 Apr 1948–4 Jul 1955	Sir Bhopal Singh
(from 1 Apr 1949, maharajpramukh)	

Governors

1 Nov 1956–16 Apr 1962	Gurumukh Nihal Singh
16 Apr 1962–16 Apr 1967	Sampurnanand
16 Apr 1967–1 Jul 1972	Sardar Hukam Singh
1 Jul 1972–15 Feb 1977	Sardar Jogendra Singh
15 Feb 1977–11 May 1977	Vedpal Tyagi (acting)
17 May 1977–8 Aug 1981	Raghukul Tilak
8 Aug 1981–6 Mar 1982	K.D. Sharma (acting)
6 Mar 1982–4 Jan 1985	Om Prakash Mehra
20 Nov 1985–15 Oct 1987	Vasantrao Patil
20 Feb 1988–3 Feb 1990	Sukhdev Prasad
3 Feb 1990–14 Feb 1990	Milap Chand Jain (acting)
14 Feb 1990–26 Aug 1991	Debi Prasad Chattopadhyaya
26 Aug 1991–5 Feb 1992	Swarup Singh (acting)
5 Feb 1992–31 May 1993	Marri Channa Reddy
31 May 1993–30 Jun 1993	Dhanik Lal Mandal (acting)
30 Jun 1993–1 May 1998	Bali Ram Bhagat
1 May 1998–24 May 1998	Darbara Singh
25 May 1998–16 Jan 1999	Navrang Lal Tibrewal (acting)
16 Jan 1999–14 May 2003	Anshuman Singh
14 May 2003–22 Sep 2003	Nirmal Chandra Jain
22 Sep 2003–14 Jan 2004	Kailashpati Mishra
14 Jan 2004–1 Nov 2004	Madan Lal Khurana
1 Nov 2004–8 Nov 2004	Thanjavelu Rajeshwar
8 Nov 2004–	Pratibha Patil

Chief Ministers

25 Mar 1948–18 Apr 1948	Gokul Lal Asawa
18 Apr 1948–7 Apr 1949	Manikya Lal Verma
7 Apr 1949–6 Jan 1951	Hiralal Shastri
6 Jan 1951–26 Apr 1951	Cadambi Seshachar Venkatachari (acting)
26 Apr 1951–3 Mar 1952	Jai Narayan Vyas
3 Mar 1952–1 Nov 1952	Tikaram Palliwal
1 Nov 1952–13 Nov 1954	Jai Narayan Vyas
13 Nov 1954–13 Mar 1967	Mohan Lal Sukhadia
26 Apr 1967–9 Jul 1971	Mohan Lal Sukhadia
9 Jul 1971–11 Oct 1973	Barkatullah Khan

23 Oct 1973–22 Jun 1977	Harideo Joshi
22 Jun 1977–16 Feb 1980	Bhairon Singh Shekhawat
6 Jun 1980–14 Jul 1981	Jagannath Pahadia
14 Jul 1981–23 Feb 1985	Shiv Charan Mathur
23 Feb 1985–10 Mar 1985	Heera Lal Devpura
10 Mar 1985–20 Jan 1988	Harideo Joshi
20 Jan 1988–4 Dec 1989	Shiv Charan Mathur
4 Dec 1989–4 Mar 1990	Harideo Joshi
4 Mar 1990–15 Dec 1992	Bhairon Singh Shekhawat
4 Dec 1993–1 Dec 1998	Bhairon Singh Shekhawat
1 Dec 1998–8 Dec 2003	Ashok Gehlot
8 Dec 2003–	Vasundhara Raje

Matsya
Matsya Union formed by merger of former princely states of Alwar, Bharatpur, Dholpur, and Karauli

Chief Minister

18 Mar 1948–15 May 1949	Shobha Ram

Ajmer

Chief Minister

24 Mar 1952–1956	Hari Bhau Upadhyay

Sikkim

16 May 1975   State

Governors

16 May 1975–10 Jan 1981	Bipen Bihari Lal
10 Jan 1981–16 Jun 1984	Homi J.H. Taleyarkhan
16 Jun 1984–31 May 1985	Kona Prabhakara Rao
31 May 1985–21 Nov 1985	Bhishma Narain Singh
21 Nov 1985–2 Mar 1989	Thanjavelu Rajeshwar
2 Mar 1989–8 Feb 1990	S.K. Bhatnagar
8 Feb 1990–21 Sep 1994	R.H. Tahiliani
21 Sep 1994–12 Nov 1995	P. Shiv Shanker
12 Nov 1995–10 Mar 1996	K.V. Raghunatha Reddy
10 Mar 1996–18 May 2001	Chaudhury Randhir Singh
18 May 2001–25 Oct 2002	Kidar Nath Sahani
25 Oct 2002–	V. Rama Rao

Chief Ministers

16 May 1975–18 Aug 1979	Kazi Lhendup Dorji
18 Oct 1979–11 May 1984	Nar Bahadur Bhandari
11 May 1984–25 May 1984	B.B. Gurung
8 Mar 1985–18 May 1994	Nar Bahadur Bhandari
18 May 1994–12 Dec 1994	Sanchaman Limboo
12 Dec 1994–	Pawan Chamling

Tamil Nadu

15 Aug 1947	Madras province
26 Jan 1950	State (until 1956: Part A)
14 Jan 1969	Renamed Tamil Nadu

Governors

15 Aug 1947–7 Sep 1948	Sir Archibald Edward Nye
7 Sep 1948–12 Mar 1952	Sir Krishnakumarsinhji Bhavsinhji
12 Mar 1952–10 Dec 1956	Sri Prakasa
10 Dec 1956–30 Sep 1957	Anapparambul Joseph John
24 Jan 1958–4 May 1964	Bishnuram Medhi
4 May 1964–26 Jun 1966	Jayachamarajendra Wodeyar
26 Jun 1966–27 May 1971	Sardar Ujjal Singh
27 May 1971–16 Jun 1976	Kodardas Kalidas Shah
16 Jun 1976–8 Apr 1977	Mohan Lal Sukhadia
8 Apr 1977–27 Apr 1977	C.P.N. Singh (acting)
27 Apr 1977–4 Nov 1980	Prabhudas Balubhai Patwari
4 Nov 1980–3 Sep 1982	Sadiq Ali
3 Sep 1982–17 Feb 1988	Sundar Lal Khurana
17 Feb 1988–24 May 1990	P.C. Alexander
24 May 1990–15 Feb 1991	Surjit Singh Barnala
15 Feb 1991–31 May 1993	Bhishma Narain Singh
31 May 1993–2 Dec 1996	Marri Channa Reddy
2 Dec 1996–25 Jan 1997	Krishan Kant
25 Jan 1997–3 Jul 2001	Fathima Beevi
3 Jul 2001–18 Jan 2002	Chakravarti Rangarajan
18 Jan 2002–3 Nov 2004	P.S. Ramamohan Rao
3 Nov 2004–	Surjit Singh Barnala

Chief Ministers

15 Aug 1947–6 Apr 1949	Amandur Ramaswami Reddiar
6 Apr 1949–10 Apr 1952	Poosapati S. Kumaraswamy Raja
10 Apr 1952–13 Apr 1954	Chakravarti Rajagopalachari
13 Apr 1954–2 Oct 1963	Kumaraswami Kamaraj
2 Oct 1963–4 Mar 1967	M. Bhaktavatsalam
4 Mar 1967–3 Feb 1969	C.N. Annadurai
10 Feb 1969–31 Jan 1976	Kalaignar Muthuvel Karunanidhi
30 Jun 1977–17 Feb 1980	Marudur Gopala Ramachandran
9 Jun 1980–24 Dec 1987	Marudur Gopala Ramachandran
7 Jan 1988–30 Jan 1988	Janaki Ramachandran
27 Jan 1989–30 Jan 1991	Kalaignar Muthuvel Karunanidhi
24 Jun 1991–13 May 1996	Jayaram Jayalalitha
13 May 1996–14 May 2001	Kalaignar Muthuvel Karunanidhi
14 May 2001–21 Sep 2001	Jayaram Jayalalitha
21 Sep 2001–2 Mar 2002	O. Paneerselvam
2 Mar 2002–	Jayaram Jayalalitha

Tripura

15 Oct 1949	Province
26 Jan 1950	Part C state
1 Nov 1956	Union territory
21 Jan 1972	State

Chief Commissioners

15 Oct 1949–1951	R.K. Ray
1951–1955	Venkatasubrami Nanjappa
1955–1956	H.L. Atal
1956–1958	Kalka Prasad Bhargawa
1958–1962	N.M. Patnaik
15 Nov 1962–17 Jan 1967	Shanti Priya Mukherjee
17 Jan 1967–5 Nov 1967	U.N. Sharma
5 Nov 1967–31 Jan 1970	D.K. Bhattacharya
31 Jan 1970–8 Aug 1971	Anthony Lancelot Dias
8 Aug 1971–21 Jan 1972	Baleshwar Prasad

Governors

21 Jan 1972–22 Sep 1973	Braj Kumar Nehru
22 Sep 1973–10 Aug 1980	Lallan Prasad Singh
10 Aug 1980–14 Aug 1981	Prakash Chandra Mehotra
14 Aug 1981–14 Jun 1984	S.M.H. Burney
14 Jun 1984–12 Jul 1989	K.V. Krishna Rao
12 Jul 1989–12 Feb 1990	Sultan Singh
12 Feb 1990–15 Aug 1993	K.V. Raghunatha Reddy
15 Aug 1993–16 Jun 1995	Romesh Bhandari
16 Jun 1995–23 Jun 2000	Siddheswar Prasad
23 Jun 2000–2 Jun 2003	Krishna Mohan Seth
2 Jun 2003–	Dinesh Nandan Sahay

Chief Ministers

1 Jul 1963–1 Nov 1971	Sachindra Lal Singh
20 Mar 1972–1 Apr 1977	Sukhamoy Sen Gupta
1 Apr 1977–26 Jul 1977	Prafullah Kuma Das
26 Jul 1977– 5 Nov 1977	Radhika Ranjan Gupta
5 Jan 1978–5 Feb 1988	Nripen Chakraborty
5 Feb 1988–19 Feb 1992	Sudhir Ranjan Majumdar
19 Feb 1992–11 Mar 1993	Samir Ranjan Barman
10 Apr 1993–11 Mar 1998	Dasarath Deb
11 Mar 1998–	Manik Sarkar

Uttar Pradesh

15 Aug 1947   United province
26 Jan 1950   Uttar Pradesh state (until 1956: Part A)

Governors

15 Aug 1947–2 Mar 1949	Sarojini Naidu
3 Mar 1949–2 May 1949	Bidhubhusan Malik (acting)
2 May 1949–2 Jun 1952	Sir Hormasji Peroshaw Mody
2 Jun 1952–10 Jun 1957	Kanaiyalal Maneklal Munshi
10 Jun 1957–1 Jul 1960	Varahagiri Venkata Giri
1 Jul 1960–16 Apr 1962	Burgula Ramakrishna Rao
16 Apr 1962–1 May 1967	Biswanath Das
1 May 1967–1 Jul 1972	Bezawada Gopala Reddy
1 Jul 1972–14 Nov 1972	Shashi Kanta Verma (acting)
14 Nov 1972–25 Oct 1974	Akbar Ali Khan
25 Oct 1974–2 Oct 1977	Marri Channa Reddy
2 Oct 1977–28 Feb 1980	Ganpatrao Devji Tapase
28 Feb 1980–31 Mar 1985	C.P.N. Singh
31 Mar 1985–12 Feb 1990	Mohammed Usman Arif
12 Feb 1990–27 May 1993	B. Satyanarayan Reddy
27 May 1993–3 May 1996	Motilal Vora
3 May 1996–19 Sep 1996	Mohammed Shafi Qureshi
19 Sep 1996–17 Mar 1998	Romesh Bhandari
17 Mar 1998–20 Apr 1998	Mohammed Shafi Qureshi
20 Apr 1998–24 Nov 2000	Suraj Bhan
24 Nov 2000–2 Jul 2004	Vishnu Kant Shastri
2 Jul 2004–8 Jul 2004	Sudarshan Agarwal
8 Jul 2004–	Thanjavelu Rajeshwar

Chief Ministers

15 Aug 1947–28 Dec 1954	Govind Ballabh Pant
28 Dec 1954–7 Dec 1960	Sampurnanand
7 Dec 1960–2 Oct 1963	Chandra Bhanu Gupta
2 Oct 1963–14 Mar 1967	Sucheta Kriplani
14 Mar 1967–3 Apr 1967	Chandra Bhanu Gupta
3 Apr 1967–17 Feb 1968	Charan Singh
26 Feb 1969–18 Feb 1970	Chandra Bhanu Gupta
18 Feb 1970–2 Oct 1970	Charan Singh
18 Oct 1970–4 Apr 1971	Tribhuvan Narain Singh
4 Apr 1971–12 Jun 1973	Kamlapati Tripathi
8 Nov 1973–30 Nov 1975	Hemwati Nandan Bahuguna
21 Jan 1976–30 Apr 1977	Narain Dutt Tiwari
23 Jun 1977–28 Feb 1979	Ram Naresh Yadav
28 Feb 1979–17 Feb 1980	Banarsi Das
9 Jun 1980–19 Jul 1982	Vishwanath Pratap Singh
19 Jul 1982–3 Aug 1984	Sripati Mishra
3 Aug 1984–24 Sep 1985	Narain Dutt Tiwari
24 Sep 1985–25 Jun 1988	Bir Bahadur Singh

25 Jun 1988–5 Dec 1989	Narain Dutt Tiwari
5 Dec 1989–24 Jun 1991	Mulayam Singh Yadav
24 Jun 1991–6 Dec 1992	Kalyan Singh
5 Dec 1993–3 Jun 1995	Mulayam Singh Yadav
3 Jun 1995–18 Oct 1995	Mayawati
21 Mar 1997–21 Sep 1997	Mayawati
21 Sep 1997–21 Feb 1998	Kalyan Singh
21 Feb 1998–23 Feb 1998	Jagadambika Pal
23 Feb 1998–12 Nov 1999	Kalyan Singh
12 Nov 1999–28 Oct 2000	Ram Prakash Gupta
28 Oct 2000–8 Mar 2002	Rajnath Singh
3 May 2002–29 Aug 2003	Mayawati
29 Aug 2003–	Mulayam Singh Yadav

Uttaranchal

9 Nov 2000   State created from part of Uttar Pradesh

Governors

9 Nov 2000–8 Jan 2003	Surjit Singh Barnala
8 Jan 2003–	Sudarshan Agarwal

Chief Ministers

9 Nov 2000–30 Oct 2001	Nityanand Swamy
30 Oct 2001–2 Mar 2002	Bhagat Singh Koshiyari
2 Mar 2002–	Narain Dutt Tiwari

West Bengal

15 Aug 1947	Province
26 Jan 1950	State (until 1956: Part A)

Governors

15 Aug 1947–21 Jun 1948	Chakravarti Rajagopalachari
21 Jun 1948–1 Nov 1951	Kailash Nathi Katju
1 Nov 1951–8 Aug 1956	Harendra Coomar Mookerjee
8 Aug 1956–3 Nov 1956	Phani Bhusan Chakraborty
3 Nov 1956–1 Jun 1967	Padmaja Naidu
1 Jun 1967–1 Apr 1969	Dharma Vira
1 Apr 1969–19 Sep 1969	Deep Narayan Sinha
19 Sep 1969–21 Aug 1971	Shanti Swaroop Dhavan
21 Aug 1971–6 Nov 1977	Anthony Lancelot Dias
6 Nov 1977–12 Sep 1981	Tribhuvana Narayana Singh
12 Sep 1981–10 Oct 1983	Bhairab Dutt Pande
10 Oct 1983–16 Aug 1984	Anant Prasad Sharma
16 Aug 1984–1 Oct 1984	Satish Chandra
1 Oct 1984–12 Aug 1986	Uma Shankar Dikshit
12 Aug 1986–20 Mar 1989	Nurul Hasan
20 Mar 1989–7 Feb 1990	Thanjavelu Rajeshwar
7 Feb 1990–12 Jul 1993	Nurul Hasan
13 Jul 1993–14 Aug 1993	B. Satyanarayan Reddy
14 Aug 1993–27 Apr 1998	K.V. Raghunatha Reddy
27 Apr 1998–18 May 1999	A.R. Kidwai
18 May 1999–4 Dec 1999	Shyamal Kumar Sen
4 Dec 1999–14 Dec 2004	Viren J. Shah
14 Dec 2004–	Gopalkrishna Gandhi

Chief Ministers

15 Aug 1947–14 Jan 1948	Prafulla Ghosh
14 Jan 1948– 1 Jul 1962	Bidhan Chandra Roy
8 Jul 1962–15 Mar 1967	Prafulla Sen
15 Mar 1967–2 Nov 1967	Ajoy Kumar Mukherjee
2 Nov 1967–20 Feb 1968	Prafulla Ghosh
25 Feb 1969–19 Mar 1970	Ajoy Kumar Mukherjee
2 Apr 1971–28 Jun 1971	Prafulla Ghosh
19 Mar 1972–21 Jun 1977	Siddharta Shankar Ray
21 Jun 1977–6 Nov 2000	Jyoti Basu
6 Nov 2000–	Buddhadev Bhattacharya

Delhi

15 Aug 1947	Province
26 Jan 1950	Part C state
1 Nov 1956	Union territory
1 Feb 1992	National Capital Territory of Delhi

Lieutenant Governors

1 Nov 1966–1970	Adity Nath Jha
1970–1971	M.C. Pimputkar
1971–1974	Baleshwar Prasad
1974–1978	Krishan Chand
1978–1979	Dalip Rai Kohli
Feb 1980–1981	Jagmohan
1981–Sep 1982	Sundar Lal Khurana
Sep 1982–Mar 1984	Jagmohan
Mar 1984–Nov 1984	P.G. Gavai
Nov 1984–Nov 1985	Mohan M.K. Wali
Nov 1985–Aug 1988	Harkishan Lal Kapoor
Aug 1988–Dec 1989	Romesh Bhandari
Dec 1989–Dec 1990	Arjun Singh
Dec 1990–1992	Markandey Singh
4 May 1992–4 Jan 1997	Prasannabhai Karunashankar Dave
4 Jan 1997–20 Apr 1998	Tejendra Khanna
20 Apr 1998–9 Jun 2004	Vijai Kapoor
9 Jun 2004–	B.L. Joshi

Chief Ministers

17 Mar 1952–12 Feb 1955	Chaudhary Brahm Prakash
12 Feb 1955–Nov 1956	G.N. Singh
1993–26 Feb 1996	Madan Lal Khurana
26 Feb 1996–12 Oct 1998	Sahib Singh Verma
12 Oct 1998–3 Dec 1998	Sushma Swaraj
3 Dec 1998–	Sheila Dikshit

Andaman and Nicobar Islands

15 Aug 1947	Province
26 Jan 1950	Part D territory
1 Nov 1956	Union Territory

Lieutenant Governors

12 Nov 1982–3 Dec 1985	Manohar L. Kampani
4 Dec 1985–Dec 1989	Tirath Singh Oberoi
Dec 1989–24 Feb 1990	Romesh Bhandari
25 Feb 1990–Dec 1990	Ranjit Singh Dayal
Dec 1990–18 Mar 1993	Surjit Singh Barnala
19 Mar 1993–18 Mar 1996	Vakkom Purushothaman
19 Mar 1996–25 May 2001	Ishwari Prasad Gupta
26 May 2001–4 Jan 2004	Nagendra Nath Jha
5 Jan 2004–	Ram Kapse

Chandigarh

1 Nov 1996   Union territory created from part of Punjab

Chief Commissioners

1 Nov 1966–31 Oct 1968	M.S. Randhava
31 Oct 1968–8 Apr 1969	Damodar Dass
8 Apr 1969–1 Sep 1972	B.P. Bagchi
1 Sep 1972–Dec 1975	Mohan Prakash Mathur
Dec 1975–15 Jun 1976	G.P. Gupta
15 Jun 1976–Jun 1978	T.N. Chaturvedi
Jun 1978–19 Jul 1980	J.C. Agrawal
19 Jul 1980–8 Mar 1982	B.S. Sarao
8 Mar 1982–2 Jun 1984	Krishna Banerji
2 Jun 1984–2 Aug 1984	The Governor of Punjab (administrator)
2 Aug 1984–30 May 1985	Krishna Banerji
30 May 1985–	The Governor of Punjab (administrators)

Dadra and Nagar Haveli

2 Aug 1954	End of Portuguese rule
11 Aug 1961	Union territory

Administrators

1962–2 Sep 1963	Tumkur Sivasankar
2 Sep 1963–8 Dec 1964	M.R. Sachdev
12 Dec 1964–24 Feb 1965	Hari Sharma
24 Feb 1965–18 Apr 1967	Kashinath Raghunath Damle
18 Apr 1967–16 Nov 1972	Nakul Sen
16 Nov 1972–16 Nov 1977	S.K. Banerjee
16 Nov 1977–31 Mar 1981	Pratap Singh Gill
31 Mar 1981–30 Aug 1982	Jagmohan
30 Aug 1982–24 Feb 1983	Idris Hasan Latif (acting)
24 Feb 1983–4 Jul 1984	Kershasp Tehmurasp Satarawala
4 Jul 1984–24 Sep 1984	Idris Hasan Latif (acting)
24 Sep 1984–18 Jul 1989	Gopal Singh
18 Jul 1989–25 Mar 1991	Khurshed Alam Khan
25 Mar 1991–16 Mar 1992	Bhanu Prakash Singh
16 Mar 1992–28 Mar 1994	K.S. Baidwan
28 Mar 1994–15 Jul 1995	Ramesh Chandra
15 Jul 1995–26 Jun 1998	S.P. Aggarwal
26 Jun 1998–23 Feb 1999	Ramesh Negi (acting)
23 Feb 1999–23 Apr 1999	Sanat Kaul
23 Apr 1999–19 Jul 1999	Ramesh Negi (acting)
19 Jul 1999–	O.P. Kelkar

Daman and Diu

6 May 1962	Part of Goa, Daman, and Diu Union territory (see Goa)
30 May 1987	Separate Union territory

Administrators

30 May 1987–   The Administrators of Dadra and Nagar Haveli

Lakshadweep

1 Nov 1956	Laccadive, Minicoy, and Amindivi Islands Union territory (separated from Madras [see Tamil Nadu])
1 Nov 1973	Renamed Lakshadweep

Administrators

1 Nov 1956–7 Nov 1956	U.R. Panicker
8 Nov 1956–21 Sep 1958	S. Moni
22 Sep 1958–5 Dec 1961	C.K. Balakrishna Nair
6 Dec 1961–8 Apr 1965	M. Ramunny
9 Apr 1965–31 Oct 1969	C.H. Nayar
1 Nov 1969–30 Apr 1973	K.D. Menon
22 May 1973–21 Jun 1975	W. Shaiza
22 Jun 1975–14 Feb 1977	M.C. Verma
21 Feb 1977–30 Jul 1978	S.D. Lakhar
31 Jul 1978–15 Jun 1981	P.M. Nair
15 Jun 1981–21 Jul 1982	Pradip Mehra
21 Jul 1982–9 Jul 1985	Omesh Saigal
9 Jul 1985–8 Sep 1987	J. Sagar
8 Sep 1987–31 Jan 1990	Wajahat Habibullah
1 Feb 1990–1 May 1990	Pradip Singh
2 May 1990–3 May 1992	S.P. Aggarwal
4 May 1992–9 Sep 1994	Satish Chandra
9 Sep 1994–14 Jun 1996	G.S. Chima
1 Aug 1996–1 Jun 1999	Rajeev Talwar
1 Jun 1999–20 Aug 1999	R.K. Verma
21 Aug 1999–30 Apr 2001	Chaman Lal
30 Apr 2001–19 Jun 2001	R.K. Verma
19 Jun 2001–	K.S. Mehra

Pondicherry

I Nov 1954	French India becomes de facto part of India
16 Aug 1962	De jure transfer to India
2 Jan 1963	Pondicherry Union territory

High Commissioners

I Nov 1954–1957	Kewal Singh
1957–1958	M.K. Kripalani
1958–1958*	L.R.S. Singh
1960	A.S. Bam
1961–1961*	Sarat Kumar Dutta

Lieutenant Governors

14 Oct 1963–14 Oct 1968	S.L. Sailam
14 Oct 1968–8 Nov 1972	Basappa Danappa Jatti
8 Nov 1972–30 Aug 1976	Cheddy Lal
30 Aug 1976–1 Nov 1980	Bidesh T. Kulkarni
I Nov 1980–16 Apr 1981	Ram Kishore Vyas
16 Apr 1981–27 Jul 1981	Sadiq Ali
27 Jul 1981–15 May 1982	R.N. Haldipur
15 May 1982–5 Aug 1983	Kizhekethil Mathew Chandy
19 Aug 1983–18 Jun 1984	Kona Prabhakara Rao
18 Jun 1984–1 Oct 1984	Sundar Lal Khurana
I Oct 1984–22 Jun 1988	Thiru Tribhuvan Prasad Tewary
22 Jun 1988–19 Feb 1990	Ranjit Singh Dayal
19 Feb 1990–19 Dec 1990	Chandrawati
19 Dec 1990–6 Feb 1993	Swarup Singh
6 Feb 1993–31 May 1993	Bhishma Narain Singh
31 May 1993–2 May 1995	Marri Channa Reddy
2 May 1995–23 Apr 1998	Rajendra Kumari Bajpai
23 Apr 1998–31 Jul 2002	Rajani Rai
31 Jul 2002–27 Oct 2003	K.R. Malkani
31 Oct 2003–5 Jan 2004	P.S. Ramamohan Rao (administrator)
5 Jan 2004–7 Jul 2004	Nagendra Nath Jha
7 Jul 2004–	M.M. Lakhera

Chief Ministers

I Jul 1963–11 Sep 1964	Edouard Goubert
11 Sep 1964–9 Apr 1967	V. Venkatasubha Reddiar
9 Apr 1967–6 Mar 1968	M.O. Hasan Farook Maricar
6 Mar 1968–18 Sep 1968	V. Venkatasubha Reddiar
17 Mar 1969–3 Jan 1974	M.O. Hasan Farook Maricar
6 Mar 1974–28 Mar 1974	Subramanyan Ramaswamy
2 Jul 1977–12 Nov 1978	Subramanyan Ramaswamy
16 Jan 1980–24 Jun 1983	D. Ramachandran
16 Mar 1985–19 Jan 1989	M.O. Hasan Farook Maricar
5 Mar 1990–12 Jan 1991	D. Ramachandran
4 Jul 1991–14 May 1996	V. Vaithilingam
26 May 1996–18 Mar 2000	R.V. Janakiraman
22 Mar 2000–27 Oct 2001	P. Shanmugam
27 Oct 2001–	N. Rangaswamy

Index